THE COOK'S GARDEN

*Growing and Using
the Best-Tasting Vegetable Varieties*

by

Shepherd and Ellen Ogden

Illustrated by
Karl Stuecklen

WINGS BOOKS
New York • Avenel, New Jersey

This 1993 edition is published by Wings Books,
distributed by Outlet Book Company, Inc., a Random House Company,
40 Engelhard Avenue, Avenel, New Jersey 07001, by arrangement
with Rodale Press.

Random House
New York • Toronto • London • Sydney • Auckland

Printed and bound in the United States of America

Library of Congress Cataloging-in-Publication Data
    Ogden, Shepherd.
        The cook's garden : growing and using the best-tasting
    vegetable varieties / by Shepherd and Ellen Ogden : illustrated by
    Karl Stuecklen.
            p.   cm.
        Rev. ed. of: The cook's garden. c1989.
        Includes index.
        ISBN 0-517-09286-7
        1. Vegetable gardening.   2. Vegetables—Varieties.   3. Organic
    gardening.   4. Cookery (Vegetables)   I. Ogden, Ellen.   II. Ogden,
    Shepherd.   Cook's garden.   III. Rodale Press.   IV. Title.
    SB324.3.042   1993
    635—dc20   92-39250
                                                                          CIP

8 7 6 5 4 3 2 1

For Shepherd's grandfather, Big Sam, who got him started in gardening.

CONTENTS

PART I

THE KITCHEN-GARDEN CONNECTION

*M*ost varieties of vegetables in America are wonders of plant breeding—uniform in size and shape, high yielding, disease-resistant hybrids. They're great for commercial growers and shippers and for the supermarkets that sell them. They would be great for home gardeners, too, if old-fashioned qualities like taste and texture didn't have to be sacrificed in the breeding process.

But in far too many cases, sacrifices in eating quality have been made to serve the needs of large growers, who want durable varieties that can be mechanically harvested and transported long distances. Gardeners don't need to ship their vegetables anywhere but into the kitchen, but since farmers buy more seed, most large seed companies have changed their offerings over the years to serve the commercial grower.

The trouble is that when these varieties are grown in home gardens, they taste a lot like the ones you can buy at the market, which is to say, they don't taste as good as they could. Tomatoes are an excellent example. An "interior ripening gene" that's partly responsible for the good taste of vine-ripened tomatoes has been bred out of many commercial varieties because it also made them too delicate to ship well. Even grown in the home kitchen garden and given loving care, these varieties aren't going to have that wonderful tomato flavor. It just isn't in their genes anymore.

We began as market gardeners a decade ago looking for crops we could grow that were better than what was available at the local supermarket. We soon realized that only by finding the best-tasting varieties, giving them the best care, and harvesting them at their prime would we be able to bring our customers produce like they could get from their own gardens. In ten years of looking for better vegetables, we have discovered many excellent new varieties and rediscovered some great old ones. In every case, these varieties are the ones that have retained their natural goodness and haven't succumbed to the demands of big growers and shippers.

Along the way, we've come to be known as growers of "gourmet" vegetables. I suppose that's fine, but it's not really the way we think of ourselves. Our emphasis, and the emphasis of this book, is on eating well, not just eating differently. Culinary gardening, as we like to think of it, is no fad; it's plain good sense. For any kitchen use there is a best vegetable, a best variety; it's just a matter of knowing which to grow and how to grow it to perfection. If you're going to have a garden, you might as well enjoy it—make it a place of beauty, fun, diversity, and just plain good eating; that's something no one can sell you.

Growing the Best

There are really only a few steps to growing great-tasting vegetables. One is choosing the best varieties, and much of this book is devoted to helping you find those. But there are also a few tips and tricks you can use to enhance the quality of your harvest.

Choose the site for your garden with care. If possible, avoid a "microclimate" that's particularly harsh for your area. In the north this means low-lying, frost-prone areas that collect cold air on clear, still nights and northern slopes that hold their snow cover late into spring; in hot, dry climates the reverse would be true—low spots on a gentle northern slope will require less water and will temper the effects of the sun during the hottest part of the year.

In general, it's a good idea to have the garden as close to the house as you can, both for the convenience of working in it during spare moments and for the ease of harvest. You'll probably find that having your garden right at hand will mean you use more of its produce in the kitchen.

The first thing I usually tell new gardeners who come to us for seeds or plants is, "Start small." The second thing I tell them is, "Plant in raised beds." Experienced gardeners already know the folly of having a garden bigger than they can easily care for. But many long-time gardeners still grow vegetables in widely spaced rows surrounded by bare ground on all sides. This requires a lot of unnecessary cultivation to keep all that unused ground free of weeds, and it lowers the productivity of your garden on a square-foot basis. If you have unlimited time and space, those things may not matter too much, but I've yet to meet the gardener who doesn't feel short of both.

Gardens planted in wide, raised beds require fewer pathways, so you need less space to grow the same amount of vegetables. You'll also be able to concentrate your fertilizer and compost applications on the areas where plants are actually growing. And since the soil in raised beds rarely gets stepped on, it stays loose and uncompacted. As a result, you can double or triple your average yields. This increase in productivity means you can grow all of your old favorites and still have space to try some of the new (and old, but overlooked) vegetable varieties in this book.

Getting Ready

Converting an existing row garden to beds is simple. Once the ground has been tilled in the spring, the only tools you'll need are a spading fork, shovel, rake, marker string, and stakes. First, decide where the beds will be, then stretch string lines around stakes to mark the perimeter of the beds. Rake soil from the pathways outside the string onto the bed inside to raise it, layering this soil with compost, manure, and any other organic materials. If your site has particularly poor drainage or thin topsoil, you can shovel additional soil from the path onto the beds, raising them even higher.

If you're starting from scratch and your garden will be less than 500 square feet, you don't even need a tiller. First, mark the location of the growing beds, then strip off the sod or other vegetation within that area. Next, remove one shovel-width of soil along the entire edge of the bed and pile it in a wheelbarrow or off to the side nearby. When that has been done, use your spading fork to loosen the bottom of the resulting foot-deep trench. Then shovel the next, adjacent strip of topsoil, along with any compost, manure, and such, on top of the loosened subsoil in the first trench. Loosen the bottom of this second trench as you did the first, and continue the process across the entire bed. (Use the soil you put aside from the first trench to fill the last one.) This process, called double digging, can make a productive garden out of any spot, no matter how inhospitable at the start.

We grow as many crops as possible from transplants. That way we can put the plants precisely where we want them. We start our transplants in 10-by-20-inch plastic trays that hold separate molded plastic "inserts" with individual, tapered growing cells. Some inserts have many small cells; others have fewer but larger cells. All the inserts fit the same size tray, so regard-

Raised beds: Mounding the soil (left); *leveling the bed*

less of the size of the plants or the number of plants per tray, all trays are still interchangeable. Both the trays and the inserts are made of inexpensive polyethylene, but they will last for a number of seasons if they are well cared for. They're easy to clean and simple to transplant from. The inserts range from 24 cells, each about the size of a small paper cup, to as many as 512 tiny, pencil-eraser-size cells.

Even if you need only a few trays, the modular form is a great help. Some gardeners start their plants in a mishmash of peat pots, foam drinking cups, or egg and milk cartons. These makeshift planting flats all work fine, but together they take up more room than they should, fall over from the weight of the plants during watering, and are a nuisance to move around. Both gardener and plants suffer as a result of the chaos.

As we discuss individual vegetables and herbs later in the book, we'll tell exactly which size cell works best for each crop. But in general we use three sizes: an insert that holds 162 plants, another that holds 98, and a third that holds 50 plants in cells the size of peat pots. For every #162 (162 cells) tray, we have two of the #98 size, and three of the #50 version. This system works well because one tray of seedlings from the #162 will fit in the two #98's and then fill the #50 trays as the plants grow. A small garden could be kept com-

Planting tray with two inserts

pletely stocked with only six trays and their inserts. The total growing space required would be less than 12 square feet.

One last type of insert we use is called a 20-row tray. This version has 20 1-inch-wide channels that are 1 inch deep running across the tray. This arrangement is very convenient if you are growing small amounts of a number of different plants because each variety can have its own row. In addition, any disease problems, such as damping-off, can be confined to individual rows and won't be spread throughout the whole tray.

For plants that outgrow the largest-size cell, we use modular pots that fit the same trays as the plug inserts. These come in two sizes: a 3½-inch size that fits 18 to a tray, and a much larger 6-inch-square size that fits 8 to a tray. Since these pots completely fill the trays, there is no wasted space, and the pots tend to hold each other up.

While the plants are growing indoors, we fertilize them with a solution made by mixing 1 tablespoon each of fish emulsion and seaweed to 1 gallon of water.

For large-scale feedings out in the garden later on, mix 1 quart of fish emulsion (we use an odorless 4-8-4) in 2 gallons of water in a pail, then add 1 quart of liquid seaweed and 2 more gallons of water. We use this solution right from the bucket with a siphon proportioner that dilutes it to the correct working strength.

Siphons are available from garden centers and mail-order catalogs for about $12 and are very handy to have around. The dilution will vary from about 12:1 to 16:1 with changes in water pressure, but that's not a problem, since you are using a relatively diluted fertilizer to start with. To use a proportioner, simply screw it onto the hose cock (or anywhere in the hose line less than 50 feet from the nozzle end), put its siphon tube into the fertilizer solution, and use the hose like normal.

If you'd rather not spend the money on a siphon proportioner, just dilute the stock solution and use a watering can. Manure or compost tea can be used instead of fish emulsion, but you should be extra careful to dilute it, because its strength will vary from batch to batch.

Planting Out

Soil conditions in raised bed gardens are usually good enough to allow closer planting than in row gardens. For example, rows of carrots need be only 2 to 4 inches apart. As the plants mature, their foliage will form a "living mulch" over the entire bed that will help fight weeds and conserve moisture.

The planting pattern can also be altered to maximize the use of growing space. We plant in what is called a hex layout, a pattern that allows us to fit as many plants in a given space as possible. For the sake of illustration, take seven coins of the same size and arrange them on the table with one in the center and the other six in a circle (or hexagon) around it. As you can see, there is almost no wasted space between the coins. This pattern is also the most efficient way to space plants.

An example from our garden is the pattern we use for lettuce. At one end of a bed, we set three plants across (one in each corner and a third centered between them); next down the bed, we set two plants equidistant from each other and from the first three. We then set three more below those two, then another two again, three, and so on, working our way lengthwise down the bed. I call this a 3:2:3 pattern, and a quick glance will show that it is identical to the pattern of the coins on the table. Triangulation and equidistant spacing are the essence of a hex layout. Depending on the size of the plants and the growing beds, you could also use a 2:1:2 layout or a 4:3:4 layout, or any other alternating pattern.

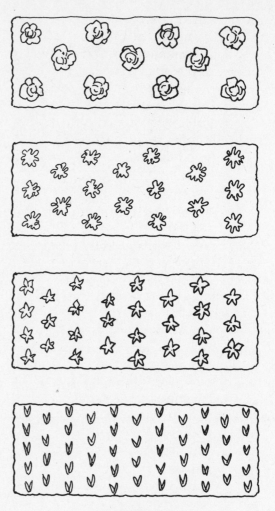

Hex layout beds

Growing Up

You can conserve even more space by getting vine crops up off the ground on trellises. Growing these crops vertically also helps control disease because it exposes the plants to more sun and wind.

Most trellised crops require extra water, though, because of the increased exposure. Overhead sprinkling is inefficient with trellised crops, but drip irrigation and moisture-conserving mulches work well and make the most effective use of the water available. Any vining crop like tomatoes, pole beans, peas, cucumbers, or melons is a good candidate for growing on a trellis.

We use two basic kinds of trellis systems: braiding and string fences. For braiding, a string is tied to the base of the plant (with a loose, nonslip knot) and then to an overhead support, leaving plenty of slack. The plant either twines around the string, like climbing beans, or is braided onto the string by hand, as with tomatoes and cucumbers. As the plant grows, the interweaving of plant and twine uses up the slack in the string.

A string fence is simply a series of horizontal strings running between posts spaced every 8 feet along the bed. We find that the strings should be no more than 6 inches apart. At the end of the season we simply pull down trellis and plants together and compost the whole lot. (Be sure to use untreated twine so it will rot completely by the following spring.)

If high productivity is your goal, make all the beds the same size so you can move trellises and cloches from bed to bed as needed throughout the season. I like beds that are about 3 feet across. With a 1-foot path, this makes a 4-foot-wide "module" —large enough to accommodate a number of different cropping plans, yet small enough to allow almost anyone to work on the entire bed without having to step in it. Furthermore, most plastic mulches and row covers come in 4-foot widths.

Interplanting—combining different plants within a single area—is another important technique in our garden. By considering how the nutrient requirements and growth habits of different plants interact, you can greatly increase both the beauty and the efficiency of the garden. For example, we mix radish and carrot seed together before planting. The radishes germinate quickly and break the surface of the soil, which helps the less vigorous carrot seedlings emerge. By the time the carrots need more space, the radishes have all been harvested. This same trick will work for other slow-germinating crops such as parsley and parsnips.

In some cases, a particular combination may also help with weed, pest, or disease control. Insects are drawn to large areas of plants they like, but interspersing their favorites with plants they find repellant will lessen their interest and their appetites. This is why some gardeners plant a circle of radishes around each hill of squash. It's an elegant concept, but the details can be complex, and only experimentation in your own garden will tell you what really works.

The most compelling reason to interplant is that it makes efficient use of sunlight, nutrients, and the gardener's time. The radish and carrot mix serves all three of these ends. So does mixing pumpkins or winter squash in your corn patch. The vine crops thrive in the shade provided by the corn and help block weeds that would otherwise grow there. They also dissuade raccoons, which don't like brushing against the spines that cover the pumpkin vines. Because both crops use the same space, your preparation and maintenance efforts go twice as far.

Other favorite interplantings of ours are cool-weather greens grown in the summer shade of trellised late peas, and early basil transplanted along the edges of the tomato and pepper beds. Every square foot that you don't need to cultivate is time and effort saved.

Intensive planting schemes make the most of a given space; succession planting—planting a new crop in the space left when you harvest an earlier crop—makes the most of the time nature gives us to grow our crops. Succession planting is also a key to getting the best and the freshest ingredients for the kitchen over the longest possible time.

The rules of successful successions: Plant frequently and harvest young. The first is especially important with single-harvest crops like salad greens that don't hold well in the garden, but the second rule—to harvest young—applies to almost all garden crops. Members of the tomato and melon/pumpkin family are exceptions, but all root and leaf crops pass their prime long before they reach maturity. So do legumes, cucurbits, and the majority of stem and bulb crops.

You can increase the length of your season through a number of techniques that temper the effects of weather on the garden, making it warmer in cold weather and cooler during the hot season. If you want to stretch the season this way, using mulches, covers, and frames, it helps to keep the growing beds as modular as possible. That way you can move your season extenders around with the crops they enhance, as they are rotated through the various growing areas.

Only a few years ago, season extenders were limited to bulky cold frames and bell jar cloches, but with the development of agricultural plastics, today's gardener has more options for protecting plants from the vagaries of weather. Polyethylene mulches that conserve soil moisture while they warm the soil; clear plastic strips that can be formed into continuous "tunnel" cloches with precut openings for ventilation; translucent spunbonded row covers so light they can be draped directly on the plants, and so diaphanous they allow rain and wind to pass through yet exclude insects: all these products are a boon to organic gardeners. In our garden, they add more than two weeks to each end of the growing season.

Plastic and biodegradable mulches come in a number of different forms and sizes. Many gardeners use opaque black plastic mulches, usually only 1 or 2 thousandths of an inch thick, that are applied to the growing bed a week or so before planting to warm the soil and conserve moisture. An extra advantage of these black films is that they stop weed growth by cutting off all light to the soil beneath them. Black plastic mulches commonly come in 3- or 4-foot widths but are available up to 20 feet wide.

For hot climates, where conserving moisture is most important, there are mulches with white or reflective surfaces that don't raise soil temperatures as much as black films. So-called biodegradable mulches are usually made either of special paper formulations or special plastics that break down quickly when exposed to sunlight.

Spunbonded floating row covers are made from a lightweight synthetic material called tricot (pronounced "tree-co"), also used by the apparel industry as an inexpensive, nonwoven fabric for lining garments. A few years ago researchers at the University of New Hampshire tried it out as a season extender for vegetables. They found that when the material was laid directly over growing plants, it not only gave a small amount of frost protection, but also kept insects from getting at the vegetables. In one study, lettuce and spinach plants survived sub-zero temperatures covered only by a floating row cover. At the same time, these tests demonstrated that floating row covers speed maturation of protected crops.

The row covers come in 62-inch-wide, 50-foot-long rolls that cost about $10. When installing the row covers, you bury the edges, leaving all the slack in the center, over the plants. The plants will take up this slack as they grow and support the cover themselves. For complete protection, you've got to bury the entire edge so no bugs can crawl underneath.

Keeping Weeds Away

Weed control is crucial to a productive garden. With intensive plantings, the first rule of cultivation is to match the tools to the plant spacing, not the other way around. We use a set of three oscillating stirrup hoes that are 3, 5, and 7 inches wide. The hoe blades are hinged where they mount to the handle so that the blade drags at about a 15-degree angle to the soil when it's pulled or pushed. This causes the blade to cut just beneath the surface, slicing off the roots of small weeds before they can become established. Stirrup hoes don't work well against large weeds, but if used regularly, they can prevent weeds from getting large in the first place.

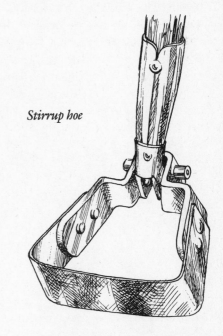

Stirrup hoe

Soon after transplanting, we cultivate with the largest-size hoe that will fit between the plants. As they grow closer together, we switch to the next smaller size; when we can no longer fit the smallest hoe between the plants without damaging them, we stop cultivating and let the "living mulch" of the plant canopy take over until harvest. We like stirrup hoes because they do not dig too deeply or bring up weed seeds that are down too far to germinate, and also because you can work much more quickly with a hoe that cuts in both directions.

The hex layout we use for transplanted crops makes cultivation a snap. As you'll notice once the plants are in, these patterns actually create rows diagonally across the growing beds. It's a simple matter to work along one side—pulling the hoe toward yourself, diagonally across the bed—and then back down the other side. By cultivating both diagonals, you loosen the soil and uproot the weeds on all sides of the plants. There is no in-row weeding

necessary. For example, you can cultivate a 25-foot-long bed of lettuce planted on a 3:2:3 layout in less than ten minutes.

With direct-seeded vegetables that don't transplant well, such as salad greens and root crops, be sure to set your rows a consistent distance apart. In that way you can make a quick and easy pass with the hoe to take care of any weeds that spring up between the rows. To mark out evenly spaced rows, we made a rakelike implement from scrap lumber. The tines, or markers, are set at whatever distance we want to space the rows. More sophisticated versions of this marker are available from mail-order catalogs.

Cultivation pattern for hex layout beds

Prime Harvest

When is the best time to harvest a given vegetable? That depends on how you plan to use it. If you want to sauté patty-pan squash, or use it to make tempura, you should obviously harvest when your squashes are young, thus being most tender and a good size for preparing whole. But if you're going to stuff them, let them grow until they are a size that is suitable for the dish and their skin is thick enough to survive baking without collapsing in a pool of mush in the baking dish.

This principle is true for all your crops. You're growing them to eat, so you might as well harvest at just the stage where it is ideal for your intended use. Plants go through stages of growth, and their culinary qualities are different at each stage. For fresh use, harvest your vegetables at their expansive peak, as soon as they are fully developed, but before the plant has turned the corner of metabolic maturity.

Take carrots, for example. Young, or as some call them, baby carrots are a real treat—sweet, tender, and juicy. But if you harvest them when they're too young, you'll be disappointed by their lack of flavor and color. They won't have developed the carrot's specific characteristics—orange coloring (in most varieties) and sweetness (due to the storage of sugars in the root). For a period of time as the carrot is maturing, color and sweetness will increase. But after a certain point, the plant will turn a corner of maturity and begin to become more fibrous.

The trick with carrots, and with most vegetables, is simple. Watch them closely, sample them often, and harvest when they're in prime condition. Throughout the book, we'll offer tips on when to harvest specific vegetables and herbs, but experience and experimentation remain the best teachers.

Special Treatment

Beyond the basics of giving your plants the best possible growing conditions, there are a few techniques that can be used to increase yield and quality. The best of these is pruning and thinning. Decreasing the number of fruits on a plant, such as a melon vine, allows the plant to put all of its energy into ripening the remaining fruits. This lowers the stress on the plant and increases the quality of the harvest. Northern gardeners know that trimming tomato plants a month before frost benefits the fruits that remain. The same principle applies to thinning root crops. When long-rooted carrots are sown too thickly, the roots intertwine, and the plants are forced to compete for nutrients. The resulting stress deforms the carrots and ruins their flavor and texture.

Some vegetables are improved by blanching. Blanch plants by excluding light from the part to be harvested, to temper its flavor and make it more tender, or to make it grow larger. Any gardener who grows potatoes knows the basics of blanching. We hill the plants to protect the tubers from light, and as they grow, we continue hilling to stimulate the formation of more and more tubers.

Blanching isn't just for potatoes, though. Leeks, scallions, and celery can be hilled to increase the length of the stem and to make it less fibrous. Hilled asparagus will turn out tender and white, and hilled carrots have crowns as orange and sweet as the rest of the roots.

Many salad greens are blanched to mellow their flavor; in fact, many of them develop their distinctive taste only after blanching. The heads can be tied up like cauliflower or covered with a nursery pot to block out sunlight. This technique can be used for a number of plants, including dandelion, rhubarb, asparagus, radicchio, and sea kale. With some plants, the roots or crowns are dug up and then resprouted in a root cellar to produce a blanched head that is very tender.

Two final techniques that deserve mention are used by salad gardeners to provide a continuous supply of tender greens for the salad bowl: growing seedling crops and cut-and-come-again harvesting. Seedling crops are usually fast-growing, leafy greens that are harvested just after the first true leaves have formed. They make very intensive use of space and yield tasty salad fixings. Some vegetables that work well as seedling crops are arugula, cress, *mâché,* mustard, chervil, purslane, lettuce, endive, chicory, spinach, and radish.

Cut-and-come-again culture is similar to growing seedling crops, except that the plants are allowed to grow to 6 inches or so before they are cut, after which they are watered, fertilized, and allowed to regrow. A well-managed planting of cut-and-come-again greens can yield up to four cuttings before the quality begins to deteriorate. Most of the same plants that work for seedling plantings can also be grown in this way, as can dill, fennel, beet greens, and parsley.

With good basic gardening techniques like these, you can't help but have a great garden. Now let's look at some of the varieties we've discovered over the years— the pick of the vegetable kingdom—and get into a little more detail about each of the crops.

PART II

THE BEST OF THE GARDEN

No two seasons are the same. One year the tomatoes do well, the next year the spinach and greens, the next might be the year of the melon. Whatever the conditions, your chances of having peak produce for the kitchen are best if you grow a wide range of crops. Not only will your garden be a more productive place, but it will be more beautiful as well—a tapestry of edible treasures in every season and every light.

In the section that follows, you'll find some crops that you may not have grown before and some new varieties of the old standbys, crops you've grown for years. Remember, you don't need to give up any of those old favorites to have room for these new and different crops—just use the space in your garden more efficiently by using the intensive planting methods we covered in Part I, and you'll have the room to grow a wider range of vegetables, herbs, and salad greens. Your garden—and your kitchen—will never be the same again.

We have organized the following discussion of individual crops alphabetically for easy reference. With each vegetable entry (except corn), you'll find a Variety Source Chart to make your seed ordering easier. (You won't find a chart with the corn chapter, simply because corn varieties are so specific to climatic regions; you'll do best if you buy corn seed on the advice of expert gardeners in your locale.) The charts are fully indexed to the Seed Source List at the back of the book. In addition to source codes, the charts present varietal information from the text in tabular form to help make comparisons easier.

You won't always find every variety that is mentioned in the text listed in the accompanying chart. There are many more names than there are true varieties. We have listed in the chart only what we consider to be the main variety name, not all its variants and copies. The welter of names, incidentally, derives as much from modern marketing as it does from modern plant science. Where the variation has some basis in plant science, it will generally be in color or adaptation to particular seasons or climatic regions. More often, though, the variance in name has to do with the reluctance of any seed company to sell a variety under the same name as its competitors; the variety will be the same, all right, but the name will be different to make it seem unique. Almost always, however, there's a clue to kinship, so we simplified things by eliminating unnecessary duplication in the charts.

BEANS

Have you ever been in a fancy food shop and seen *haricots verts* for sale? Sounds fancy, doesn't it? The price for these small, tender vegetables is usually fancy, too: about $6 a pound. But those two French words (at $3 apiece) translate into English as simply "beans, green." Let the gourmets spend their money on overpriced beans; if you're a gardener you can save the $6 and grow your own. It's just a matter of choosing the right variety and picking at the right time.

I'll bet you own a "frencher." It's that little open box housing the parallel blades on the end of your potato peeler. It slices green beans into thin slivers, and it exists for the sole purpose of making snap beans like French beans. Obviously, it would be easier to grow the correct beans in the first place, then skip the slicing. In fact, that's the whole point of growing *haricots verts* and why they were bred: to be used whole, but while they are still tiny, thin, and tender. These tender, stringless bean varieties, sometimes called "filet beans," are picked when the pods reach 3- to 6-inch length and ⅛- to ¼-inch thickness.

There are some other types of beans you might have overlooked, too: flat Italian snap beans, yellow beans, purple beans, and even curly beans. Then there are "flageolet" beans, a French shelling type equivalent in use to the American lima beans, but better adapted to the cool growing conditions in much of the northern United States. None of these beans were bred for farmers; they were bred for cooks. And none of them are any harder to grow than the more common types.

Growing

Beans (and peas) occupy the middle niche in our garden rotation. After the brassicas, lettuces, and squashes have lowered the nitrogen content of newly manured areas during their season of occupancy, we plant legumes to rebuild the nitrogen reserves. Then, in the third season, we grow root crops, herbs, and ornamentals. Our early season legume crop is peas, of course, and in the high summer we grow beans of all kinds and descriptions.

Most of the varieties we like are bush beans, direct seeded into the growing beds around the frost-free date. We either plant two rows per bed, with a small, quick-growing crop such as greens down the center of the bed between them; or we seed a single row of beans down the center of the bed and transplant a crop of lettuce down both sides. In either case, we thin the beans to 6 inches as soon as the first true leaves appear.

Beets and onions both work well planted with beans, but you can also put a late-planted, heat-tolerant green like *mâchè* down the center and let the beans shade it as they mature. For best results, wait until the beans are well up before planting the companion crop, so you can get in a few cultivations first. Then, by the time growth of the *mâchè* stops your cultivation, there will be enough leaf cover over the bed to inhibit the weeds.

We usually start one bed's worth of beans in #50 plug trays around May 1, in case we have an early spring; they are ready to go out in about three weeks, and we cover them immediately after planting with a floating row cover. They may end up only a week or so earlier than those direct seeded on the frost-free date, but to us that week is worth it.

Harvesting

Beans require periodic cultivation, but stay out of the bean patch when the foliage is wet. The water on the leaves is a perfect place for disease bacteria to live, and you spread the disease from leaf to leaf when you brush against the plants.

If you want the kind of beans that inspire fancy French names and premium prices, you not only need to plant the right varieties, you need to harvest them when they're young. The right varieties were bred for length and slimness, and if they grow too large, they will become tough and stringy. The perfect size is ⅛ inch thick, about the thickness of clothesline. Length is not the determining factor. There should be no sign of seeds swelling in the pods. In this they are similar to snow peas, and they are expensive for the same reason—it takes a lot to make a pound.

Ideally, filet beans should be picked daily to keep them producing in a big way, though new varieties just coming on the scene will hold longer on the vine. Daily picking may *sound* like a lot of trouble, but filet beans are easier to prepare than regular beans because they need only to have the stems cut off before they are cooked.

Regular snap beans can be picked young like filets, but they won't be as slim or tender, nor will they taste quite as good. There is a special sweet, "beany" taste to the true *haricots verts* varieties that's not in the snap beans, even when they're young.

The Best Varieties

Filet Beans

The two traditional varieties of filet beans are FIN DES BAGNOLS and TRIOMPHE DE FARCY. FDB, as we call it, is a little earlier and more vigorous; TDF is just as good and has the advantage of being a bit mottled in color, which makes the beans easier to see when you're picking. Improved strains of these two favorites are now making their way into this country. AIGUILLON is a new Fin des Bagnols type, and ETALON was bred out of Triomphe de Farcy; both are higher yielding than their forebears, but they still require daily harvest for best results. The highest yielding standard filet type in recent trials at the Rodale Research Center in Pennsylvania was CAMILE.

There has been a flurry of new varieties as well, most of which are called *haricots nain filet/mangetouts,* which just means "bush beans you can harvest as filets or snap beans." These varieties don't require such close attention to get good quality. If you ignore the harvest for a few days and the beans get big, they are still usable as snap beans. For the busy gardener who still wants the best, this is an attractive option. The best that we have tried is a new variety called FINAUD. Two others

(continued on page 22)

VARIETY SOURCE CHART

BEANS

Variety	When to Plant	When to Harvest	What to Harvest	Comments	Sources*
Bush/Snap Beans					
BUERRE DE ROCQUENFORT	After all danger of frost is past	Just as seeds begin to form	Pods 4″–8″ long	Yellow-podded snap bean (wax bean); good for cool areas	HG/ WD/CG
DRAGON TONGUE (DRAGON LANGERIE, TONGUE OF FIRE)	After all danger of frost is past	Just as seeds begin to form	Pods 4″–8″ long	Horticultural type	SB/JS/ CG/PT

(continued)

BEANS

Variety	When to Plant	When to Harvest	What to Harvest	Comments	Sources*
Bush/Snap Beans—*continued*					
FRENCH HORTICULTURAL	After all danger of frost is past	When pod separates from bean	Large oval beans	Heirloom shelling and dry bean; many variations available	Widely available
MAJOR	After all danger of frost is past	Just as seeds begin to form	Pods 4"–8" long	Yellow-podded snap bean with near-flat thinness	LM
ROC D'OR	After all danger of frost is past	Just as seeds begin to form	Pods 4"–8" long	Another good yellow-podded bean (wax bean)	SS/NG/ ST/JS
ROYAL BURGUNDY	After all danger of frost is past	Just as seeds begin to form	Pods 4"–8" long	Purple snap bean (green after cooking); great flavor	Widely available
Bush/Filet Beans					
AIGUILLON	After all danger of frost is past	When pod diameter reaches ⅛"	Seedless pods, 4"–8" long	Improved form of FIN DES BAGNOLS gives higher yields	LM
ARAMIS	After all danger of frost is past	When pod diameter reaches ⅛"	Seedless pods, 4"–8" long	Exceptional taste	WD
BAHALORES	After all danger of frost is past	When pod diameter reaches ⅛"	Seedless pods, 4"–8" long	—	SB/PT
CAMILE	After all danger of frost is past	When pod diameter reaches ⅛"	Seedless pods, 4"–8" long	Highest yielding filet type; needs regular harvesting	CG
DELINEL	After all danger of frost is past	When pod diameter reaches ⅛"	Seedless pods, 4"–8" long	Filet/mangetout type does not need to be harvested so frequently	NG
ETALON	After all danger of frost is past	When pod diameter reaches ⅛"	Seedless pods, 4"–8" long	Improved form of TRIOMPHE DE FARCY gives higher yields	LM
FINAUD	After all danger of frost is past	When pod diameter reaches ⅛"	Slim, 4"–8" green pods	Doesn't need as much care as other filets to get top quality	CG

BEANS

Variety	When to Plant	When to Harvest	What to Harvest	Comments	Sources*
FIN DES BAGNOLS	After all danger of frost is past	When pod diameter reaches ⅛"	Seedless pods, 4"–8" long	Traditional heirloom French variety; requires daily harvest	HG/ CG/LM
TRIOMPHE DE FARCY	After all danger of frost is past	When pod diameter reaches ⅛"	Seedless pods, 4"–8" long	Heirloom; pods have purple mottling; harvest daily	HG/JS/ CG
VERNANDON	After all danger of frost is past	When pod diameter reaches ⅛"	Seedless pods, 4"–8" long	Filet/mangetout type does not need to be harvested so frequently	WD
Bush/Flageolet Beans					
CHEVERBEL	After all danger of frost is past	When beans separate from pod	Fresh green shelled beans	Pods are also usable as snap beans when young	TM
CHEVRIER	After all danger of frost is past	When beans separate from pod	Fresh green shelled beans	Flageolets are better suited to the north than lima beans	HG/CG
FLAVEOL	After all danger of frost is past	When beans separate from pod	Fresh green shelled beans	Developed from the CHEVRIER variety; pods edible when young	LM
Pole/Snap Beans					
BLUE COCO	After all danger of frost is past	Just as seeds begin to form	Purple pods	Early purple pole type	SB
BLUE LAKE	After all danger of frost is past	Just before seeds form	Straight round stringless pods	Good pole variety for filet beans if picked young	Widely available
FORTEX	After all danger of frost is past	Just as seeds begin to form	Round green pods	Good pole variety for filet beans	JS
GREEN ANNELINO	After all danger of frost is past	Just as seeds begin to form	Curved, flattish pods	Curled pods with very good flavor	LM
ROMANO	After all danger of frost is past	Just as seeds begin to form	Flattish pods, 6"–10" long	Very good flavor; later than bush types but higher yielding	Widely available

(continued)

| | VARIETY SOURCE CHART—*Continued* | | | | |

BEANS

Variety	When to Plant	When to Harvest	What to Harvest	Comments	Sources*
Pole/Snap Beans—*continued*					
TRIONFO VIOLETTO	After all danger of frost is past	Just as seeds begin to form	Long, thin, purple pods, 6"-10" long	Climbing purple snap bean	CG
YELLOW ANNELINO	After all danger of frost is past	Just as seeds begin to form	Curved, flattish pods	Same as green, but pale yellow in color	LM
Runner Beans					
PAINTED LADY	After all danger of frost is past	Just before seeds form	Long green pods	Bi-color flowers are edible and make a good salad garnish	TM
SCARLET RUNNER	After all danger of frost is past	Just as seeds begin to form	Slim, flattish pods	Harvest young for best quality plants; quite ornamental	Widely available

*Listings correspond to seed companies included under Seed Source List at the back of the book.

that have performed well in our trial gardens are DELINEL and VERNANDON.

Snap Beans

There are several other types of bush beans worth growing. Many southerners are familiar with yellow wax or butter beans, but here in New England they still cause a stir when we bring them into our market from the garden. This is especially true of the DRAGON TONGUE wax bean, a golden flat-podded variety with violet stripes. These beans are truly outrageous looking, but also tender and juicy, even when large. They have a marvelous beany taste that isn't subdued by moderate cooking, though the stripes fade a bit. This variety also goes by the name DRAGON LANGERIE. There are also purple bush beans like ROYAL BURGUNDY or PURPLE TEEPEE that make a wonderful dish when mixed with golden-colored BUERRE DE ROCQUENFORT, MAJOR or ROC D'OR wax beans and covered with vinaigrette dressing. Just as with squashes, a little variety can be a big help in ending the midsummer blahs in the kitchen and garden. If you're growing 100 feet of bush beans, it's not much trouble to plant 25-foot rows of four different kinds rather than a single 100-foot row of plain green beans.

Flageolets

Flageolets are grown for shucking fresh when they're young or drying when they reach maturity. They're better adapted than limas to the cool sections of the United States because they are much earlier, but even southerners should give them a try because of their rich yet delicate taste. Culture is the same as for other bush beans. Harvest them for shelling as soon as the beans themselves begin to separate from the pod. You can feel this by squeezing the pod—there will be a tiny bit of give before you feel the bean inside. Shuck out a couple to check further. The beans should not feel moist on the surface, and the meat of the pod should have shrunk back from the bean and callused over. Since some flageolets are white and some green, color is not a good indicator of maturity.

To dry flageolets, wait until the pods have turned a brownish color, pull the plants, and hang the entire bush in a dry, dark place. Once the beans have hardened, spread a tarp and beat the plants against it to loosen the pods. These can then be shucked to remove the beans. Store like regular dried beans.

Pole Beans

We grow our pole beans up strings suspended from 5-foot-high trellises, the same ones we use for our peas. We direct-seed the pole beans 1 inch apart along the base of the trellis, then thin to 6 inches once they have put out their first true leaves. All we do is wrap the growing plants around the string once and they begin to climb on their own. After that, we leave them alone until harvest, except for an occasional weeding and cultivation. The same harvest rule holds true for pole beans as bush beans: Pick them when they're young and you'll get better beans with less kitchen work. Since pole beans will continue to produce until frost, keeping them picked is crucial to overall yields.

The Italians love pole beans, and they have a host of varieties that deserve to be better known and more widely grown: ROMANO, the flat snap bean with an unforgettable beany taste; TRIONFO VIOLETTO, a climbing purple bean with tender, stringless pods; GREEN and YELLOW ANNELINO, two hard-to-find Italian pole beans with the taste of ROMANO beans and unique, curlicue-shaped pods. We have had good crops of each. Two pole types that are grown as a substitute for filet beans are the old favorite BLUE LAKE and a new, fine-tasting introduction named FORTEX. There is also the famous FRENCH HORTICULTURAL bean, and dozens of kinds of runner beans, such as SCARLET RUNNER, RED KNIGHT, and PAINTED LADY. Experiment with a few each season; pole beans don't take up a lot of room, and the rewards are tasty.

BEETS

Beets were originally grown for their leaves, and if you've ever eaten them lightly steamed, then topped with a bit of lemon and butter, it should be no surprise why. The beets we grow today were all bred from "leaf beets" to provide a larger, sweeter root. At first, beets were long and thin, but over centuries of domestication, round roots were favored, and most of the common varieties today are both round and red. Nevertheless, there are still long, or carrot-rooted, beets available, as well as gold and white beets that are not only "color fast" (they don't bleed when cooked), but incredibly sweet. Ellen makes a great beet, *mâchè,* and onion salad, a traditional favorite from many years ago. It uses the non-bleeding Dutch white beet instead of a red variety and it looks as good as it tastes, a perfect example of using the right variety for the right dish.

Growing

Beets, like carrots, are best grown on "old land" that is well drained and well prepared, but not too rich.

A few seasons back, I went over to a friend's house, and in front was a new vegetable garden. It was a great spot for a garden—deep, rock-free river-bottom land. Walking past it, I couldn't help but notice a row of waist-high plants with strangely familiar leaves. "Oh, those are beets," said my friend when I asked. "They don't taste very good."

It turned out he had put a whole truckload of manure on the garden! Next to the beets, which were the size of cantaloupes, was a row of carrots. They too were waist high, with hairy roots the size of rolling pins. The root crops probably would have grown fine with no manure at all in that soil. If they had waited a year, after manuring, they would have had an exceptional garden.

We put beets in the third part of our rotation, so that the manure applied two falls ago has had a chance to turn into humus, a perfect source of the slow-release nutrients root vegetables need. We plant four rows of beets per bed: a row of small, quick-growing "baby beets" on both sides and a row each of the carrot-rooted pickling type and the mixed golden and white beets in the center, where foot traffic won't compact the soil and inhibit their growth. This proportion gives a good mix of beets and greens for the table.

Try to seed the beets as sparsely as you can. Even then, you'll have to thin the rows, as each beet seed is actually a fruit with up to eight seeds, each capable of growing into a mature plant. If you like, you can place the seeds individually in a 4-3-4 pattern, skip the thinning, and harvest a clump of beets from each spot.

For a super-early crop in spring, we use a variation of this method. We start beets indoors six to eight weeks before the last frost in a #162 tray, one seed to a cell, and transplant into the growing bed in a 4-3-4 layout a month before the last frost. We cover the bed with a floating row cover

immediately after setting the plants. Each cell planted will produce a small bunch of beets about 60 days after transplanting. Early varieties like REPLATA and CROSBY'S EGYPTIAN work best.

If you're going to harvest round types when they are still young, you need to thin your row-grown beets to only 2 or 3 inches apart. The long-rooted types can be grown to maturity at this spacing. Just thin as you harvest. For larger roots, increase the spacing, up to 6 inches apart.

After thinning, there is little to do but keep the beets cultivated, and watered if the weather is dry. Beets like consistent moisture, but alternating wet and dry periods will cause rings in the roots and can lead to cracking. If you have a very dry spell, get some water on them every week or two to keep them growing.

Keep an eye out for pests. Leaf miners, tiny insects that tunnel between the upper and lower leaf surfaces, can be a real problem because there is no good way to get at them once they're inside the leaf. Once an attack is under way, about the only way to control growth of the population is to strip off the infested leaves and burn them. In our garden, the leaf miners show up in the first week of June and attack our beets and chard. They're generally gone within the month.

We take a different approach to keeping them off each of these crops. With chard, we delay planting until June. This way, we get the crop in midsummer, when other greens are hard to come by, and the miners miss out on it. Our first beet crop, planted at the end of April, gets covered with a floating row cover after planting, and this keeps the parents of the leaf miners from laying their eggs on the plants.

Harvesting

Pick your beets when you're ready to use them. If baby beets for the crudité platter are your pleasure, harvest as soon as they begin to round out, and steam them lightly. If you're going to grate them for relish or to add to a salad, let them get a bit larger so they'll be easier to handle. Taste and texture are at their peak when the beets reach golf-ball size, although the white and golden varieties will stay relatively tender up to the size of a baseball.

The carrot-rooted beets will grow up out of the ground as they mature. To keep the crowns sweet and tender, either harvest just as they begin to emerge from the ground, or hill soil around them. They can get just as big as a normal main-crop carrot with no loss of quality.

Special beet varieties for baby beet production should be picked as soon as they fill out, at about the size of a Ping-Pong ball. Pick them even if they aren't perfect; most of the varieties used for baby beet production are early types, and they quickly become woody as they mature.

The Best Varieties

Our favorite for baby beets used to be LITTLE BALL, but after a few years of trials, we switched to a new Dutch variety called DWERGINA. The heirloom variety CROSBY'S EGYPTIAN (also known as FLAT EGYPTIAN and FLAT BLACK EGYPTIAN) works well for an early crop grown from transplants. This variety grows almost entirely on top of the ground and is very uniform when small, though it roughens as it matures.

REPLATA also grows well from transplants, but it can be left to mature an additional month or so beyond the "baby" stage as a standard table beet. This is a valuable trait because it lets you stretch the harvest from a single planting.

For salad beets that won't bleed onto your other ingredients, there are really only two good varieties that we know of: BURPEE'S GOLDEN and ALBINA VEREDUNA. Seed for golden beets is readily available, but the plants are not as widely grown as they should be. While these varieties are weak germinators, they are well worth growing. Golden beets have exceptionally fine tops with golden ribs on smooth leaves that can be used directly in the salad when young or for color in a mix of steamed greens. The roots are a beautiful, deep golden color, fine-textured and very sweet. Because the roots don't bleed, these beets are ideal for an accent dish, and they can be grated over other dishes as a finishing touch.

ALBINA VEREDUNA beets are not so boldly colored, and they are best used where beet taste is needed without either the deep color of standard red beets or the bright color of the golden beet. They're very sweet and fine textured, particularly when harvested young. The greens are also good in salads or steamed like Swiss chard. I've seen SNOW WHITE, ALBINO WHITE, and ALBINA VEREDUNA listed as separate varieties, but the differences are minimal.

The carrot-rooted beets available today are all closely related. The first of

VARIETY SOURCE CHART

BEETS

Variety	When to Plant	When to Harvest	What to Harvest	Comments	Sources*
ALBINA VEREDUNA (ALBINO WHITE, SNOW WHITE)	ASAP in spring in succession	When roots are 1″–3″ in diameter	Roots and leaves	Roots top-shaped, sweet; true albino beet; will not bleed when cut or cooked	ST/CG/ TM/SB
BURPEE'S GOLDEN	ASAP in spring in succession	When roots are 1″–3″ in diameter	Roots and leaves	Roots globe-shaped or top-shaped; good tasting and sweet; will not bleed when cut or cooked	Widely Available
DWERGINA	ASAP in spring in succession	When roots are 1″–3″ in diameter	Roots	Roots globe-shaped; good for baby beets, but can be left to mature	JS/CG
FORMANOVA (CYLINDRA)	ASAP in spring in succession	When roots reach ½″ in diameter	Roots	Long, cylindrical roots (to 2″ × 6″); yields uniform slices over full length	Widely available
LITTLE BALL	ASAP in spring in succession	When roots reach 1″ in diameter	Roots	Roots globe-shaped; quick-growing variety for baby beets; harvest early	ST/SS/ WD/SB/ BP/PT
LONG SEASON	90 days before first frost	Before killing frost	Roots	Large, top-shaped beets stay tender even at maturity; good for storing	ST/CG/ HM/SB
MACGREGOR'S FAVORITE	ASAP in spring in succession	Once tops reach 6″ in length	Roots and leaves	Grown primarily for beautiful, deep purple, lancelike leaves; roots sweet, too.	CG/NG
REPLATA/ CROSBY'S EGYPTIAN	ASAP in spring	When roots reach 1″ in diameter	Roots	Roots flat to globe-shaped; sow in flats or plugs in early spring for early crop	CG

*Listings correspond to seed companies included under Seed Source List at the back of the book.

these to be available in this country in recent years was CYLINDRA, and many seed houses still list it. A few years ago, however, an improved strain called FORMANOVA was developed and has replaced CYLINDRA in many listings. For the home gardener, the difference may be academic. This long-rooted beet actually has many antecedents (a half-dozen long, red varieties are listed in *The Vegetable Garden,* a book published in 1885). In general, this type of beet is very sweet and has good texture. Perhaps its most important characteristic is that it slices uniformly (due to its cylindrical shape), and it is easier to peel after cooking than a regular beet. Once the crown is cut off, it slips out of its skin with just a slight squeeze at the root end.

One last favorite we would recommend is LONG SEASON. This is a late variety, and though it grows to incredible proportions, it never loses its sweet flavor and fine texture. We've had beets that weighed in at 4 pounds, but were as sweet as a baby.

A few seasons ago, we got an emergency call from one of the restaurants we supply, asking for a case of beets. We sent them eight LONG SEASON beets, which without the tops weighed in at 20 pounds.

Twenty minutes later we got an irate call from the chef, who wasn't expecting such large beets. "Try them," I said. "If you don't like them, we won't bill you." The next day the chef called back, not to complain but to order more of the beets. "I can't believe it," he said. "We got 44 meals out of eight beets, and it only took about 15 minutes to prepare them." Now he takes a case a week.

BROCCOLI AND CAULIFLOWER

Broccoli and cauliflower were both selected from their ancestor, the wild cabbage, for the production of flowering shoots. In fact, the term broccoli—coined by Italian gardeners—originally applied to flowering shoots of the whole family. Now, because selective breeding has emphasized their differences, we know them as different crops.

Basically, there are two kinds of broccoli: the heading types and the sprouting types. The heading types, which form a large central head, are relatively recent developments, and most of the currently popular American varieties are Japanese hybrids. Sprouting broccoli, instead of forming a large mass of florets at the end of the plant's terminal shoot, form many smaller shoots that rise from the leaf axils (like brussels sprouts). There are green, purple, and white forms of sprouting broccoli, though only the green is well known here at present.

To the Italians, the distinction between cauliflower and broccoli was originally one of color. If it was white, they called it cauliflower, and if it was colored, it was broccoli. Cauliflower is the most demanding member of the cabbage family. It is more high-strung and prone to failure if stressed, so you've got to be careful about keeping it cool, well fed, well watered, and well drained. It is no coincidence that some of the best cauliflower is grown in the mild, ocean-tempered climate of Long Island.

Growing

The key to quality crops—for this whole family of plants—is quick growth, without checks or stress. The ground should be fertile and well prepared. Moisture should be abundant but the drainage free, so that the roots won't be sitting in water. We put out our broccoli and cauliflower in beds that were manured the previous fall and then cover-cropped to hold down weeds.

We use annual ryegrass for a winter cover and buckwheat for a summer one. Both of these are vigorous plants that will choke out weeds and provide a lot of organic matter when turned under. You should ask your county extension agent what cover crops are best for your area, though, as each region of the country is different. Even after the broccoli and cauliflower are established, don't allow weeds to get into the bed. The roots of all brassica plants are relatively shallow, and pulling large weeds nearby can disturb them and check the growth of the plants.

If you buy your seedlings at a local garden center, be sure to avoid plants with thick stems and short petioles (leaf stems). Those are signs that the transplants were crowded, subjected to cold growing conditions, or didn't get enough nitrogen, all of which will lead to "buttoning," the formation of tiny, premature heads. Young broccoli and cauliflower are quite hardy, but once they reach the four- or five-leaf stage, as little as a week of temperatures below 40°F can trigger buttoning. Many cauliflower varieties will not head at all if the temperature is below 44°F, and can be permanently damaged by temperatures in the mid-twenties.

To get plants that are well along into the garden yet avoid cold stress and the damage of flea beetles, we start our plants in #162 trays four to six weeks before the frost-free date. This gets them into the ground just as the weather settles down. We cover the beds with a floating row cover immediately after transplanting. With proper timing the plants will have a chance to establish themselves before any weeding is necessary. In our garden we set transplants out around the first of May, cover them, and let them grow until mid-June. We then remove the covers and give the bed a thorough weeding.

The floating row covers also protect newly set transplants from root maggots. In our garden, the parent generation of the maggot—a fly resembling the common housefly—is only around until the middle of May. Plants set out after that time are rarely bothered. This pest seems to attack any member of the mustard family, but is especially drawn to broccoli.

Intensive gardeners can set the plants 18 inches on center, which means that a 2:1:2 layout (described in Part I) will work with a 3-foot bed. Make sure your soil is fertile if you are going to put in this many plants. Brassicas are prime candidates for interplanting because of their size. When first set out, they may need a space only 6 inches across, but by harvest time, the largest will be almost 2 feet across. This extra space can be used to grow another, quicker maturing crop.

Most cole crops can be direct seeded in the garden, sowing the seed ¼ inch deep in rows 18 to 36 inches apart (depending on whether you will have a path between the rows). For a spring crop in cool climates, seed about 3 weeks before the frost-free date. For a fall crop, seed 10 to 12 weeks before the first fall frosts. Overwintering crops in mild areas should be timed to reach about 4 to 6 inches tall before winter sets in; larger plants are more likely to run to seed in spring before producing a head.

The major pest and disease problems with cole crops are flea beetles, root maggots, cabbageworms, and a disease called club root. They are also sometimes attacked by cutworms, aphids, and slugs (but then, so is almost every other vegetable!).

Cabbageworms are the caterpillar form of the small white butterfly seen flitting above the garden in midsummer. When Shepherd was a child, he and his friends swatted the butterflies with old tennis rackets in his grandfather's market garden for a nickel apiece. Having them on the payroll worked wonders, but they also handpicked any eggs and worms they saw. Handpicking is still effective, but so is *Bacillus thuringiensis* (Bt), a naturally occurring bacterium that infects and kills many kinds of soft-bodied caterpillars. Bt is commercially cultured and is available in both liquid and powdered form under a number of different trade names, including Dipel and Thuricide.

It is important to apply Bt when you first see the worms, because the bacteria require three or four days to do their work, and the caterpillars do a lot of damage before they lose their appetite. Reapply BT every seven to ten days if the butterflies are still laying eggs.

Club root is caused by a soil-borne fungus, and is best dealt with by maintaining a strict rotation plan so that no member of the cabbage family is planted in the same soil more than once in four years. The disease is favored by soil with a low pH, so adding lime to acid soils—to get the soil up to the neutral point—may help.

Harvesting

Harvest heading broccoli before the florets show any sign of opening. Even a peek of yellow from within the floret or a loosening of the many small buds is a sure sign that the moment has arrived. Cut the stems about 4 inches below the base of the floret, leaving the rest of the plant to produce new shoots. Most of the new, central-heading types are best removed from the garden after harvest and replaced by another crop.

Sprouting broccoli (and some of the older heading types) will continue to produce over a long season if cut just below the floret. This stimulates the formation of new shoots. Most of the sprouting types are fully hardy to U.S. Department of Agriculture (USDA) Zone 6, and can be grown right through the winter in warm-winter climates.

Cauliflower should be harvested after the head is fully formed, but before the "curds" begin to separate and resemble grains of rice. As a rule of thumb, wait until the heads reach at least 6 inches in diameter. Cut below the head with a sharp knife, leaving enough of the wrapper leaves to protect the head from breaking.

The Best Varieties of Broccoli

Heading Types

The heading broccolis, as noted previously, are one of the two kinds of broccoli. Most popular in America are Japanese hybrid varieties of heading broccoli. Very uniform, these new hybrids produce single heads of up to 9 inches across on the plant's terminal shoot.

Some notable varieties of this type are PREMIUM CROP, CRUISER, EMPEROR, and GREEN COMET. This last will produce a good crop of cut-and-come-again secondary shoots after the central head is cut, a characteristic also of most of the earlier, nonhybrid, heading broccoli varieties like the WALTHAM strains. The varieties DE CICCO and ITALIAN GREEN SPROUTING are even closer to the original sprouting types, and whereas they don't produce a very large head, they will continue to produce side shoots over a very long period.

At the other end of the spectrum of heading broccoli are a couple of intermediate varieties more closely related to cauliflowers. These are not widely grown in this country, but deserve a place in just about every garden for both their beauty and their yield of fine-tasting spears. The taste has a bit more depth than that of cauliflower, but less "greenness" than broccoli, and the texture is midway between the two. The best of these is ROMANESCO. It forms a large central head, but is otherwise totally unlike common broccoli, both in form and color. The large chartreuse heads resemble the ascending spiral of a conch shell, with each individual floret made of tightly closed flowers in this same arrangement. The overall effect is striking. Seen from above, the spirals of florets interweave like ripples in a quiet pool.

ROMANESCO *broccoli*

ROMANESCO is a long-season plant, grown over the winter in Italy and California. In areas colder than USDA Zone 6, it should be started indoors in flats during April to be set out after the hard frosts of spring. As with all the broccoli

BROCCOLI AND CAULIFLOWER

Variety	When to Plant	When to Harvest	What to Harvest	Comments	Sources*
Broccoli					
BRONZINO (D'ALBENGA)	Midspring	Early fall, before heads flower	Central heads	Similar to ROMANESCO but earlier; does not "head" as reliably	CG
CALABRESE (CALABRIA, ITALIAN GREEN SPROUTING)	Midspring	Summer (60 days from transplant)	Central heads and side shoots	Open-pollinated	ST/CG
CRUISER HYBRID	Midspring	Summer (58 days from transplant)	Central heads	Tolerant of wet conditions	VB/ST
DE CICCO	Midspring	Summer (60 days from transplant)	Side shoots	Cut head when small, then side shoots will grow	HP/JS/LM
EMPEROR HYBRID	Midspring	Summer (58 days from transplant)	Central heads	More side shoots than other central heading hybrids	ST/JS
GREEN COMET HYBRID	Midspring	Summer (55 days from transplant)	Central heads and side shoots	Produces lots of side shoots after main head is cut	HP/TM/BP/VB/PT
PREMIUM CROP HYBRID	Midspring	Summer (82 days from transplant)	Central heads	Cut before flowering few side shoots	Widely available
PURPLE SPROUTING	Midspring	Fall/winter	Side shoots	Hardier than other broccoli; has no central head; cut-and-come-again	CG/TM/LM
ROMANESCO	Midspring	Late fall	Large central heads	Very late variety; beautiful, with rich broccoli taste	CG/SB/SS/LM/AL
WHITE SPROUTING	Midspring	Fall/winter	Side shoots	Similar to PURPLE SPROUTING but with creamy white sprouts. Has no central head.	CG/SB/TM/LM

(continued)

VARIETY SOURCE CHART—*Continued*

BROCCOLI AND CAULIFLOWER

Variety	When to Plant	When to Harvest	What to Harvest	Comments	Sources*
Broccoli Raab					
QUARANTINA HYBRID	Spring	2 months after planting	Small plants with sprouts	More uniform and productive than old kinds; strong flavor	CG
SPRING RAAB (RAPINE)	Spring	2 months after planting	Small plants with sprouts	Strong flavor; raab is actually a turnip, not a broccoli!	Widely available
Cauliflower					
ALERT HYBRID	Early spring/ midsummer	Early summer/ early fall	Central heads	Good for succession with SNOW CROWN	ST
ANDES HYBRID	Early spring/ midsummer	Early summer/ early fall	Central heads	Good heat and cold tolerance; does not need tying to blanch	ST/JS/ TM
SICILIAN VIOLET	Spring	Fall (80-90 days)	Central heads	Fine curds, cream to purple color; old Italian heirloom type	CG/LM
SNOW CROWN HYBRID	Early spring/ midsummer	Late spring or fall	Central heads	Widely adapted home garden hybrid; relatively easy to grow; blanch before harvest	Widely available
VIOLET QUEEN HYBRID	Early spring/ midsummer	Late spring or fall	Central heads	Deep purple head resembles broccoli more than cauliflower	CG/JS/ SB

*Listings correspond to seed companies included under Seed Source List at the back of the book.

planted during the egg-laying season of the cabbage maggot fly, we cover the bed immediately after transplanting with a floating row cover. You can also discourage this pest by sprinkling wood ash around the base of the plants to kill the eggs, or by placing tar paper collars around the plants to prevent the fly from laying. The cover accomplishes this aim just as well, and also gives the plants a bit of protection from the irregular spring weather and the damage of flea beetles.

Treat ROMANESCO just like brussels sprouts, which have a similar growth period and habit. Allow at least 2 feet between plants, and keep the bed well cultivated and watered throughout the season. You can harvest the heads at any stage, but be sure to pick them before they begin to flower. You can also pick the florets one by one, but the heads are so spectacular, it's a shame to do so. At our produce stand, ROMANESCO is in demand as much for the crudité platter as for the plate, because it tastes just as good raw as cooked.

There is an earlier and slightly smaller strain called BRONZINO or D'ALBENGA. Its coloring tends more toward yellow or bronze, and we have found it to be a bit less consistent in form and more likely to deteriorate when stressed. Its earliness may be important in short-season areas where even spring plantings of ROMANESCO will not be ready until late fall. A hard freeze can ruin the crop, because these broccoli are not nearly as hardy as brussels sprouts.

Sprouting Types

Instead of forming a large mass of florets at the end of the plant's terminal shoot, sprouting broccoli forms many smaller shoots that rise from the leaf axils, like brussels sprouts. There are green, purple, and white forms of sprouting broccoli. Only the green is well known here at present, under the name CALABRESE or CALABRIA. You also can find PURPLE SPROUTING and WHITE SPROUTING varieties.

Sprouting broccoli is easy to grow in mild climates. Planted in early fall, it grows slowly over the winter months, then begins

to produce a multitude of flowering shoots as spring unfolds. It will continue to produce sprouts over a long period if kept cut. As with regular broccoli, it should be harvested before the florets show any sign of opening. Any peek of yellow from within the floret or loosening of the many small buds is a sign to harvest immediately. Cut off the stems about 4 inches below the base of the floret, leaving the rest of the plant to produce new shoots.

In cold climates, seed sprouting broccoli indoors in spring and set out as early as the ground can be worked. As with the other members of the cabbage family, it should be covered with an insect barrier if the cabbage fly is about. We put floating row covers over all brassicas transplanted before May 15.

Broccoli Raab

A member of the mustard family that is often mistaken for broccoli is spring raab, or rapini. It is not really a broccoli at all, but was selected from turnips (also a cabbage relative) for its shoots and flowers. Although the sprouts do resemble small heads of broccoli, the gardener who grows it will find soon enough that it does not hold long in the garden, but bolts to seed and then is useless.

Raab should be direct seeded in rows 8 inches on center in spring or fall for a quick crop of small florets (with the few small leaves that surround the sprout). It is steamed in the same fashion as kale. The Italians are also responsible for this vegetable, and they have many kinds. A good variety is QUARANTINA. Other strains are available on seed racks and in a number of catalogs simply as SPRING RAAB or RAPINE.

The Best Varieties of Cauliflower

There are two types of cauliflower: white and purple. Most everybody knows white cauliflower, but the purple types aren't yet widely grown. The latter taste more like broccoli when the plants are young, but once a frost or two touches them, their flavor changes, and they begin to taste like the familiar white cauliflower.

White Cauliflower

We've had good luck with SNOW CROWN, a hybrid that can withstand temperatures down to 20°F and still form a good head. Some other good candidates are ANDES, which has shown good adaption to both spring and fall cropping areas, and ALERT, one of the self-blanching types, where the leaves grow upright and shade the heads so the curds stay white and tender.

With cauliflowers, it's always best if you can find one that is especially well adapted to growing conditions in your region. Check with local nurseries, or try to find a seed company that specializes in varieties for your area. You'll be surprised at how many regional seed catalogs there are out there. Your local extension agent should be able to help you find one.

Purple Cauliflower

Purple cauliflower can be thought of as heading purple broccoli. This is especially true of the newer, hybrid varieties, which have a central heart of purple florets on green stems that open yellow as they flower, just like broccoli. The older forms, such as SICILIAN VIOLET, more closely resemble traditional cauliflower, though with a golden violet cast to the fine-textured curds. The texture is similar to Romanesco broccoli, but without the spiral form. Planting for this variety should be timed so that it matures during cool, but not frosty, weather. We grow it as an early crop here because our fall weather tends to be unreliable. It does not need blanching.

The new hybrid purple cauliflowers are grown like broccoli and thus do not need blanching. The major difference from regular broccoli is in the color, which makes them excellent for eating raw as a crudité. (If cooked for more than a couple of minutes, the spears will turn green, which is a good key for home processors—when the spears change color, they have been cooked long enough to kill spoilage bacteria.) One of the best of these hybrids is VIOLET QUEEN, which has a broccoli-like flavor and is relatively pest and disease resistant.

BRUSSELS SPROUTS

*I*t's unclear exactly how brussels sprouts came into cultivation. They grow like collards but form small, cabbagelike heads at each leaf axil (the spot where the leaf joins the stem). The gardener who first noticed this tendency and began to save plants with tightened and more numerous sprouts is unknown, but the plant we now call brussels sprouts is testimony to his plant-breeding skills.

Growing

Brussels sprouts are generally started a little later than other members of the cabbage family because the touch of the first fall frost seems to improve the flavor so much. If the plants mature before frost, the sprouts will be loose and bitter. We set our brussels sprouts closer than normal—a foot and a half apart—because we think crowding the plants helps keep the sprouts tight.

You need to keep the weeds at bay, but otherwise, once the plants are established, they can pretty much take care of themselves. Keep an eye out for flea beetles right after the sprouts are transplanted, as they can really set the plants back. A few weeks before the first frost, remove all the leaves that have partially formed sprouts at their base.

VARIETY SOURCE CHART

BRUSSELS SPROUTS

Variety	When to Plant	When to Harvest	What to Harvest	Comments	Sources*
DOLMIC HYBRID	Spring	Fall (best after frost)	Small heads in leaf axils	Early hybrid oval sprouts easier to pick than dwarf types	ST/CG
JADE CROSS	Spring	Fall (best after frost)	Small heads in leaf axils	Hardy dwarf type; flavor not as good as tall kinds	Widely available
LONG ISLAND IMPROVED	Spring	Fall (best after frost)	Small heads in leaf axils	Open-pollinated variety	HP/ST/PT
OLIVER HYBRID	Spring	Fall (best after frost)	Small heads in leaf axils	Very early (90 days from transplant)	BP/JS
RUBINE	Early spring	Late fall	Small heads in leaf axils	Very late, large variety with red sprouts	CG/SB/WD
STIEKEMA	Spring	Fall (best after frost)	Small heads in leaf axils	Tall variety with teardrop-shaped heads; good flavor	WD/SB

*Listings correspond to seed companies included under Seed Source List at the back of the book.

Harvesting

The best way to control maturity is topping the plants. If you cut the top 6 inches off the plant four to six weeks before your anticipated harvest date, all the sprouts will mature uniformly, and they'll store better.

If you want to pick your sprouts a few at a time over a long period, leave the tops on. A hormone secreted at the tip of the plant will inhibit maturity of the sprouts nearest it, stretching your harvest over the longest possible time.

The Best Varieties

There are two types of brussels sprouts—a tall kind with small, teardrop-shaped sprouts spread out along the stem, and a dwarf type that bears larger, rounder, and more closely packed sprouts. Tradition has it that the tall varieties have better flavor. The dwarf types are earlier, however.

The standard varieties JADE CROSS and LONG ISLAND IMPROVED are widely available dwarf types. LUNET is one of the first of the new, tall European hybrids to become available in this country, and we have had great luck with it. DOLMIC is similar, but two weeks earlier. Two other good varieties are OLIVER, an extra early hybrid, and RUBINE, a very late variety with deep red sprouts that look like miniature red cabbages.

CABBAGES

*T*he cabbage family stands as one of the greatest tributes to gardeners in the plant world. Almost all the common garden members of this family—cabbage, broccoli, cauliflower, brussels sprouts, kale, and kohlrabi—are descendents of a single species, *Brassica oleracea*, which is a ragged-looking wild cabbage native to Europe and Asia. Through centuries of selection, gardeners took that single plant and gave expression to each of its characteristics, developing separate vegetables that accentuated its leaves, its flowers, even its stem. The vision that guided the long process of domestication has been handed down through generations of gardeners, along with the seed that each spring since pre-

history has been planted and cared for, then harvested so the cycle could continue.

It is characteristic of cabbage family members that as the plants grow, the petioles, or stems of new leaves, get shorter and shorter. Cabbages themselves were selected for later leaves that fold inward and a petiole that shrinks to almost nothing. The combination of these two traits causes cabbages to form their familiar heads.

Growing

The ancestor of our modern cabbages was a seaside plant, and to this day the garden version likes cool, moist conditions. What this means for the home gardener—

whatever the climate—is that plantings should be timed to mature during cool weather. Head formation is the critical period and hot weather or other stress at that time can lead to a radical drop in the quality of the harvest. Here in the North, we can grow cabbage in the summer, but in warmer climates it usually does best as either a spring or fall crop. In the South and frost-free areas of California, cabbage is grown as a winter crop.

We plant our cabbages in beds that were manured the previous fall, so the soil will be rich but not too rank. Some nitro-

VARIETY SOURCE CHART

CABBAGES

Variety	When to Plant	When to Harvest	What to Harvest	Comments	Sources*
EARLY JERSEY WAKEFIELD	Spring	Summer (about 60 days)	Conical heads	Very early; small; good flavor; good for intensive gardens	VB/CG/HM
RED ACRE	Spring	Summer (76 days from transplant)	Heads	Open-pollinated red variety	HP/BP
RUBY BALL HYBRID	Spring	Summer (about 70 days)	Heads	Widely adapted and easily grown; red with good flavor	Widely available
SALARITE	Spring	Summer (about 60 days)	Loose heads	Salad type; small; good flavor; good for intensive gardens	ST/CG
SAVOY KING HYBRID (QUINTAL D'ALSACE)	Spring	Summer (about 80 days)	Curly heads	Very high yielding	HP/TM
SHAMROCK	Spring	Summer (9-10 weeks	Heads	Large heads hold well without splitting; sweet and juicy	TM/CG
SPIVOY HYBRID	Spring	Summer or fall (about 90 days)	Conical heads	Small, conical savoy type; good for intensive gardens	TM/CG/PK

*Listings correspond to seed companies included under Seed Source List at the back of the book.

gen is necessary for good yields and quality, but too much can cause the heads to split. It won't do any good to try and make up for an early lack by feeding the plants just as they mature. A lot of the nutrients used for that last growth don't come from the roots, but rather from nutrients captured earlier in the season and stored in the plant. Rich, well-drained soil high in organic matter is the best assurance of good results.

Crowding will lower the average head size, but where soil fertility is adequate, it will increase overall yields. It will also increase the compounds that give cabbage its characteristic flavor. Whether this is desirable is a matter of personal taste.

Harvesting

Cabbages can be harvested anytime after the heads have formed and are hard and solid to the touch. To harvest, cut the heads off just above the root crown with a sharp knife. The base may resprout with five or six little buds, and if you remove all but one, it will develop into a small head. We prefer to pull the plants and start another crop.

The Best Varieties

Early spring cabbages are relatively mild, as are all red cabbages; late green storage types and savoy cabbages are the strongest in flavor.

Our favorite for taste is EARLY JERSEY WAKEFIELD, a very early cabbage that forms small, pointed heads. This is a very old variety that has stood the test of time. The 2- to 3-pound heads can grow as close as a foot apart in intensive gardens and will produce an enormous amount of very tasty eating in only a little more than two months.

For red cabbage, our favorites are RUBY BALL and RED ACRE, two red varieties. They're very similar, but RED ACRE is a little later and larger. A good early green with succulent leaves and a broad habit is SALARITE. One of the earliest cabbages, it has excellent flavor fresh or steamed. An early, small savoy hybrid with a pointed head is called SPIVOY. It can be planted closely and matures early, yet it holds well after maturing, so you can extend the harvest over a longer period. For a later, larger savoy cabbage, try SAVOY KING, or QUINTAL D'ALSACE.

CARROTS

Carrots have been cultivated for nearly 1,000 years. The earliest carrots were as purple as beets, due to the presence of anthocyanin, the compound responsible for the red or violet coloring of beets, lettuce, and beans. Once early gardeners had bred the purple color out of carrots, the roots were yellow; you still see an occasional yellow root in just about any planting of carrots, a genetic reversion to the carrot's ancestry. About 400 years ago, the Dutch began breeding the orange carrot we know, and over time developed four basic types: Early Scarlet Horn, which still survives as a variety, Early Half Long, Late Half Long, and Long Orange. All of today's common carrot varieties are descendants of these four types.

We like our carrots sweet. Sweetness varies with variety, stage of maturity, climate, and soil. But flavor in carrots is a double-edged sword. The "carroty" taste derives from substances that, in excess, yield a harsh or bitter taste. Like the effect of salt on a meal, too little of these substances makes a carrot bland, and too much will cause a resinous taste.

The texture of carrots is simpler. It's natural for a carrot to have a tender outer layer of flesh surrounding a tough and fibrous core. Although most people want their carrots crisp, they don't want them to be fibrous. For generations, breeders have sought to get rid of the tough core. A good carrot is also expected to have a thin, smooth skin, free of hairs and wrinkles so that it is easy to clean and doesn't need peeling. Carrots like this are hard to find, except in your own garden.

Growing

Carrots are among the most productive crops per square foot of garden space that you can grow, and as long as their basic needs are met, one of the easiest. Carrot seedlings are not strong enough to force their way through compacted or rocky soil; roots will be stunted in compacted soil and will grow crooked or forked if the soil is rocky.

Unless you are lucky enough to have a foot of loose, mellow topsoil in your garden, both the yield and quality of your carrot harvest will be improved by making a raised bed for them. See Part I for details. Scrape up loose soil from the pathways to gain the added depth you need to grow long, smooth carrots.

We seed five rows of carrots in each 3-foot-wide bed. Mix radish seed with the carrot seed before sowing (we use about 30 percent by volume). The radishes germinate quickly, loosening the soil so the carrots don't have any trouble breaking the surface. The emerging radishes mark the row, too, so we can cultivate even before the carrots are up. When we harvest the radishes, we pull up enough carrots along with them to thin the carrot rows. Carrots are usually sown thickly to guarantee a good stand, but with the help of the radishes, you can sow them a lot more thinly and save yourself some trouble.

Because walking on the garden paths causes soil compaction, we plant round or short carrots on the edges of the bed. Their small size means they don't need a deep soil to develop, so we save the loose center of the bed for longer varieties. Plant the edge rows first, and it will be easier to keep the spacing of all five rows more consistent. Regular spacing of the rows is important to ease of cultivation later on.

Next, plant a row of baby carrots on each side of the round carrots. Baby carrots are mature when they are 4 to 6 inches long, and are perfectly cylindrical. These kinds are bred to be very sweet, and they develop their color and flavor early. That is what distinguishes them from main crop varieties, which should be left to mature for the best quality.

The center rows are planted to a main crop variety, which can grow to full size in the soft soil there. In our garden, however, they often get pulled before they mature because the customers at our stand, used to supermarket produce, can't get enough of this supposedly unglamorous vegetable. Carrots are one of the secret performers in our market garden and rank only behind lettuce and maybe radicchio as what used to be called "mortgage burners"—crops that produce a lot of very salable produce in a very small space.

Cultivate as soon as the radishes are up. We use the narrowest of our stirrup hoes (described in Part I) for this, though any hoes from 3 to 5 inches wide can be used. You can make quick work of the job if the rows are straight and evenly spaced.

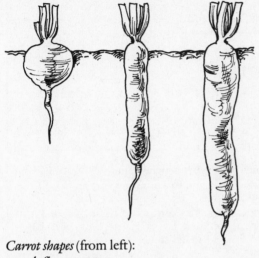

Carrot shapes (from left):
round, finger, mature

I hold the hoe along my left side (being right-handed), with my left hand down as low as I can reach on the handle and my right hand, palm up, pulling the handle toward me against the pivot of my left hand. I walk the length of the bed with the hoe dragging between the two outside rows on the near side. When I reach the end of the bed, I come back down the other side and do the same thing. It takes six passes to do the whole bed: four between rows, then once along the two outside edges. Here I use a wider hoe (7 inches) to clean up behind my footsteps.

Pest control for our carrot crop has been limited to picking occasional parsleyworms off the tops and keeping the carrot rust fly from laying eggs. This second pest looks something like a housefly, and it lays its eggs at the base of the plants in early spring; they hatch into larvae that bore into the roots, ruining them. In our garden, they bother only the early crops, planted before May 15. We used to postpone planting until that date, but we now control this pest by putting down a floating row cover immediately after seeding. We secure it well along the edges and leave it on until it is time to harvest the radishes. We then weed and cultivate thoroughly. Once the radishes are gone, we cultivate regularly until the carrots close over the row.

Harvesting

Instead of thinning our carrots, we prefer to harvest them. Varieties that color-up early are usable as soon as they reach the size of your little finger. Crowding is not a problem if they are sown thinly along with radishes. Carrots should be harvested young for the best texture and taste. As soon as they start to develop their mature color and shape, you can begin to use the thinnings. The best baby carrots are usually the forcing, pickling, and canning types; look for references to this in the name of the variety or its description. Once again, don't worry about lowering overall yields; if the crop is harvested early, you have time for more successions. This means you plant more, but take care of each crop for less time; you will be better off having 10 pounds of something that tastes good than 12 pounds of something that is only so-so.

The Best Varieties

For round carrots, we use PLANET. They are ready to harvest as soon as they reach the size of a marble but will get to

VARIETY SOURCE CHART

CARROTS

Variety	When to Plant	When to Harvest	What to Harvest	Comments	Sources*
A-PLUS HYBRID	As soon as ground can be worked	When roots reach 7" long	Long, tapered orange roots	Extra high vitamin A content	JS/PT/ ST/BP
MINICOR	ASAP in spring in succession	Once roots color-up	Cylindrical roots up to 1" × 6"	Very early to get color and flavor; Try FINCOR in dry areas	JS/ST/ CG/LM
MOKUM HYBRID	ASAP in spring in succession	Once roots color-up	Tapered roots, 4"–8" at maturity	Very high-quality roots; tops detach easily, so dig up roots	CG/TM
PARIS MARKET (EARLY FRENCH FRAME)	ASAP in spring	When roots reach 1" diameter	Round orange roots	—	LM
PARMEX HYBRID	ASAP in spring in succession	Once roots color-up	Round roots, 1"–2" in diameter	Hybrid round PLANET type; good for crudités, stews, and pickling	JS
PLANET	ASAP in spring in succession	Once roots color-up	Round roots, 1"–2" in diameter	Good for shallow soils; use for crudités, stews, and pickling	ST/CG/ SS/SB
RONDINO HYBRID	ASAP in spring in succession	Once roots color-up	Cylindrical roots, 6"–8" long	Very uniform; stores well; stronger tops than MOKUM	JS
TOUCHON	ASAP in spring in succession	Once roots color-up	Slightly tapered roots, 6"– 10" long	Open-pollinated NANTES type with good color and flavor	CG/LM/ ST/SB/ NG

*Listings correspond to seed companies included under Seed Source List at the back of the book.

the size of a golf ball without losing their sweetness (though they will get tougher). The ideal is to harvest once they have lost all the taper in the root and it has receded into the bottom of the carrot; at this point it should be about the size of a cherry tomato. Other good-tasting round carrots are PARIS MARKET and PARMEX, a new

Dutch variety. EARLY FRENCH FRAME is not round, but it is short enough to be suitable for shallow soils or even containers.

Our "finger" carrots are MOKUM and MINICOR. We did tests of about a dozen baby varieties and found these to be the favorites of the kids who came by our produce stand. The carrot trial beds were right behind our produce stand, and while their parents were shopping, we'd take the kids around back and let them taste as many as they liked. They loved being part of the flavor trials, and by the end of the summer, we had a good idea which carrots were tastiest.

Our main-crop carrot is TOUCHON. It is fine flavored and crisp, even if harvested early, but it can grow to full maturity without losing its quality. Two other good main-crop carrots, renowned for their taste and texture, are RONDINO and A-PLUS. The latter is a new hybrid with high sugar and vitamin A content.

CHICORY

*C*hicory is a crop that's been grown in this country for a very long time. The chicory you see growing wild by the side of the road "escaped" from colonial gardens and is now fully at home in North America. It is a variety of *Cichorium intybus,* a perennial species that includes virtually every kind of chicory grown for consumption except the endives and escaroles. The latter are varieties of *Cichorium indivia,* a leafy biennial, somewhat resembling lettuce. Thus all the garden chicories belong to two closely related species. Though chicory has been cultivated for centuries, only recently have breeders begun to release varieties that are free of the limitations that prevented this large group of salad plants from being more widely grown.

From a gardener's perspective, there are several types of chicory. All are cool-weather crops, but each type has slightly different needs. Endive and escarole are grown much like lettuce, but the three types of perennial chicory—Belgian endive (or forcing chicory), spring cutting chicory, and rosette chicory, and the red and green heading types known as radicchio—require different treatment.

Endive

Endive—known also these days as "frisee" (pronounced free-zay)—has deeply cut, feathery foliage; escarole has broad leaves, like lettuce. The only difference between them is leaf shape. We'll use the word endive for both.

Growing

These are bitter plants by nature. What you want is a head that has only a hint of bitterness—a taste that's cleansing, not biting—and the way to get that is to make sure that your plants mature during cool weather.

In very mild climates endive is grown as a winter crop. Northern gardeners have to try to grow a crop in spring or fall, between the extreme hot and the extreme cold. Because our spring weather is very unreliable, we start our endive in #162 plugs in mid-March and set them out with the first lettuce as soon as the ground can be worked (usually around April 15). A floating row cover gives them just enough protection from the last hard frosts of spring. Heads are ready to blanch by the time temperatures climb into the eighties. Where spring is friendlier, you can direct seed ¼ to ½ inch deep in rows 8 to 12 inches apart as soon as the ground can be worked. Growing from seed to table will require at least two months, plus a week or two for blanching (see Part I).

For the fall crop, we seed in mid-June so the heads mature shortly after Labor Day. Light frost while the heads are blanching isn't a problem, but a hard frost will ruin them. Count back ten weeks from the average date of your first fall frost to schedule your planting.

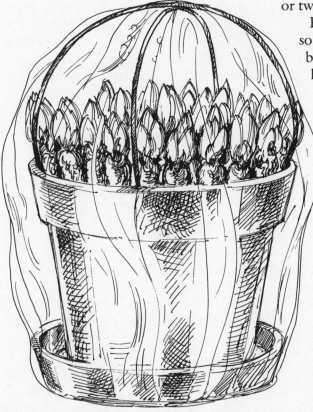

Belgian endive being forced in pot, covered with plastic

Harvesting

Endive is blanched for a week to ten days before harvest to lessen its natural bitterness. When the heads are full, gather up the leaves in one hand and put a wide rubber band, twist tie, or strip of cloth around the bunch about halfway up. If you have a large enough flower pot you can just place it over the entire head. Be sure the head is dry at the start, though, or it may rot.

The Best Varieties

One of our favorite varieties is called RICCIUTISSIMA or FINE CURLED ("Ricci" means curly, and "tissima" means very much so). Three other of the traditional varieties are DE MEAUX, an old variety for hot climates, DE RUFFEC, which tolerates cold, wet conditions, and PANACLIERE, which has a cream-colored—not white—heart after blanching, with a hint of red in the leaf veins. Newer introductions of each type are generally not as fine leaved, but are better adapted to different climates and growing schedules.

When a new type is developed it usually has some shred of the ancestor variety's name included within its own, so you can get some idea of its general characteristics even before you've planted it. A good example is the old and widely grown variety, RONDE VERTE A COEUR PLEIN, which translates as "round green full heart." Today, seed catalogs overflow with variations of this one variety, all traceable to it through their names: BATAVIAN FULL HEART, FULL HEART WINTER, FLORIDA FULL HEART, FLORIDA DEEP HEART, and BROAD BATAVIAN FULL HEARTED.

Place names also modify the naming of many varieties, without modifying the nature of the plant. In France, two of the traditional varieties of escarole are CORNET D'ANJOU and CORNET DE BOURDEAUX. As the names indicate, they are two regional adaptions of the same original variety whose head resembled the mouth of a horn ("cornet" means horn).

There are a number of varieties that fall somewhere between the two, with relatively large leaves that are puckered and cut on the margins, but whose midribs are larger than curly endive. One of these, GROSSE POMMANT SEULE, is another granddaddy plant, and its descendants are widely available. A good, cold-tolerant variety that can be found in many American catalogs is SALAD KING. If you're growing just one endive to see if the schedule suits you, this would be a good choice because of its adaptability.

Belgian Endive

Belgian endive, also called witloof chicory (witloof is Dutch for "white leaf"), is grown as a root vegetable. The roots are "forced" to produce the small, elongated heads that make a delicate and expensive salad fixing. Growing Belgian endive is an involved process, but not a difficult one.

Growing

Belgian endive is grown as you would any other root vegetable. The seeds should be sown ¼ to ½ inch deep in rows 8 to 12 inches apart. Thin the plants to 4 to 6 inches apart after the first true leaves develop. Soil that grows good carrots will

CHICORY

Variety	When to Plant	When to Harvest	What to Harvest	Comments	Sources*
Chicory (*C. intybus*)					
CATALONIA FRASTILIGATA	Mid- to late summer	Following spring	Leaves and stems	Can also be succession-sown throughout summer for cutting	No current source
CATALOGNA	Late spring or late summer	Second spring	First growth in spring	Blanch new shoots in spring to mellow strong flavor	CG
DENTARELLA	Mid- to late summer	Following spring	Young leaves and stems	May be blanched to mellow strong flavor	CG
GRUMOLO (CERIOLO)	Late spring or late summer	Fall or spring	Small rosettes of leaves	For fall harvest; cut back to 1″ after first frost	LM/CG
PUNTARELLA (CATALONIA DI GALATINA)	Mid- to late summer	Following spring	Second growth stems in spring	Cut back first growth and allow to regrow; peel and steam	LM/CG
ROBIN WITLOOF	120 days before frost	Just before killing frost	Roots for forcing	Store roots for winter forcing (see text); pink shoots	CG
SAN PASQUALE	Mid- to late summer	Following spring	Young leaves	Can also be succession-sown throughout summer for cutting	No current source
SPADONA	Early spring to late summer	When leaves are only 4″–6″ long	Individual leaves	Grow like GRUMOLO or as part of annual mesclun mix	CG
SUGARLOF (PAIN DE SUCRE)	Midspring or mid-summer	Fall or winter	Cylindrical heads	Resembles large cos lettuce; use blanched heart	CG/LM
ZOOM WITLOOF HYBRID	120 days before first frost	Just before killing frost	Roots for forcing	Store roots for winter forcing (see text); pale, cream-colored shoots	CG/LM
Endive (*C. indivia*)					
CORNET D'ANJOU/ CORNET DE BOURDEAUX	Late spring	Late summer/ early fall	Heads, 8″–12″ in diameter	Broadleaf type; lettucelike heads	CG/LM

(continued)

CHICORY

Variety	When to Plant	When to Harvest	What to Harvest	Comments	Sources*
Endive (*C. indivia*)—*continued*					
DE MEAUX	Early spring to late summer	Anytime before bolting	Leaves or whole heads	Use in mesclun mix or blanch mature heads	No current source
DE RUFFEC (AND VARIATIONS)	Early spring to late summer	Anytime before bolting	Leaves or whole heads	Use in mesclun mix when small, or blanch heads at maturity	HM/NG
FINE CURLED (FRISEE, RICCIUTISSIMA)	Early spring to late summer	Anytime before bolting	Leaves or whole heads	Use in mesclun mix when small, or blanch heads at maturity	CG/LM
FULL HEART	Early spring to mid-summer	Early summer or fall	Leaves or whole heads	Intermediate, between FINE CURLED and CORNET types	Widely available
GROSSE POMMANT SEULE	Early spring to late summer	Anytime before bolting	Young leaves or whole heads	Use in meslun mix when small or blanch heads at maturity	No current source
PANACLIERE (PINKSTAR)	Early spring to late summer	Anytime before bolting	Leaves or full heads	Use in mesclun mix when small or blanch heads at maturity	NG
SALAD KING	Midsummer	Fall	Whole heads or single leaves	Well adapted to fall conditions; disease resistant	ST
Radicchio (*C. intybus*)					
ADRIA	Early to midsummer	Early fall	Small round red heads	Does not need cutting back	ST
AUGUSTO	Midspring	Late summer	Small, round, red heads	Similar to GUILIO; plant in succession with it	JS/CG
CASTELFRANCO	Midspring or late summer	Fall or spring	Small, loose heads	Green outside, marbled white and pink inside	LM/CG
CESARE	Early summer	Early fall	Small, round, red heads	Similar to GUILIO; plant in succession with it	HM

| VARIETY SOURCE CHART |

CHICORY

Variety	When to Plant	When to Harvest	What to Harvest	Comments	Sources*
CHIOGGA	Midspring or mid-summer	Fall or spring	Small, round heads	Similar to CASTEL-FRANCO, but more compact heads	LM
GUILIO	Early spring	Midsummer	Small, round, red heads	New type, red throughout growth period	JS/CG
MARINA	Midspring	Early fall	Small red heads	—	BP
OTELLO	Mid- to late summer	Late fall into winter	Small, round, red heads	For fall cropping in mild climates	No current source
PALLA ROSSA	Early spring	Mid- to late summer	Small, loose heads	Larger, looser heads than RED VERONA or GUILIO; good for spring	CG/LM
PRIMA ROSSA	Early spring	Early to midsummer	Small loose red heads	Does not need cutting back to produce a head	No current source
RED VERONA	Late spring or late summer	Late fall or spring	Small, round, red heads	For fall harvest, cut back to 1″ at first frost; reheads	LM/CG
RED TREVISO	Late spring or late summer	Late fall or spring	Small, pointed, red heads	Same culture as RED VERONA, but not as hardy	LM/CG

*Listings correspond to seed companies included under Seed Source List at the back of the book.

grow good Belgian endive. Seeding to root harvest takes about 120 days. Remove any seed stalks that form, but don't harvest the tops.

After a few light fall frosts, or when the plants' growth slows, dig the roots and trim the foliage to within an inch of the crown. The best roots for forcing are 8 to 10 inches long and about an inch across at the crown. Don't bother with smaller roots as they don't have enough reserves to produce a decent head. Store the roots in damp sand or sawdust in a cool spot that stays just above freezing.

Forcing stimulates plants to grow out of season by raising the temperature with supplemental heat. To force the witloof heads, or "chicons," you'll need a forcing box or pot at least 12 inches deep and a dark, humid spot that can be held at a constant 50° to 60°F. Put a couple of inches of loose stones or other drainage material in the bottom of the pot, then stand the root crowns up in the pot so they are butting right up against each other. Cover the roots with sand or clean soil up to 4 inches above the crown. Belgian endive needs high humidity, but plenty of air circulation. Water the roots lightly, and keep them in total darkness. The chicons will be loose if the temperature rises above 60°F.

Harvesting

In about three weeks, you'll see new tops start to push through the top of the sand. Harvest by cutting the tops off just above the crown. Water them again and set the pot back in the dark. Strong roots can produce three good crops of these sprouts before they must be discarded and another set taken from storage to be forced. With good planning of successions, a continuous supply of Belgian endive can be grown in a very small space.

The Best Varieties

Many sources of seed for Belgian endive simply list it as WITLOOF or WITLOOF IMPROVED. Of course, every seedsman would like to think that a particular variety has been improved by his attention, but the surest success will be had with one of the new hybrids that does not need to be covered for forcing. These hybrids can be treated just like the older types mentioned above, except that it is not necessary to cover the roots with soil when forcing. Thus, they can be easily grown in a flower pot or planter placed in a cool pantry, or even under the sink. To exclude light you can bend coathangers wigwam-style over the pot and then drape a black plastic garbage bag (with holes cut for ventilation) over the whole affair.

Spring Chicory

At our house, we have a perennial salad bed, much the way some gardeners have an asparagus or rhubarb bed. We grow perennial salad greens there, out of

Spring chicory with fiber pot removed

the normal rotation that is used for annual crops. Cutting chicory is a mainstay of the bed, along with sorrel, good King Henry, and dandelion.

Spring cutting chicory is a crisp, mild salad green that's overwintered in the garden and harvested early in the spring. Some varieties, most notably PUNTARELLA, produce hollow spring shoots that resemble asparagus when they break through the soil.

Growing

Sow seeds 90 days before the first fall frost (but not later than September 1). Place seeds ¼ to ½ inch deep in rows 12 inches apart. If you'll be growing a permanent bed of chicories, you might want to start the plants in a plug tray or peat pots just to make placement of the plants easier; if so, set them a foot apart each way. Keep the bed as free of weeds as you can until the first hard freeze of fall, then mulch deeply to protect the crowns from freezing.

Harvesting

Early in the spring, remove the mulch. The plants will probably have started to grow already. Cut them back to an inch above the crowns (and enjoy the relatively mild shoots in a spring salad). In about three weeks, the plants will have regrown. You can blanch the new shoots under a flower pot, just like endive, to tone down the bitterness. Before they get more than 6 inches tall, harvest the young leaves.

PUNTARELLA types should be allowed to grow until they send up a central seed stalk. Cut this first stalk at ground level, and the plant will send up a flurry of replacements, which can then be harvested. Don't let these shoots get more than 8 inches tall or they'll be woody and hollow. Strip the leaves from the shoots and you've got a crisp, juicy, and slightly bitter addition to salads and crudité platters. Or try steaming the stalks lightly and serving them as you would asparagus.

The Best Varieties

The rosette chicories are all variations on one variety, known variously as GRUMOLO, or CERIOLO. Spring cutting varieties range from SPADONA, a smooth-leaf variety also known as "Lingua di Cane" or dog's tongue chicory, to SAN PASQUALE, with pale green leaves that are indented like dandelions varieties DENTARELLA and CATALONIA FRASTILIGATA, which have darker leaves. Only the variety called PUNTARELLA, or CATALONIA DI GALATINA, produces the tender shoots known as "puntarelles." If a catalog or seed packet doesn't identify the variety beyond calling it CATALOGNA or RADICHETTA, it is hard to know just which of these you might be getting. In this situation, you should look elsewhere, though locating a number of these varieties can be difficult.

Radicchio

Tradition has it that an Italian farmer, finding he had no market for his crop of fall heading chicory, harrowed it into the ground in disgust. Early the next spring, as he walked his fields in preparation for spring plowing, he noticed that the root crowns had sprouted tiny red heads. He took some home for his wife to make salad, and a new crop was born.

Radicchio (pronounced "rah-dik-ee-oh") is a kind of chicory that forms small, tightly packed, mostly red heads that weigh a ¼ to ½ pound apiece. Radicchio is prized for its strikingly beautiful red and white color and unusual, slightly bitter taste.

Growing

Some gardeners new to growing radicchio are disappointed because their "Italian red radicchio lettuce," which they expected to be a small red plant, is a huge green monster with hairy leaves and an unbearably bitter flavor. The problem is simply that they don't understand the plant's growth cycle. The old-fashioned radicchio varieties don't get their red coloration until the weather turns cool, and only then if the large plants are cut back and allowed to resprout.

In Italy, radicchio is sown in summer for a fall or winter harvest. In the parts of the United States where winters are mild, this schedule should hold. But although radicchio needs cool weather to turn it red, it is not really frost-hardy. So in most of the North, radicchio should be sown in the spring and harvested in early fall.

Sow radicchio ¼ to ½ inch deep in rows 1 foot apart. Thin the plants to 1 foot apart in the row, and let them grow unimpeded until the fall frost date. Then cut them back to an inch above the ground. When they resprout—within the next 4 to 6 weeks—the heads will not only be red, but small and well packed. We've found that in bad years, when the plants may not make a head before the tops are damaged by hard frost, we are likely to have a cold winter with plenty of snow. That helps them overwinter for harvest in the spring.

If you live in an area that gets early freezes, you can sow radicchio in a cold frame around the middle of June for a fall harvest, and in mid- to late August for a spring harvest. Leave the sash off the frame until hard frost, and then cut the plants back. Harvest as the heads form.

You can also grow radicchio like Belgian endive: Sow in late spring, dig the roots after frost, and force in the darkness as needed. Grown this way, the color of the heads will be a beautiful pinkish white instead of the normal deep burgundy.

With increased interest in radicchio, breeders have developed a number of new strains that are suitable for spring and summer harvest, and these new types are much easier to grow. They have the traditional red coloring throughout their growth cycle, and have been selected for reliable heading during the hot part of the year. Sow in #162 plug trays and treat the same as lettuce from first planting to last. The early varieties take about 80 days to mature from seed sown in midspring and can be set out 8 to 12 inches apart in the bed, depending on how large a plant you want.

Harvesting

Harvest radicchio when the heads have begun to firm up: Determine this by thumping them with your finger. Cut the head above the crown and the stump will resprout, either immediately or in the spring, giving you a second harvest. Remove the outer leaves until the heart (where the veins of the leaves are blanched white) is exposed.

The Best Varieties

The traditional Italian varieties of radicchio were developed hundreds of years ago, and as long as the crops were produced and consumed locally, little work was done to change the traits that made them successful in their home region. But now, increased interest in fresh salads has caused these beautiful plants to pop up in gardens around the world, and the range of varieties being offered is increasing. Just about every seed catalog you pick up has at least one variety of radicchio, and some catalogs offer a very broad selection.

The three traditional Italian radicchio varieties are RED VERONA, which forms round, baseball-size heads that are deep burgundy with white veins; CASTELFRANCO, a larger, looser, round-headed type whose leaves are marbled with white and pink on a pale green background; and RED TREVISO, the mildest of the three, which has a pointed head like its relative Belgian endive, but with larger, longer, and pink to red leaves. VERONA was selected from TREVISO for its tendency to form tight, round heads, and CASTELFRANCO is thought to be the result of a cross between TREVISO and a green leaf variety.

RED TREVISO and RED VERONA grow green through the summer and need cutting back with the approach of cool weather to form heads here in the north. CASTELFRANCO grows more like a lettuce, maintaining its basic color from the moment it breaks ground. As the head forms, the heart becomes blanched and the color contrasts heighten.

Some newer varieties will form a head without being cut back. Our favorite is a Dutch variety named GUILIO. While the heads are normal size, the plants are quite compact, which makes the variety ideal for intensive plantings. Other varieties of this type are AUGUSTO, sown in June for an August harvest; CESARE, which can be planted in July for harvest in September and October; and OTELLO, which is meant for August sowing and harvest from November through February. Using these new varieties in succession plantings, it is possible to harvest radicchio six months of the year, even here in the mountains of Vermont. All of these varieties are the traditional round, red VERONA type.

Other spring radicchio varieties that will head up without special treatment are PRIMA ROSSA and PALLA ROSSA, both of which form a relatively loose head with a pinkish heart, MARINA, and ADRIA. There is also a new form of the RED TREVISO chicory, called ROBIN, bred especially for forcing like witloof. Finally, there is a variety known as CHIOGGA, which is similar to CASTELFRANCO, but has a firmer, more closely packed head.

Sugarlof Chicory

Sugarlof chicory makes very large romaine-lettuce-type heads weighing up to 2 pounds. Both sugarlof chicory and romaine lettuce are grown in their native

Italy as late summer crops sown for winter and spring harvest. Both are naturally self-blanching, and thus easy to grow in a Mediterranean climate. In areas where winter temperatures fall below the twenties, though, this schedule may need to be modified.

SUGARLOF requires from 90 to 120 days to mature, and since it needs cool weather to develop the best flavor, we begin planting June 1. This is a large plant and should be 18 inches from any neighbors. Some varieties will bolt if sown while the days are still lengthening (before June 20). Harvest before hard frost when the heads firm up—just like romaine lettuce. Only the inner parts of the head are used, because the outer leaves are very bitter, even in the fall. This vegetable is also known by its French name, PAIN DE SUCRE.

CORN

Why do people want to grow sweet corn in the first place? It takes up a lot of room, is greedy for nutrients, prone to weeds, and vulnerable to frost, wind, hail, and raccoons.

Why go to all this trouble? Simply because the sweet corn you buy never tastes as good as the sweet corn you grow, even if you buy it at a garden stand. The period of peak flavor for corn is measured in minutes, not hours. The faster you can run from the garden to the kitchen with a dozen ears, the better the corn will taste. Gardeners have found that the new super-sweet types of sweet corn hold their flavor longer, but that is only a matter of de-

gree; the best corn is still the freshest, and the freshest still is the corn in your own kitchen garden.

Growing

Wait until the soil is fully warmed up before planting your corn. Because our season is so short, we plant our corn about a week before the frost-free date. At a soil temperature of 50°F or more, germination takes only about a week. The sensitive growing tip of the plant doesn't actually emerge from the ground until the corn is almost 6 inches tall, so even if the tops get nipped by frost, the plants will regrow. All we will have lost is a week's growth. But again, if you don't have to, don't push it; wait until the soil is fully warmed up.

Plant at least three varieties—one early, one midseason, and one late. Sow all three at the same time, putting the seed an inch deep in the soil. Since corn is pollinated by the wind, each variety (or each succession) should be planted in blocks of three or four rows, not single (or even double) rows. That way, when the pollen is ready, the silks of the same variety are in proximity and will be fully pollinated. Poorly filled ears are the result of insufficient pollination.

Intensive gardeners can plant three rows per 3-foot bed, with the plants 18 inches apart. Just make sure the soil is very fertile because corn is a greedy feeder, and if it doesn't get enough nutrients, yields will be disappointing. Work in three bushels or so of aged manure or compost per 100 square feet of bed.

If you are short of compost or manure, plant your corn in hills. Mound the soil into hills spaced 2 to 3 feet apart along the bed. Add a shovelful of compost to each hill, and sow each with four to six seeds, thinning to the four most vigorous as soon as the growing tip emerges. This will give you a hill of four plants every 3 feet and ensure that there is pollen available to each plant in the group.

Row gardeners should put their rows at least 30 inches apart, and thin the plants to 8- to 12-inch spacings within the rows. Remember to plant at least four rows side by side for good pollination, even if it means you end up with four short rows.

Keep your corn well cultivated early on, as it is slow to get started and you don't want to waste valuable nutrients growing weeds. If you time it right, two or three passes with the hoe or tiller (at two-week intervals) should be enough. You can use a mulch, but be sure to wait until the ground has warmed or you may slow things down by shading the soil from the heat of the sun.

If you do decide to try the new supersweet corn, be sure to isolate it to prevent cross-pollination. Do this by placing it at least 100 feet from your other corn plantings or by sowing it at least ten days before or after your other corn plantings (so the two types are not releasing pollen at the same time). If you don't do this, the ears will be tough and starchy, like field corn.

Moreover, you should delay planting until soil temperatures reach at least 60°F, and don't plant as deep—1 inch is plenty—as regular corn. To germinate, the shrunken seed kernels of supersweets need to absorb almost twice as much water as the regular types. Finally, harvest on time; the ears should be ready three weeks after half the plants are showing silk.

Harvesting

Proper timing of the harvest is crucial to the quality of the sweet corn you bring to the table. Just as the tip of a carrot blunts as it matures and the seam on a pea pod folds in at its peak of ripeness, so, too, an ear of corn changes shape as it matures. Feel the tip (not just the top of the sides) of the husk, and if the cob, with its kernels, is blunt and filled to the tip, then the ear is ready. Once you learn the trick, you'll be able to tell at a glance if your sweet corn is ready for the table.

For fresh use, you always want to harvest a plant just as it reaches the apex of its growth cycle. So pick your corn just as the kernels have swollen to their maximum size, but before they've begun to harden. (Remember—the kernels are seeds!) If they squirt like a grapefruit in response to being poked, the ear is ready, bursting with flavor as well as with the milky sap that gives good sweet corn its creamy texture.

The Best Varieties

The best sweet corn, like the best melon, comes from varieties that are well adapted to your region. Your best sources of information are experienced local gardeners and your extension agent.

But even then you will have to decide between standard sweet corn and the new genetic supersweet varieties. "Normal sugary," or "su," varieties are the kinds gardeners have been growing for years, and they quickly lose both their flavor and texture after harvest. "Sugar enhanced" varieties, which have an "se"-type gene, are tender and a bit sweeter than normal types, and the conversion of sugar to starch is somewhat slower. These varieties usually have the identifying letters SE (sugar enhanced) or EH (standing for "Everlasting Heritage") in or following their names. "Shrunken gene" varieties (so named because varieties with this genetic makeup have shrunken seed kernels) are the sweetest and are slowest to lose their flavor. The terms "supersweet" or "extrasweet" usually appear in the name or description of these varieties.

How sweet is supersweet? Standard field corn, which is fed to livestock, picked at the right stage, is about 4 percent sugar. Standard sweet corn, which humans eat, is more than twice as sweet—10 percent sucrose—but it loses half those sugars within 24 hours of picking and is back to no better than cattle corn. But the sweetest of the sweet, those with the "sh2," or "shrunken gene," can be as high as 37 percent sugar! Even two days after picking, these supersweet corns will still have almost 30 percent sugar. There is a problem with their flavor, though: They taste more like sugar than like corn, and when fresh they can be watery, instead of creamy like old-fashioned sweet corn.

CUCUMBERS

*C*ucumbers are a garden staple, grown in half of all vegetable gardens. But they have been around so long that few people get excited about them. When the fruits are ready, we cut them into quarters, and into the salad bowl or pickle jar they go. We never give them a thought. But we should, because there is more to cucumbers than most gardeners realize.

The cultivation of cucumbers predates written history. Even in tropical Asia, where the plant is thought to have originated, it is not known to exist in a wild state. As is usually the case with long-cultivated plants, there once was an enormous range of varieties. Unfortunately, the demands of commercial growers and their methods have reduced the choices available to the home gardener. So, it's up to you to track down the unusual varieties. Cucumbers make an ideal garden snack food due to their low calorie content, juiciness, and a mildly acerbic flavor that is both thirst quenching and refreshing.

Growing

Cucumbers are very sensitive to frost. Whether you start with seed sown directly in the garden, or as we do, with transplants started a few weeks earlier in #50 trays, they should not go in the garden until the ground is thoroughly warm. There is not much point in pushing the season, because they grow so quickly that even here in the land of the green tomato, they mature in plenty of time to beat the first fall frosts. Once the heat of early summer comes on, the vines grow like they are racing for the edge of the earth.

We grow cucumbers in the first part of our rotation to give them all the benefit of the previous fall's manuring. If you've ever seen how vigorously a cucumber plant grows out of the side of a compost pile, you'll appreciate that plentiful nitrogen, phosphorus, and potassium produce large, rambling plants, loaded with juicy fruits. Yet cucumbers are more restrained than summer squash and can be grown on adjacent beds without taking over the entire surface of the garden. Once the vines begin to "run" and the growing tips reach to the edge of the bed, train the plants by turning the tips out of the path and back onto the bed. Better yet, provide a trellis for them to climb. In addition to improved air circulation around the plants, which helps fight disease, this also spares room to grow cool-weather crops on the edges of the bed, where they will be shaded from the midday sun by the lush foliage of the cucumbers.

As said, we start our cucumber (and squash) plants a couple of weeks before the last frost in #50 plug trays, then set them out a week or so after the anticipated frost-free date. All the members of this family resent transplanting, and they are less drought tolerant if allowed to become even slightly root-bound in the pot. But for us, the advantage of being able to precisely place each plant, already germinated and growing well, outweighs the risks. No matter what size your garden, being able to protect the young plants from cold weather is a big help.

We like to put cucumbers on a high bed so that they get the extra drainage and warmth from the sun that all the members of this tropical plant family thrive on. Just rake up the sides of the bed until it is 8 inches or so above the adjacent path; it should be half as wide but twice as tall as a normal bed.

We cover the bed with black polyethylene mulch to help retain moisture and to heighten the effect of the sun. Poke a hole in the plastic at 1-foot intervals. Into each hole pour a cup or so of transplant solution, made from fish emulsion and liquid seaweed (manure tea will work just as well, but make sure it is *weak!*). Then we plop a transplant right down into the soupy soil, and pull a bit of drier soil from under the mulch to hill up around the plant. We don't firm the soil around the plants because air will be excluded by the settling process. The stems are very tender; if damaged by rough handling, the plants may just give up the ghost and collapse into a heap of limp leaves.

As soon as we set out our cucumbers, we cover them with a floating row cover to protect them from drying winds, freak late frosts, and visits by the cucumber beetle. We have found that once they have four or five leaves and are growing vigorously, the plants are less vulnerable to the beetles. The critical time is shortly after germination, when the plants are just putting out their first true leaves. At that stage, it takes only a few of these voracious insects to strip a plant so completely that it doesn't have the photosynthetic capacity to keep growing. When the first female flowers appear, we remove the covers to make way for pollinating bees. The new parthenocarpic cucumbers will fruit without being fertilized, and you can leave the covers on until the plants outgrow them or you need to put up a trellis.

You can save a lot of space by trellising cucumbers. Most of the long, burpless, and oriental types need to be grown off the ground if you want straight fruits; otherwise, you'll end up with a collection of the oddest corkscrew cukes you've ever seen. Trellising also increases yields and discourages rots, molds, and fungi in humid summer climates by improving air circulation. Also, it is a lot easier to see insects and their eggs if the leaves are held up by a trellis rather than when they are sprawled all over the ground.

Finally, prompt harvest keeps the vines producing. Trellised fruits are easier to find at harvest time, so few escape notice and overripen. All this makes tending your cukes less trouble and helps you get the best possible quality. You can find a number of good trellis designs in general gardening books, or you can buy one readymade. Keep one thing in mind: A bumper crop of cukes weighs more than you might think, so make sure it's sturdy.

Harvesting

The cucumber fruit is an overdeveloped ovary attached to the plant's female flowers. If you look closely at a growing cucumber vine, you will notice that the male flowers grow on a stalk, and the females are attached directly to the vine by the cucumber itself. Cornichons, the "gourmet" delicacy that non-gardeners pay so dearly for in the supermarket import section, are harvested when they are the size of your little finger, just as soon as the flower drops off. There is no technical difference between these cucumbers and other, more traditional varieties. In fact, you can harvest cornichons at any time from any favorite cucumber variety. There are, however, varieties bred especially to produce the spiny little fruits that you see in those expensive jars. If you want to grow a real cornichon for pickling, just locate one of these special varieties and put a few plants at the end of your cucumber row.

The single thing you need to know about harvesting young cucumbers: *Keep*

CUCUMBERS

Variety	When to Plant	When to Harvest	What to Harvest	Comments	Sources*
ARMENIAN	Frost-free date	1″–2″ in diameter	Long pale green ridged fruits	Ridges make fruits quite attractive when sliced	BP/LM/SS
BURPLESS HYBRID	Frost-free date	1″–1½″ in diameter, 10″–12″ long	Fruits	High yielding; good tasting; tolerant of poor conditions	BP/PK/PT/CG
EURO-AMERICAN HYBRID	Frost-free date	1″–1½″ in diameter, 8″–10″ long	Long green fruits	Mild flavor; very uniform; should be peeled	PK/PT
LEMON (CRYSTAL APPLE)	Frost-free date	1″–2″ in diameter	Round, pale yellow fruits	Productive; good tasting; use whole for crudités or pickling	LM/CG/JS
SUYO LONG	Frost-free date	15″–20″ long	Long, thin, deeply ridged fruits	Ridges make it good-looking slicer; likes hot weather	JS/PT
SWEET SUCCESS HYBRID	Frost-free date	1″–2″ in diameter, 10″–12″ long	Long green fruits	Will set fruit without pollination, so can be grown seedless	HM/PT/NG

Pickling Cucumbers

Variety	When to Plant	When to Harvest	What to Harvest	Comments	Sources*
DE BOURBONNE	Frost-free date	½″ in diameter, 3″–4″ long	Small, spiny fruits	Known in France as cornichons; pickle whole in brine	LM/CG
FIN DE MEAUX	Frost-free date	½″–1″ in diameter, 3″–5″ long	Small, spiny fruits	Larger and longer than DE BOURBONNE	SB
VERT PETIT DE PARIS	Frost-free date	1″ in diameter, 3″–4″ long	Small blocky fruits	Less spiny than other cornichons; good for bread and butter pickles	LM

*Listings correspond to seed companies included under Seed Source List at the back of the book.

them picked. A small cucumber is better for pickling because it can soak up the flavorings without losing its structure. Pick the fruits when they are the size of your little finger, and let the brine or syrup become the liquid that fills out the fruit. Cucumbers can double in size within only a few days, so you've got to keep a close eye on them if you want to get the best quality: firm texture, few seeds, and the proper size for pickling whole.

For fresh use, cucumbers should be filled out. The problem is telling when the fruit is fully swollen and juicy, but has not yet begun to thicken its skin or harden its seeds. One trick is to run your fingers along the skin, and when you can no longer feel the little dimple where the spines protrude, the fruit is at its peak.

The Best Varieties

The same compounds that make some immature cucumbers bitter and astringent are responsible for the problems some people have digesting this vegetable. In properly matured fruits, these compounds are mostly in the skin, so gardeners who love cucumbers but have sensitive stomachs should peel them. With the development of the new burpless cucumbers, this is no longer necessary, and in the process of removing the "burp," breeders have also helped the flavor of fresh cukes. If you haven't already tried a few of these new varieties, make a little room for them. We have had good luck with BURPLESS, SWEET SUCCESS, and EURO-AMERICAN.

LEMON, or CRYSTAL APPLE cucumbers, are less puckery by nature than the conventional kinds. They are small, round, pale yellow fruits that grow to about tennis-ball size under good conditions. As they near maturity, their color darkens to a lemon shade. We like to pick them small—about golf-ball size—and eat them fresh like plums. These tiny cukes make excellent pickles, too.

For the best pickles, though, plant true cornichon varieties like DE BOURBONNE and FIN DE MEAUX; both have prominent spines and are harvested when they are only 2 or 3 inches long and less than ½ inch thick. VERT PETIT DE PARIS (Small Green Paris) is larger and blockier, more like our own American picklers. The ability of these cornichon varieties to stay thin and maintain a uniform size when small is why they make such great pickles, whatever the recipe.

We have not grown the long oriental or Armenian cucumbers, but they come highly recommended by fellow gardeners. SUYO LONG and the variety known simply as ARMENIAN are both vigorous plants that bear thin-skinned, flavorful fruits. Remember, though, that they should be grown on a trellis for best results, as they tend to curve if they are allowed to run on the ground.

EGGPLANTS

*E*ggplants are not widely grown in this country, either commercially or in home gardens. In fact, even okra is more popular. That's too bad, because they are interesting and beautiful plants, and the wide range of varieties available for home gardens makes the supermarket selection look silly. Although eggplants are a hot-weather crop, requiring even more heat over a longer period than peppers and tomatoes, they are not difficult to grow.

Growing

We start our eggplants almost a month before our tomatoes because they grow more slowly. We start them in #162 plug trays. After a month or so, when the plants have developed their first true leaves, we pot them up to a #50 plug. When their roots fill the cell in this larger plug (you can check by gently lifting the plants), move them to 4-inch pots. You can prevent legginess in eggplants by not giving them any more heat than they have light to use for photosynthesis; otherwise, they will stretch toward whatever light there is and become spindly. Since eggplants need to be kept warm, you may have to use grow lights if you live in a cloudy climate and don't have access to a greenhouse.

Eggplants should not be set out in the garden until all danger of frost is past.

Ideally, you should wait until nighttime temperatures are consistently above 50°F, because the plants will be set back by temperatures in the low forties. Harden the plants for a few days by moving them outside to a protected spot on warm afternoons.

Raised beds have better drainage and get more exposure to the sun, so the soil is as warm as possible. Black plastic mulch will help both yields and quality by warming the soil even further while moderating soil moisture. After laying the mulch, we make a crosswise slit every 18 inches down the center of the bed, then reach through the opening and pull back a bit of soil to make a hollow. We put in a small handful of colloidal phosphate, cover that with two heaping handfuls of compost, and mix the amendments around. Then we smooth the soil over the area to leave a level surface under the opening. When it is time to plant, we make up a watering can of fertilizer solution (see Part I). We pour a cup or so of the mix into each hole to make a soil soup. Plants are set directly into the wet soil, and dry soil is pulled around them. Work gently so that the stems aren't damaged.

Immediately after planting, we put a floating row cover over the beds to give them a buffer against our cool mountain winds and to keep out insects until the plants are well established. Once the plants are in full flower, the covers should be removed so that insects can get to the blossoms and pollinate them.

The biggest problem we have with eggplants is weather. Eggplants seem more resistant to the blights that affect all of our outdoor tomato plantings, and we have had almost no problems with disease. Colorado potato beetles are the biggest pest on established eggplants, but they can be easily handpicked, and their egg clusters are easy to find on the undersides of the leaves. (Even if you don't like the fruits, it might be worth growing a few eggplants just to attract the beetles away from your potatoes.)

Harvesting

Eggplants can be harvested anytime after they are about one-third grown, and frequent picking will stimulate the plants to continue setting fruit. Clip the fruit stem with scissors or pruning shears to avoid tearing the joint where it meets the main stem of the plant. Handle the fruits gently, as they bruise easily. There is no point in leaving malformed or otherwise defective fruits on the plant, as they just inhibit the formation of new fruits.

The Best Varieties

Small eggplants are especially good for grilling and tempura. For best results, grow genetic dwarfs SLIM JIM or LITTLE FINGERS, two sturdy varieties that bear clusters of thumb-size lavender fruits close to the stem. Early, productive, and quite ornamental, they are good choices for container plantings. Harvest as soon as the color and shape of the fruits have developed.

For stuffing, we grow the larger, round varieties and let them mature fully so the skins can withstand cooking without becoming soggy. VIOLETTE DI FIRENZE is my

EGGPLANTS

Variety	When to Plant	When to Harvest	What to Harvest	Comments	Sources*
BABY WHITE	8–12 weeks before last frost	When fruits are 1″–2″ in diameter	Round to oval white fruits	Asian-type fruit for soups and stews	SB
BIANCA OVALE	8–12 weeks before last frost	When fruits are 2″ × 4″	Egg-shaped white fruits	Harvest at maturity (before they turn yellow); good for containers	CG
BRIDE HYBRID	8–12 weeks before last frost	When fruits are 2″ × 8″	White fruits with lavender	Color like VIOLETTE DI FIRENZE, but long and thin	LM
CASPER	8–12 weeks before last frost	When fruits are 2½″ × 6″	Oblong, white fruits	Larger form of white eggplant; milder flavor	SB/ST
EASTER EGG HYBRID	8–12 weeks before last frost	When fruits are 2″ × 4″	Egg-shaped, white fruits	Similar to BIANCA OVALE; same as OSTEREI	PT
FARMER'S LONG	8–12 weeks before last frost	When fruits are 2″ × 12″	Long, thin, red-purple fruits	Good for uniform slices	LM
LISTADA DI GANDIA	8–12 weeks before last frost	When fruits are 4″–6″ in diameter	White and lavender globe fruits	Similar to VIOLETTE DI FIRENZE	SB
LITTLE FINGERS	8–12 weeks before last frost	When fruits are ½″ in diameter	Small cylindrical fruits	Good variety for "baby eggplants"	HM
ROSSA BIANCA	8–12 weeks before last frost	When fruits are 4″–6″ in diameter	White and lavender globe fruits	Similar to VIOLETTE DI FIRENZE	SB/LM
SLIM JIM	8–12 weeks before last frost	When fruits are 1″ × 4″	Small lavender fruits	Early high-yielding type; good for containers	CG
VIOLETTE DI FIRENZE	8–12 weeks before last frost	When fruits are 4″–6″ in diameter	White and lavender globe fruits	Italian heirloom; primitive plants; large but variable fruits	CG/PT

*Listings correspond to seed companies included under Seed Source List at the back of the book.

favorite. The plants are very primitive looking, covered with supple black thorns on the stems and foliage. The softball-size fruits vary in color from a rich, shiny lavender to white; they vary in shape from oblong to round, sometimes ribbed with lavender stripes reaching down from the cap. ROSSA BIANCA and LISTADA DI GANDIA are other good varieties of this type.

Intermediate between these two types is BRIDE. This Asian variety bears 10-inch-long fruits in clusters on compact plants; it is a light lavender, with stripes of white running out from underneath the cap. Another long variety that is a bit earlier, with slightly longer, thinner, reddish purple fruits, is FARMER'S LONG.

White eggplants generally have a milder and fuller flavor than the purple types. Their fruits range from the size of a quarter up to the size of traditional purple varieties. One good Italian variety is BIANCA OVALE. The plants are vigorous and bear over a long period; the fruits can be harvested small, at which point they resemble hen's eggs, or left to grow larger. As they mature, the color changes from a very pale green to white and then to a creamy yellow. Other white varieties to try are WHITE BEAUTY, EASTER EGG, and CASPER.

There are also eggplants, such as BABY WHITE, that are especially good pickled or used whole in stews. They are best harvested while white; young green fruits will not have developed full flavor, and older yellow fruits may be seedy.

HERBS

Herbs play a big part in our cooking, so they play a big part in our gardening, too. Fresh herbs are markedly superior to the dried herbs available in stores, and most of them are valuable ornamentals as well. While we have a permanent herb border, we grow so many now that our plantings spill out into other parts of the garden, where they add to both the beauty and the bounty.

The term "herb" is not like a lot of the other garden terms we've been dealing with. We've mostly been talking about groups of plants that are related to one another, and that require similar conditions and treatment to thrive. A tomato is a tomato. No matter what the variety,

it's going to need the same sort of care and feeding.

Herbs, on the other hand, are plants that have been grouped together purely because they're used in similar ways. Culinary herbs might not have anything more in common than that they are all used to flavor other foods. Since the term covers so many types of plants, we'll treat most of the growing information individually.

There are annual, biennial, and perennial plants that we grow as herbs. The best techniques for each type are slightly different. Frost-hardy annuals, and herbs that grow quickly or bolt to seed if transplanted, should be sown directly in the garden as soon as the soil can be worked in spring. Tender annuals will have to wait for the frost-free date, or be started inside for transplanting after the weather has settled. For a good harvest in their first season, perennials should be started in late winter for transplanting in early spring. Seeded in early summer, they can be harvested for the first time in their second year. Biennials are sown in early spring and may yield a harvest of leaves in the first season, but they must be carried through the winter and allowed a second season of growth before they'll produce seeds.

Most herbs are at their best, and will keep the longest, when harvested just as the dew dries on a sunny morning. That's when the leaves are the most turgid. For fresh use, just rinse and dry; they will keep a few days in the refrigerator's crisper. Dried herbs keep their color and flavor best if dried and stored in the dark. If drying takes longer than two or three days (a common problem in humid climates), you may want to use a solar dryer or spread the herbs on a cookie sheet in a gas oven with just the pilot light on. Small amounts can be very conveniently dried that way with what would otherwise be wasted gas.

Parsley, basil, and dill are the three big herbs in our garden. We also like a lot of thyme, rosemary, and tarragon. Experience has taught us that not all strains of an herb are the same. As with vegetables, different varieties may be better for different uses. While one type is good for garnishing, another may hold up better to cooking, while a third may make the best herb vinegar.

Here's a rundown of the most common herbs and how we grow them.

Parsley (*Petroselinum crispum*)

Parsley is probably the most widely grown herb, although some people think of it as merely a garnish. In fact, the gentle flavor of this biennial herb makes a good addition to sauces, grilled meats, and poultry. Both the curly and flat-leaf (Italian) parsley are used in cooking.

Growing

Parsley is easy to grow and quite hardy once it's established, but the seeds are slow to germinate and the plants don't compete well with weeds. For this reason, we start our summer crop in #162 plugs, 8 to 12 weeks before the last killing frost. Even with bottom heat, germination can take a week or two. Once they've been hardened off, the plants will survive a moderate frost, but too much cold weather makes them think they've been through a winter, and being biennials, they will run to seed.

Whatever kind of container you use, set the plants out before the main taproot begins to swell (lift it out of the container to check). After this happens, they do not transplant well. We set the plants in a 3:2:3 pattern like lettuce. If you plan to keep them through the winter, they should be in the perennial area of the garden so that they won't interfere with fall cleanup.

To keep yourself in parsley throughout the snow-free season, mulch a few plants from the current summer's crop with straw or leaves after the first hard frosts of fall so they'll winter over. In the spring you'll get an early harvest of leaves before the plants run to seed, and by then your spring transplants will be ready to cut. For best results, direct seed the plants for overwintering in early summer, and don't cut them until they are mulched in the fall.

Harvesting

Parsley grows up to 18 inches, but you can cut plants anytime. For a continuous harvest, snip only the older, outer leaves and leave the center to develop.

The Best Varieties

There are a large number of curly parsley varieties, and the tendency among breeders has been to emphasize the fineness of the foliage and the length of the petioles (or leaf stalks). Long petioles make for easy harvesting, and the finely curled leaves are better looking as a garnish. The traditional variety for American gardens is MOSS CURLED, and there are numerous variations, including MOSS CURLED, DOUBLE CURLED, TRIPLE CURLED, EXTRA TRIPLE CURLED, MOSS CURLED DARK GREEN, and even CHAMPION MOSS CURLED. These are all very similar to the untrained eye. The variety we grow, BRAVOUR, is particularly cold tolerant, as are DARKI and BANQUET. We've also been testing a new Dutch variety, called TRIPLEX, which so far looks very good.

Flat-leaf, or Italian, parsley lacks the eye appeal of the curly types, but has much more flavor. Rather than using it for a garnish, try drying the leaves for winter seasoning, or using it fresh in soups, stews, and salads. Though there are a few selections of this basic and wonderful herb, they are all quite similar. The variety we grow is called CATALOGNO.

VARIETY SOURCE CHART

HERBS

Variety	When to Plant	When to Harvest	What to Harvest	Comments	Sources*
Basil					
CAMPHOR	After all danger of frost is past	Just before flowering	Leaves and flower buds	Gray-green leaves and a strong camphor scent	CP
CINNAMON	After all danger of frost is past	Just before flowering	Leaves and flower buds	Dark foliage; ornamental makes good jelly	CG/SB/ SS/PK/ PT

(continued)

HERBS

Variety	When to Plant	When to Harvest	What to Harvest	Comments	Sources*
Basil—*continued*					
FINE GREEN (PICCOLO VERDE FINO)	After all danger of frost is past	Just before flowering	Leaves and flower buds	Best for salad as small leaves don't need chopping	CG/NG/ SS/PK
GREEN BOUQUET	After all danger of frost is past	Just before flowering	Leaves and flower buds	Super-compact small leaf type; good for containers	BP/TM
GREEN RUFFLES	After all danger of frost is past	Just before flowering	Leaves and flower buds	Green form of purple ruffles	CG/BP/ PT
HOLY (SACRED)	After all danger of frost is past	Just before flowering	Leaves and flower buds	Hairy leaves; primarily ornamental or for potpourri	CP/NG/ PK
LEMON	After all danger of frost is past	Just before flowering	Leaves and flower buds	Resents transplanting; good for chicken and seafood	Widely available
LICORICE	After all danger of frost is past	Just before flowering	Leaves and flower buds	Quite ornamental and hardier than most basils	CG/SS/ PK/JS/ PT
MAMMOTH	After all danger of frost is past	Just before flowering	Leaves and flower buds	Best variety for drying and long cooking	CG
MEXICAN	After all danger of frost is past	Just before flowering	Leaves and flower buds	Huge leaves; similar to CINNAMON, but coarser plant type	CP
NAPOLEATANO	After all danger of frost is past	Just before flowering	Leaves and flower buds	Lettuce-leaf type, like MAMMOTH, but leaves a bit smaller	SS/PK
OPAL	After all danger of frost is past	Just before flowering	Leaves and flower buds	Deep purple foliage is ornamental; makes good vinegar	CG/LM/ NG/SB/ HG
PERUVIAN	After all danger of frost is past	Just before flowering	Leaves and flower buds	Wild type—sparse foliage and medicinal aroma	CP
PURPLE RUFFLES	After all danger of frost is past	Just before flowering	Leaves and flower buds	Improved "opal" type; larger leaves; more consistent color	CG/NG/ BP/PK/ PT

HERBS

Variety	When to Plant	When to Harvest	What to Harvest	Comments	Sources*
SPICY GLOBE	After all danger of frost is past	Just before flowering	Leaves and flower buds	Super-compact small-leaf type with strong aroma	PK
SWEET GENOVESE	After all danger of frost is past	Just before flowering	Leaves and flower buds	Best pesto type; productive	CG/SS/ JS
Calendula					
BON BON	4–6 weeks before last frost	Just as flowers open	Flowers and flower petals	Dwarf variety	ST
KABLOUNA	4–6 weeks before last frost	Just after flowers open	Flowers and flower petals	Dwarf variety; orange, yellow and golden	PT/SS
Celery					
DINANT	8–12 weeks before last frost	Once foliage is 6"–8" long	Stems and leaves	Stronger flavor than stalk celery; cut and come again	NG
Chives					
COMMON	Early spring/ midsummer	Anytime	Leaves and flowers	Flowers make a good garnish; leaves can be frozen	Widely available
GARLIC (CHINESE)	Early spring, or divide plants	Anytime	Leaves and flowers	Slight garlic flavor; freeze leaves for winter use	Widely available
GROLAU	Midsummer for winter use	Anytime	Leaves	Special strain for greenhouse and windowsill; productive	CG/NG/ TM
Dill					
BOUQUET	Midspring/ in succession	When foliage is 6"–8"; seed heads	Leaves, flower heads, seeds	Compact cultivar of the common dill	HM/ LM/ NG/PK
COMMON	Midspring/ in succession	When foliage is 6"–8"; seed heads	Leaves, flower heads, seeds	—	Widely available

(continued)

HERBS

Variety	When to Plant	When to Harvest	What to Harvest	Comments	Sources*
Dill—*continued*					
INDIAN	Midspring in succession	Foliage anytime, seeds when ripe	Leaves, flowerheads, seeds	Slightly more bitter than regular dill; for Indian cooking	CP
MAMMOTH (LONG ISLAND)	Midspring/ in succession	When foliage is 6″–8″; seed heads	Leaves, flowers, seeds	Tall strain; highly productive	LM/WD
TETRA (DUKAT)	Midspring/ in succession	When foliage is 6″–8″	Leaves	Dwarf form; good for cut-and-come-again harvest of leaves	CG
Fennel					
REDLEAF (BRONZE)	Midspring/ in succession	When foliage is 6″–8″	Leaves	Grows just like dill; foliage an ornamental deep bronze	CG/LM/ NG/SB
SICILIAN	Midspring/ in succession	When foliage is 6″–8″	Leaves (or bulbs, if they form)	Strong aroma, pale green foliage; summer plantings may bulb	CG/SB
ZEFA FINO	Midsummer	When bulbs reach 2″ across	Bulb at base of plant	Needs adequate moisture and cool temperatures at maturity	JS
Lavender					
HIDCOTE	Seed indoors in spring	When flowers open	Flowers	Dark blue cultivar; flowers make good garnish	TM
JEAN DAVIS	Seed indoors in spring	When flowers open	Flowers	Light pink to white cultivar; good for garnish and potpourri	CP
MUNSTEAD	Seed indoors in spring	When flowers open	Flowers	Dwarf lavender; all varieties slow to germinate and grow	TM/PK/ PT
TWICKLE	Seed indoors in spring	When flowers open	Flowers	Ornamental foliage; not as hardy as other types	NG/CP

HERBS

Variety	When to Plant	When to Harvest	What to Harvest	Comments	Sources*
Nasturtium					
CANARY CREEPER	After all danger of frost is past	Anytime after plant is 6"–8"	Leaves and flowers	Unique, palmate leaves and birdlike yellow flowers	CG/BP
GLEAM	After all danger of frost is past	When flowers open	Leaves and flowers	Dwarf type; too much nitrogen makes all leaves, no flowers	BP
WHIRLYBIRD	After all danger of frost is past	When flowers open	Leaves and flowers	Dwarf form; low nitrogen gives poor foliage but many flowers	CG/SS/ BP/PK/ GS
Oregano					
COMMON	Early spring	When flowers open	Flower heads for drying	Flowers good for drying (use GREEK for cooking)	Widely available
GOLDEN	Early spring	Anytime	Leaves	Ornamental foliage with good aroma if GREEK not available	CP
GREEK	Early spring	Just before flowering	Leaves	Known by its low habit and white flowers; best for cooking	Widely available
MEXICAN	Late spring	Just before flowering	Leaves	Not a true oregano and not as hardy; grow as an annual	PK
SEEDLESS	Not applicable	Buy plants anytime	Leaves	Hardy to 10°F, strong flavor, sweeter than GREEK	CP
Parsley					
BANQUET	Midsummer	When growth starts in spring	Individual leaves and stems	Good strain for over-wintering; can also be spring sown	HM

(continued)

HERBS

Variety	When to Plant	When to Harvest	What to Harvest	Comments	Sources*
Parsley—*continued*					
BRAVOUR	Seed indoors in early spring	Anytime after plant is 6"-8"	Individual leaves and stems	Good leaf form for garnish	CG/ST/ CG
CATALOGNO	Early spring	When plant reaches 6"-8"	Individual leaves and stems	Stronger flavor than curly type; best for cooking and drying	Widely available
DARKI	Late spring/ midsummer	When plants reach 6"-8"	Individual leaves and stems	Good cold tolerance; good leaf form for garnish	ST/TM
MOSS CURLED	Early spring	When plants reach 6"-8"	Individual leaves and stems	Heirloom variety with many strains in culture	WD/ VB/GS
TRIPLEX	Midspring	When plants reach 6"-8"	Individual leaves and stems	Improved form of MOSS CURLED	CG/SB/ PT
Rosemary					
COMMON	8-12 weeks before last frost	Just before flowering	Leaves and tips of shoots	Very poor germination; buy plants to get best varieties	Widely available
Sage					
ANNUAL CLARY	Early spring indoors	When flowers open	Flowering shoots	*Salvia hormonium;* use flowers for garnish bouquets	CG/ST/ NG/ TM/
CLARY (S. SCLAREA)	Late spring	Before flowering	Leaves	Large plant	CP/NG
COMMON	Early spring	Just before flowers open	Leaves	Slow to get started, so start indoors	Widely available
GOLDEN	Not applicable	Just before flowers open	Leaves	Primarily ornamental	CP/NG
HOLT'S MAMMOTH	Take cuttings in spring	Just before flowers open	Leaves	Large-leaf variety; does not come true from seed	NG/CP

VARIETY SOURCE CHART

HERBS

Variety	When to Plant	When to Harvest	What to Harvest	Comments	Sources*
PURPLE	Take cuttings in spring	Just before flowers open	Leaves and flowers	Ornamental type not as hardy	NG
TRICOLOR	Not applicable	Buy plants before flowers open	Variegated leaves	Primarily ornamental	CP/NG
Savory					
SUMMER SAVORY	Midspring	Before flowers open	Leaves	Good for squash and beans; whole plants dry well for ornament	Widely available
WINTER SAVORY	Early spring	Just before flowers open	Leaves	Perennial variety of savory	Widely available
Tarragon					
FRENCH	Start from cuttings or division	Anytime plants are vigorous	Leaves (does not flower)	Does not come from seed; buy your first plants	NG/PK
RUSSIAN	Early spring	Anytime after plant is 6″-8″	Leaves	Inferior to FRENCH tarragon	ST/WD/ VB/PT
Thyme					
CARAWAY	Start from layers or cuttings	Just before flowers open	Tips of flowering shoots	Caraway scent; good creeping plant for rock gardens/patios	NG
COMMON	Early spring	Just before flowering	Tips of flowering shoots	Slow to get started, so start indoors	Widely available
FRENCH SUMMER	Early spring	Just before flowering	Tips of flowering shoots	Improved variety of common thyme	CG/LM
GERMAN WINTER	Early spring	Just before flowering	Tips of flowering shoots	Improved variety of common thyme; hardier, for cold climates	HG/ WD/JS/ GS

(continued)

VARIETY SOURCE CHART—*Continued*

HERBS

Variety	When to Plant	When to Harvest	What to Harvest	Comments	Sources*
Thyme—*continued*					
GOLD EDGED	Not applicable	Buy plants anytime	Leaves	Ornamental, but can be used as substitute for *T. vulgaris*	CP (or local nursery)
LEMON	Start from cuttings	Just before flowers open	Tips of flowering shoots	Intriguing lemon scent; does not come from seed	NG/CP
NUTMEG	Not applicable	Buy plants anytime	Leaves	Primarily ornamental	CP
SERPOLET (MOTHER OF THYME)	Early spring	After flowers open	Tips of flowering shoots	Good flowers for garnish	Widely available
SILVER EDGED	Not applicable	Buy plants anytime	Leaves	Ornamental, but can be used as a substitute for *T. vulgaris*	CP (or local nursery)

*Listings correspond to seed companies included under Seed Source List at the back of the book.

Basil (*Ocimum* spp.)

Basil is another popular herb, and it is growing more so each year. In addition to being the essence of the classic Italian *pesto* sauce, this annual herb enlivens many other meat and vegetable dishes.

The French say that a person who is ranting and raving is "sowing the basil." According to folk myth in that country, this herb will thrive only if its sower is cursing. But we haven't felt the need to yell at our plants; most years it grows just fine without the noise.

Growing

We start our basil in #162 plugs about eight to ten weeks before the last spring frost, and transplant up to #50 plugs when the leaves touch. This gives us sturdy plants

to set out when the weather has warmed. Basil seeds germinate best at temperatures above 70°F, so you might want to use bottom heat to speed them up.

The soil mix can be kept moist by placing plastic wrap over the planting tray. Keep a close eye on them, though, because once the basil germinates, it needs both air and light. The plants will do best above 60°F, so keep them with your eggplants, peppers, and tomatoes.

We plant out in a 4:3:4 pattern. Since basil is a leaf crop, it needs good fertile soil to grow in. Don't overdo it on the nitrogen, though. The flavor of the herb comes from its essential oils; too much nitrogen will yield lush growth but a low oil content.

When frost threatens, pull the plants. Basil plants are so tender that they make good indicator plants for mapping the microclimate of your garden. On an early fall night, when just a touch of frost settles into the paths between the beds, and the settling air dams next to a hedge or wall, the damage to your basil plants will give an accurate picture of the cold spots in your garden.

To keep a pot of basil for the winter, either take a cutting from one of the garden plants in late summer and root it in a slightly moist, sterile potting medium, or seed a few pots in midsummer to mature in late fall. Don't expect the plants to put out much new growth during the dark days of winter without supplemental light.

Basil (from top): *sweet, fine-leaf, mammoth*

Harvesting

Harvest just before the flowers open. To get the biggest yields, cut the main stem just above the second set of leaves, being careful not to damage the suckers growing in the leaf joint. Fertilize with manure tea or fish emulsion immediately after harvest to stimulate new growth from the suckers, and in a few weeks you'll be able to pick again. Cut these shoots in the same fashion, and they too will resprout from their suckers.

The Best Varieties

There are many types of basil, each with its own special uses.

Basil for Salads

The best basils for salads are the small-leafed kinds (*Ocimum minimum*) and, luckily for salad lovers, these have received a lot of attention from breeders in recent years. This is partly due to the fact that they are some of the most ornamental of the basils. They take the form of dwarf shrubs, with tiny leaves in just the right proportion to their overall form. The flavor is generally good, with just enough of that characteristic basil spiciness to liven the leaves of lettuce, *mâchè,* and other mild greens. The tiny leaves do not need to be cut or shredded before adding them to the salad bowl. These dwarf basils are the best kinds to grow in containers.

There are a number of good varieties of dwarf basil, the most common being PICCOLO VERDE FINO, or, simply, FINE GREEN. More recent introductions are GREEN BOUQUET and SPICY GLOBE.

Basil for Pesto

Sweet basil (*Ocimum basilicum*) is the basil most of us are familiar with. The medium green leaves are smooth and shiny, yet slightly ridged. The flavor is stronger than the fine-leaf types, but sometimes picks up a touch of bitterness with long cooking. It is best used in salads or for making pesto.

Most American catalogs simply list it as SWEET BASIL, but there are a few elite European strains such as SWEET GENOVESE that are slower bolting and less likely to become bitter after long cooking in sauces.

A subtype of sweet basil, known as lettuce leaf basil, has much larger savoyed leaves. The leaves of NAPOLEATANO are 3 to 5 inches long and up to 2 inches wide, but there are even larger kinds. MAMMOTH basil has leaves that are large enough (up to 4 inches by 8 inches) to wrap around a filet of fish or piece of chicken.

Ornamental Basil

There are some purple-leaf basils that are so striking that they are often grown solely for their ornamental qualities. The first of these was OPAL (sometimes listed in catalogs simply as *O. basilicum* "purpurescens"). It has the same leaf shape as traditional basil, but the color of the leaves is a very deep purple that contrasts well with gray-leaf plants such as SILVER MOUND and

DUSTY MILLER. The flowers of OPAL are a soft lavender color, and the flavor, while not as good, perhaps, as the best strains of sweet basil, is acceptable. Its color makes it useful for an accent in salads and for colorful basil vinegar.

The one problem with OPAL is its lack of uniformity. In every planting there are a fairly large number of "off-type" plants in which the purple is streaked with green, a combination that is not very aesthetic. Fortunately this problem has been nearly solved in a new cultivar called PURPLE RUFFLES. This variety has sharply notched leaves that look very much like red shiso or perilla, for which it's often mistaken. There is also a GREEN RUFFLES, which is similar in all respects except color.

Scented Basil

There are a number of basils that have flavors reminiscent of other plants, like CINNAMON basil, LEMON basil, and LICORICE, or ANISE, basil. Each of these has its beauties and uses. Both CINNAMON basil and LICORICE basil are beautiful plants with darker foliage than normal sweet basil and prominent, deeply colored veins and stems. The flowers are lavender, and the characteristic aroma of each is quite strong. They can be used in place of regular sweet basil in any recipe where you might want a hint of something different.

LEMON basil can also be used to advantage in recipes where there is a lemon basis. One of our favorites is a chicken stir-fry that calls for lemon juice and bits of sorrel, with lemon basil and lemon thyme added to give depth to the lemon theme. Lemon basil resents transplanting, and it should be direct seeded. At the slightest root disturbance, it runs to seed, with an immediate decline in the production of leaves.

There are other rare and scented basils as well, but not with the culinary uses of those above. There is SACRED, or HOLY, basil, which has a strong medicinal, clove scent and hairy leaves and stems; PERUVIAN basil, which has a much sparser appearance and a medicinal flavor; MEXICAN basil, a coarser form of CINNAMON basil; and CAMPHOR basil, a gray-green variety with a hint of camphor in its scent.

Dill (*Anethum graveolens*)

The last of our "big three" herbs is dill, which we grow both for its seeds and its leaves. The feathery leaves are good in salads and as a garnish. The seeds, which have a stronger taste, are used whole or ground in many dishes and are especially good with breads, meats, and cheese.

Growing

Dill likes rich, open soil and full sun. While plants can be started indoors, it's hardly worthwhile, since the plants grow very fast. Sow seed ¼ to ½ inch deep as soon as the danger of hard frost is past. For greens, the rows can be as close to each other as 6 inches, but if you are growing dill for seed, you should allow a foot or more between rows. Rarely are many plants needed at any one time, so dill is usually sown as a companion to some other crop.

Harvesting

You can begin harvesting leaves any time after four or five appear, cutting above the first leaf joints so that the plant can resprout. After cutting, fertilize with fish emulsion or manure tea. If you are going to dry the dill leaves, get it done within a few days—using the pilot light in an oven, if necessary—or they'll lose their green color. Seal the leaves in airtight jars and store in the dark. Fresh dill leaves freeze well after a quick rinse and dry in a salad spinner.

You can also let the plants grow to their full size, which ranges from about 2 feet to more than 4 feet high, depending on the variety. For pickling, harvest immature flowerheads with a few leaves attached. If you want the seeds, let the flowers mature fully (they'll turn a light tan color), then cut the heads in the morning when the seeds are less likely to be shaken off. Place the flowers on a cloth in the sun for a day or two, and when the seed heads are dry, shake the seeds loose and winnow to remove the chaff.

The Best Varieties

Common dill is what we call all those unnamed types simply listed in catalogs as "dill." Most of these will grow to about 3 feet; they are only slightly inclined to regrow after cutting. MAMMOTH, or LONG ISLAND, dill is an heirloom variety, but we prefer BOUQUET, which is smaller and bushier. DUKAT or TETRA dill is an especially vigorous dwarf type, growing only about 2½ feet high; it is especially good for cut-and-come-again use. For authentic Indian cuisine, you'll want to try INDIAN dill (*Anethum sowa*), a slightly smaller and more bitter cousin of common dill.

Fennel (*Foeniculum* spp.)

There are basically two kinds of fennel: wild or common fennel and bulbing or Florence fennel. Both are biennials that become perennial in a favorable, Mediterranean-like climate. The physical resemblance to dill is strong, but fennel is more inclined to clump at the base and has a distinctly different, licorice aroma.

Growing

Growing fennel for salads is a snap. Direct seed after the danger of hard frost has passed, placing the rows 6 to 8 inches apart. Small, frequent sowings will provide a continuous harvest.

For bulbs, sow the seed about eight to ten weeks before the first fall frost. We find that plantings sown before mid-June are more likely to bolt before forming a bulb. What Florence fennel wants is a period of cool but frost-free weather for bulb formation. For us this is late August. In hot climates, fennel can be grown as a late winter or early spring crop.

Harvesting

Every part of the fennel plant is edible. You can cut the leaves for salad once the plants are established. To harvest fennel bulbs, cut just below the bulb, which forms at the soil line. If you let the seed stalk develop fairly well before cutting, you can use all the various stems that form as a delicious, licorice-flavored crudité.

The Best Varieties

There are many varieties of fennel available in Europe, where it is a widely grown and used vegetable, but their various adaptions and best uses are not yet well known. For salads, we prefer SICILIAN fennel. When we want a touch of color in salads we use BRONZE or REDLEAF fennel. For sweet fennel bulbs, try NEAPOLITAN, ZEFA FINO, or SUPERWADROMEN.

Oregano (*Origanum* spp.)

Every culinary garden should have some oregano growing in it. Its peppery flavor is an indispensable addition to tomato sauce and pizza, and it can also spice up many meat and vegetable dishes.

Growing

The tiny seeds should be sown thinly eight to ten weeks before the frost-free date if you want to get a harvest the first season. You can grow the plants as annuals using this schedule, but oregano is a hardy perennial, and we keep our plants going from year to year.

Mature plants need a space about 1 foot square to grow in. But if you're going to be cutting them regularly, as we do, they can be planted in a 3:2:3 pattern in the perennial herb bed. For best flavor, give oregano a sunny, well-drained location.

Harvesting

Harvest just before the plants flower. The best time is late on a sunny morning, just as the dew dries off the plants. Cut no more than one-third of the plant at any one time if you will be maintaining it as a perennial. Bunch the sprigs of oregano with a rubber band, and hang them in a dark, dry spot to dry.

The Best Varieties

There are several strains of oregano available, but the one to use for cooking is *Origanum heraclitum,* or GREEK oregano. It is distinguished from the common oregano by its low-growing habit, by its fuzzy, wedge-shaped leaves, and most of all by its white flowers. The flavor is much stronger than other types. This strain is variable. For the very best results, grow several plants from seed; pick the best plant from the lot, and from then on, propagate from cuttings taken from that plant.

COMMON oregano (*O. vulgare*) is a 2-foot-tall plant with nearly oval leaves and flowerheads composed of a number of small, lavender-to-purple flowers. It is invasive, and it lacks the strong flavor of GREEK oregano. ITALIAN oregano is similar in appearance to COMMON, except that it is not invasive (and therefore more desirable).

So-called SEEDLESS oregano is said to be as strong as the GREEK strains, but less biting. Neither CUBAN oregano nor MEXI-CAN oregano are true oregano, but both have been given the name oregano since they are used in their respective countries the way we use true oregano.

Chives (*Allium schoenoprasum*)

Chives are among our favorite herbs. They have a very mild, onionlike flavor, and can be used both as a seasoning and a garnish. The flowers, too, are quite beautiful and can also be used to garnish salads and soups.

Growing

You can start chives from seed or just divide an old plant. If you want to start from seed, sow it ¼ inch deep in flats or directly in the garden in early spring. Dividing can be done at any time during the growing season by separating an existing plant into smaller ones. Once established, each clump will need a foot or so of room.

Harvesting

With a half-dozen plants, you can cut one back (to 2 to 3 inches above the ground) each week and keep a succession of leaves and flowers available for use in salads and as a garnish. Harvest the leaves by cutting, but avoid the seed stalks because they are tougher than the leaves. Chive flowers are quite beautiful, and with a half-dozen plants you can have plants in every stage of development. Chives can be dried or frozen for winter use by the same methods used for dill.

The Best Varieties

Most companies just list "Chives," but there are a few improved varieties. GROLAU is especially well adapted for greenhouses and windowsills. We've been growing a cultivar called GIANT chives for years and like its large size. Finally, there is GARLIC chives (*Allium tuberosum*), also known as CHINESE chives. It's easily distinguished from the regular kind by its dainty white flowers and flat leaves, which have a subtle garlic flavor when used fresh.

Thyme (*Thymus* spp.)

The thymes are a large family of plants that include many culinary varieties, as well as a number of small ornamental shrubs and ground covers. Most are hardy perennials. It is one of the *fines herbes* of classic French cooking and goes with just about any kind of meat.

Growing

Thyme is usually grown from seed, though it can be easily layered by placing branches in contact with the ground. We start our plants in 20-row trays. The seed should be covered only lightly, if at all. Cover the tray to help keep the soil moist. We set the plants out when the danger of hard frost is past, giving each plant a space about 8 to 12 inches across.

Thyme does not compete well against weeds when young, so be sure to keep them at bay. Once the herb is well along, mulch is a better control than cultivation, as it keeps the low-growing foliage clean of dirt and grit.

Harvesting

Harvest just as the flowers begin to open. You can cut off the entire plant several inches above the ground and it will resprout, but if you take a second cutting you will be compromising its winter hardiness. A light shearing will put less strain on the plant, but even so, a winter mulch is helpful where there's no reliable snow cover to insulate the plants.

The Best Varieties

COMMON thyme, a ground-hugging plant with tiny leaves and inconspicuous pink flowers that bloom in late July, is what you are most likely to find listed in catalogs. But within this species there are some different cultivars. GERMAN WINTER is a hardy selection with dull green leaves that grows to about 12 inches high with a spread of about 12 inches. It is quite similar to ENGLISH thyme, which grows only two-thirds as large. FRENCH SUMMER thyme, or THYME DE PROVENCE, is not as hardy and has narrower, grayish leaves. It is sometimes confused with MOTHER OF THYME, or SERPOLET, which is the original, creeping form of culinary thyme. This is a beautiful plant, but it lacks the flavor of its cultivated descendants.

LEMON thyme, one of our favorites, has shiny green leaves and a citrus aroma; in our garden it is even hardier than the common thyme. As with many of the low-growing ornamental types, it is good for planting among flagstones, where it will release its fragrance when stepped on. Other fragrant varieties are CARAWAY and NUTMEG thyme. There are also a number of beautiful ornamental varieties such as SILVER EDGED and GOLDEN EDGED thyme; they have a nice scent but limited culinary uses.

Tarragon (*Artemisia dracunculus*)

The aniselike flavor of tarragon complements fresh salads, fish, and many meats. It is an ingredient in tartar sauce and béarnaise sauce, and is essential to some kinds of pickles.

Growing

Tarragon will survive in stony, infertile soils, but to get the best production for your kitchen garden, give it a mellow, well-drained spot. Most gardeners acquire tarragon as seedlings and plant them directly in the garden.

If the leaves begin to yellow, cut the plants and fertilize them. The plants should be divided every few years to keep them vigorous; as with most perennials, you should replant the young, outer parts of the clump and discard the center.

Harvesting

Harvest tarragon anytime after the shoots are 6 inches long. Tarragon dries well and can be frozen. For vinegar and pickles, use only the very tips of new growth.

The Best Varieties

Tarragon is one of those herbs that sometimes disappoints gardeners because the commonly sold, inferior type is mistakenly identified with its superior siblings. Many seed catalogs list tarragon, but the true FRENCH tarragon is propagated only by division and cuttings. If you buy tarragon seed, what you get is the original form, RUSSIAN tarragon, which is very easy to grow, but has only a hint of the flavor we all know and depend on for seasoning carrots, chicken, and vinegar.

Rosemary (*Rosmarinus officinalis*)

Rosemary is a tender perennial. It will be killed by temperatures below 25°F, though new varieties are under development that will survive much lower temperatures. Its uses as a seasoning and garnish are manifold, but it is perhaps at its best with lamb.

Growing

The normal germination rate for rosemary seed is only 10 to 50 percent, so it is usually less trouble to grow new plants from cuttings or by layering. Northern gardeners should bring the plants indoors for the winter; a cool, drafty room with plenty of light is ideal. Potted rosemary should not be allowed to dry out.

Harvesting

Snip sprigs as you need them. Or treat all but a few of your plants as annuals and harvest them before frost for drying. Bunch the sprigs and hang them in a dark, airy place to dry.

The Best Varieties

Like French tarragon, the best rosemary varieties are rarely propagated from seed. What most catalogs list simply as "Rosemary" will suffice for kitchen use.

Sage (*Salvia officinalis*)

One more hardy, perennial herb that has multiple uses in the kitchen is sage. Used for stuffing poultry and to flavor breads, cheeses, and sauces, sage is an essential part of any cook's garden.

Growing

Common sage is easily grown as an annual. The seed is large and should be planted ½ inch deep eight to ten weeks before the frost-free date for first-year harvest. Set the plants 1 foot apart and keep them well watered. To help sage plants overwinter, mulch them before the onset of hard freezes in fall.

Harvesting

Harvest just before the plants flower by cutting the whole plant off just above the soil line. Hang the sage in a dark, dry place for a week or two to dry. If the spot is dusty, you can dry the plants in a paper bag with a few slits cut for ventilation. Sage makes a good base for herbal wreaths, and it can be stored in that form for use in the kitchen.

The Best Varieties

Most gardeners just grow COMMON garden sage, but there are some improved cultivars that are propagated from cuttings. HOLT'S MAMMOTH sage is a large-leaf, hardy variety that is especially high yielding; once you have a plant, it can be propagated from cuttings to increase the size of your planting.

Ornamental forms of sage include GOLDEN sage, PURPLE sage, and TRICOLOR sage, which has variegated leaves. They lack the strong flavor of culinary sage. CLARY sage is a biennial variety that grows up to 4 feet tall and has prominent cream-colored blossoms. It is used as a flavoring agent for muscatel wine. ANNUAL CLARY (*S. hormonium*), sometimes also mistakenly called tricolor sage, is more closely related to the ornamental salvias; it bears a profusion of pink, blue, and white blossoms that make an excellent addition to salads as well as to fresh and dried flower arrangements.

Savory (*Satureja* spp.)

Summer savory is a small annual shrub. It reaches a height of 18 inches and has small pink-to-violet flowers that appear in July. Savory is so popular as a seasoning that its name has entered the language as a word that means good taste.

Growing

Savory needs light to germinate, so you should sow it only ¼ inch deep. Once the plants are up, thin them to 8 to 12 inches apart. You can also start the plants indoors in #98 plugs or other containers 6 to 8 weeks before the frost-free date.

Savory is a fast grower and likes a lot of water. It is not a greedy feeder, so it can be put in a spot that has not been recently manured. Next to the beans is a good spot because you can grab a handful of savory on the way from the bean patch to the kitchen where it will add that extra touch to a vinaigrette of *haricots verts*.

Harvesting

Harvest savory anytime after the plants reach 6 inches high; take just the tops, as you do with basil. As soon as the plants begin to flower, cut them off at the ground and hang them in a warm, dark place to dry. Savory leaves can also be frozen.

The Best Varieties

We have been talking about SUMMER savory (*Satureja hortensis*), but there is also a perennial cousin called WINTER savory (*S. montana*) that flowers about a month before summer savory. It grows best in the same kind of poor rocky soil that would be suitable for lavender. There is also a so-called ORNAMENTAL savory; this unrelated species is showier than the true savories, but it is less useful as a culinary herb.

Other Essential Herbs

There are a few other plants that deserve a place in the culinary garden, though not much breeding work has been done with them. In most cases, there are no named cultivars available.

Cilantro (*Coriandrum sativum*)

Coriander, known as cilantro when grown for the leaves, is a 2-foot-high annual that is used extensively in Mexican and Asian cooking. Though the juvenile foliage resembles flat-leaf parsley, there is no mistaking cilantro for any other plant in the garden; merely brushing by the foliage releases its fragrance, which to some is irresistible and to others unbearable. Grow cilantro in your salad bed, putting the seed ¼ inch deep in rows 4 to 6 inches apart; harvest when the plants are 6 to 8 inches high. Once the mature foliage (which resembles dill or fennel) begins to appear, the plants should be harvested immediately. The flavor of cilantro deteriorates rapidly as the plant flowers. The plants run to seed quickly in hot weather, so sow in succession for a continuous supply.

Cutting Celery (*Apium graveolens*)

This is a type of celery that is grown for its leaves, instead of the blanched stem. It looks very similar to Italian parsley from a distance, but it grows in more of a clump. Two varieties with which we are familiar are the Dutch ZWOLSCHE KRUL and DINANT, a French cutting celery with a very strong celery flavor to the leaves. This plant is grown and used just like parsley. It is hardy here in Vermont, and it will grow in many places where the standard stalk-type celery fails. It is a valuable addition to any herb garden.

Burnet (*Sanguisorba minor*)

Used primarily as a salad herb, burnet is easily grown from seed sown ½ inch deep outdoors in early spring. The plants need a space 12 inches across at maturity. The leaves have a faint cucumber flavor. There are no named varieties that we know of.

Hyssop (*Hyssopus officinalis*)

Like chives, hyssop is an herb that is equally at home in the perennial garden.

We grow it for its pungent, minty leaves and its flowers, which are good in salads. *Hyssopus officinalis* is the common, dark blue form; *H. alba* has white flowers, and *H. rosea,* pink flowers. It is a slow-growing perennial, so buy established plants or start seed indoors in flats in early spring. Grown as an ornamental hedge—it reaches 18 to 24 inches high—hyssop should be planted 12 inches on center. Individual plants should be set 18 to 24 inches apart so they have more room to develop.

Lavender (*Lavandula* spp.)

The culinary uses of lavender are limited to the flowers, which, like those of hyssop, are used as a garnish. We grow three varieties: MUNSTEAD, which is a selection of common English lavender; JEAN DAVIS, a cultivar with pale pink to white flowers; and HIDCOTE, with deep blue blossoms. All three are hardy in our garden, which is on the borderline between USDA Zones 3 and 4. Gardeners in milder climates than ours have more choices. There are fern-leaf varieties like TWICKLE, and ones with larger flowers like *Lavandula spicata.* It makes sense to buy established plants of these lavenders from a reputable nursery for your initial plantings.

Edible Flowers

There are a number of flowering plants sometimes considered herbs that will lend a touch of beauty to the garden, as well as provide blossoms for garnishing a special dish. Below, we mention three of special interest, but there are many more.

Borage (Borago officinalis)

This hardy annual reaches 18 inches, and covers a large area with its pendulant, wooly blossoms. Give it a moderately fertile, well-tilled spot—that is, plant it in your garden—and you will be rewarded with a profusion of blue flowers for garnishes and young, cucumber-scented leaves for salads or tea.

Calendula (Calendula officinalis)

Another carefree annual, calendulas are very hardy and can be started indoors for planting out as soon as the danger of hard frost is past. The taller kinds grow to 24 inches, but there are also new dwarf bedding calendulas that are under a foot tall. Any good garden soil with decent drainage and getting plenty of sun will do. Harvest the flowers just as they open, and use the petals, not the rough core, as a garnish in soups and salads. Two good varieties to look for are BON BON and KABLOUNA.

Nasturtium (Tropaeolum *spp.*)

Although not ordinarily thought of as a culinary herb, nasturtium flowers have a peppery taste and can be tossed into salads or used as an edible garnish.

Nasturtiums are sensitive to frost, but grow quickly once summer is under way. Both the leaves and flowers are edible, but keep in mind that one is produced at the expense of the other. Give your nasturtiums fertile ground and they will produce abundant leaves but few flowers; feed them lightly, and they will flower freely but leaf production will be lower. The leaves have a peppery taste, and the flowers are beautiful as a garnish. Direct seed

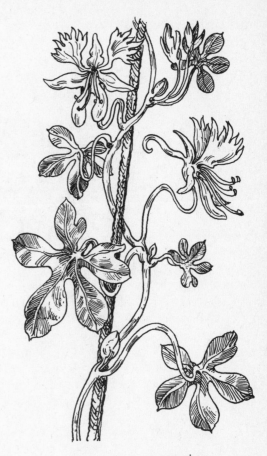

CANARY CREEPER nasturtium

after all danger of frost has passed. Dwarf forms like WHIRLYBIRD and GLEAM grow about a foot tall and 18 inches across, providing large mounds of pretty round leaves and bright orange, red, and yellow blossoms. There is a trailing type called CANARY CREEPER that has unusual five-lobed leaves and small, feathery, yellow flowers. It can grow up to 15 feet within a couple of months and makes an excellent plant for growing on a fence or arbor.

KALE AND KOHLRABI

Kale

The real eye-catchers outside our produce stand each fall are the brightly colored Japanese kales. Their deeply curled pink, white, and rose leaves stand out in high contrast to the muted grays and browns of late autumn. Not just for show, these hardy plants can also bring color and flavor to salads, soups, and cooked dishes. Other types of kale, which is essentially a nonheading form of cabbage, are less beautiful but more nutritious and can keep you supplied with fresh garden greens from the cold frame right through the winter months.

Growing

We plant kale in #98 trays in early June and set them out about July 1 in a rich, well-drained spot. You will need to handpick cabbageworms or spray with *Bacillus thuringiensis* (Bt) to keep them off the cabbages. Keep the bed well cultivated until the beginning of September.

Harvesting

Frost brings out both the color and the flavor in kale, so we don't usually harvest the plants until all the warm-season crops are done for the year. With ornamental kales, we harvest the entire plant, but they can be treated the same as the old types and can be picked leaf by leaf, as a cut-and-come-again crop.

The Best Varieties

The standard varieties of kale in this country are VATES and SCOTCH CURLED. Two heirloom English varieties known for their hardiness and good taste are COTTAGERS and PENTLAND BRIG. RUSSIAN RED, a tall, smooth-leaf type reminiscent of collards, makes a good salad crop when cut young.

Just now coming into notice are the highly bred ornamental types. The best of these are Japanese hybrids bred for the bedding plant trade. Even if not eaten, they make a very attractive base for salads, as the colors are very bright and the leaf forms visually exciting. The OSAKA series is smooth leaved, NAGOYA types are curly, and a new, deeply fringed variety called PEACOCK kale is the most beautiful of all. Each series contains white, pink, and red varieties.

Kohlrabi

One of the least known, but best tasting, members of the cabbage clan is kohlrabi. The plants produce a turniplike bulb that can be steamed or eaten raw in salads.

Growing

Since kohlrabi is a quick-growing plant (60 to 70 days), it's a good candidate for direct seeding in the garden. We plant it up to four weeks before the frost-free date so that it will germinate just about the time the cold weather is over for good.

Kohlrabi is the most cold sensitive of the brassicas. It's not ordinarily damaged by cold temperatures, but early varieties will bolt without bulbing if exposed to temperatures under 40°F for more than a day or two. Likewise, prolonged hot weather will cause the bulbs to become woody as the plant struggles to provide sap to its foliage to prevent wilting. It is also much less tolerant of transplanting than other cole crops.

Harvesting

For best quality, harvest when the bulbs are young and immature: as small as 1½ inches in diameter and no larger than 2 inches. Slice through the stem an inch below the bulb to harvest, then remove the leaves. The bulbs will keep in the refrigerator for several weeks.

The Best Varieties

The two traditional varieties are EARLY WHITE VIENNA and EARLY PURPLE VIENNA, mild-flavored types that are essentially identical except for their color. We've switched, however, to GRAND DUKE, a much more vigorous green variety, and to PURPLE DANUBE. Both are hybrids. The Danes have a number of varieties of kohlrabi, including another pair called WHITE DELIKATESSE and BLUE DELIKATESSE.

KALE AND KOHLRABI

Variety	When to Plant	When to Harvest	What to Harvest	Comments	Sources*
Kale					
COTTAGERS	Spring or fall	Summer/spring	Individual leaves and florets	Overwinter for early spring in Zone 6 or warmer	TM
PENTLAND BRIG	Spring or fall	Fall/spring	Individual leaves and florets	Overwinter for spring harvest in Zone 6 or warmer	BG
RUSSIAN RED	Spring	Summer/fall	Individual leaves or whole plant	Smooth-leaf type can be used young as part of mesclun mix	AL
Ornamental Kale					
NAGOYA HYBRID	Late spring	Fall (best after frost)	Individual leaves or whole plant	Savoy-leaved type in red, pink, and white; use for garnish	HM/CG
OSAKA HYBRID	Late spring	Fall (best after frost)	Individual leaves or whole plant	Smooth-leaf type in red, pink, and white; use for garnish	HM/CG
PEACOCK HYBRID	Late spring	Fall (best after frost)	Individual leaves or whole plant	Very finely cut, feathery leaves in red, pink, and white	HM/CG
Kohlrabi					
EARLY VIENNA	Spring or fall	Summer, late fall (60 days); when fruits are 2″ in diameter	Globular, swollen stem	Blue and white forms	Widely available
GRAND DUKE HYBRID	Spring/mid-summer	Early summer/fall	Globular, swollen stem	Pale green hybrid; uniform and disease resistant	Widely available
PURPLE DANUBE HYBRID	Spring/mid-summer	Early summer/fall	Globular, swollen stem	Blue-green equivalent to GRAND DUKE; both have good flavor	LM/JS

*Listings correspond to seed companies included under Seed Source List at the back of the book.

LEEKS

*L*eeks are the most dignified member of the onion family, and the most subtly flavored. These biennials are also one of the most beautiful plants in the garden, both during their first vegetative season, and during their second spring, when they send up a tall stalk crowned with a large spherical flower head.

Growing

We start leeks 10 to 12 weeks before the frost-free date in 20-row trays, thinning them to about three to the inch after the flag leaf unfolds. Keep the plants trimmed to 3 inches, but not below the newest leaf. We use a pair of scissors for this job. If the plants aren't kept trimmed, they might fall over and mat down when you water them, inviting diseases.

Leeks are hardier than onions, and they are less prone to bolting—sending up a seed stalk—so they can be hardened off and set out as soon as the ground can be worked in spring.

In a well-prepared bed, transplanting is a snap: Just stick your finger into the soil and plop the plant into the hole. Don't fill in the holes; wait until you've finished planting, then water the bed and let the water fill up the holes. This will settle soil around the roots of the newly planted leeks and get them off to a good start.

VARIETY SOURCE CHART

LEEKS

Variety	When to Plant	When to Harvest	What to Harvest	Comments	Sources*
ALASKA	Early spring	Late fall through winter	Blanched stems	Cold, hardy variety suitable for over-wintering	ST/WD
BLUE SOLAISE	Early spring	Late fall through winter	Blanched stems	Can be left to overwinter; harvest in early spring	CG/LM/LJ
CARENTAN	Early spring	When stem diameter reaches 1″	Blanched stems	Harvest in late summer/early fall before hard frost	WD/SS
ELECTRA	Early spring	Late fall	Blanched stems	Short plants adapted for wintering in frames and cloches	HM
GENNEVILLIERS	Early spring	When stem diameter reaches 1″	Blanched stems	Large, early leek; not frost hardy	LM
KING RICHARD	Early spring	When stem diameter reaches 1″	Blanched stems	Long, thin stems; good for "baby leeks"	PT/JS/CG
NEBRASKA	Early spring	Late fall through winter	Blanched stems	Large stems; hardy in moderate climates	JS

*Listings correspond to seed companies included under Seed Source List at the back of the book.

Leeks are usually blanched before harvest by burying the stems. Blanching forces the plant to stretch for light, which increases the amount of the lower stem that's white and tender. Setting the transplants in the bottom of a trench that is filled in as they grow is the traditional method of blanching, but it's not practical in poorly drained soils.

For a small number of leeks, "pipe" blanching works great. Once the leeks reach about an inch in diameter, clasp your hand around the stem near the ground and gather the leaves by moving your hand up the stem. Then slip a 6- to 8-inch-tall piece of 2-inch-diameter plastic pipe over each plant. If you'd rather, use a paper towel tube or a cardboard cylinder held together with paper clips. Either kind of collar will blanch the leeks without getting dirt in the leaves.

For large plantings, it may be easier to blanch the plants by hilling soil around the stems. We plant a single row of leeks down the center of a 3-foot-wide bed with a fast-growing crop of greens on each side. Once the greens have been harvested, we use the soil they were growing in to hill the leeks.

Harvesting

Leeks may be harvested at any time. When they're very small you can use them like scallions, but the taste is much milder. In the markets of Europe these baby leeks are considered a delicacy, and interest in them is growing on this side of the Atlantic.

The part of the plant you're after is the white portion of the blanched stem, but Ellen also saves the green part to use for soup stock.

The Best Varieties

Early leeks (August and September harvest) like KING RICHARD are fast growing —for a leek—and have long, thin stems an inch thick and up to a foot long. Some other good varieties of this type come from France, among them ROUEN, CAREN-TAN, and GENNEVILLIERS. They are hardy to about 20°F. They don't store well, so plant only as many as you can use fresh.

Leeks are by nature very hardy plants, and many of the later, larger varieties can survive the winter to provide a harvest before going to seed with the lengthening of the days in spring. It's important for harvest quality that they enter the winter in a juvenile state so that they have time in the spring to put out firm new growth before they mature and become tough. Our favorite winter leek is BLUE SOLAISE, another French variety. They grow very large—up to 2 inches thick—with the first leaf more than a foot off the ground. In years with good snow cover we've harvested them every month of the year, although I've sometimes had to chop the crusted snow from around the plants.

Some other good overwintering varieties are ALASKA, ELECTRA, and NEBRASKA. Winter leeks can be stored in the root cellar. Uproot the plants as gently as you can and bury them in moist sand in the root cellar. Keep temperatures in the mid-thirties, and they'll keep quite a while.

LETTUCE

We love lettuce. We grow some 50 kinds each season in our garden. That may seem like a lot, but consider that the U.S. Department of Agriculture has more than 800 varieties in its collection and that there are 275 varieties available from North American seed houses alone.

The largest class of lettuces under cultivation is butterheads. They have soft, velvety leaves ranging from maroon (pink where blanched by the outer leaves) to a pale yellow-green. They form soft, relatively loose heads. In this country they have traditionally been known as Boston or bibb-type lettuces, named for two early butterhead varieties that are still grown.

Another specific variety name that has come into the language of the garden as a type is BUTTERCRUNCH; it is still grown widely under that name, but now also signifies a kind of lettuce that forms a slightly more compact and upright head than other butterheads, with a thicker, more succulent leaf and generally a darker green color. Some sources put this type in a separate group between butterhead and cos lettuces.

Crisphead lettuce is characterized by very firm, compact heads. The American term for this type is iceberg lettuce (once again originally the name of a specific variety has come to signify a whole class). These are large, heavy heads: Supermarket lettuce is, as we all know, iceberg lettuce. The Europeans call this class batavian lettuces, and their varieties tend to be not quite as large, compact, or heavy as the American crispheads.

These lettuces do indeed have crisp, juicy leaves; most have less taste than other types, due to the blanching effect of the tight heads. The Europeans raise a number of red varieties of crisphead lettuce, but in this country that trait has been intentionally bred out of the common varieties.

A third type is the looseleaf or non-heading lettuce. This group includes most of the earliest-maturing lettuces. If given sufficient time and space, most develop large rosettes of leaves direct from the crown of the plant. It probably would be better to call them rosette lettuces. Most looseleaf varieties have tender, shiny, undulant, or toothed leaves; they come in red, green, and pale greenish yellow. These lettuces are especially good for salads because they hold dressing well on their intricate leaves and because, being unblanched, they have more flavor than heading lettuces.

Most cutting lettuces are looseleaf varieties, because this group of lettuces has the ability to resprout quickly from a cut stem. Virtually any lettuce can be cut when young for a fresh salad, however, and the use of lettuce thinnings in the salad bowl is a time-honored tradition. But true cutting lettuces are used in a cut-and-come-again fashion, giving plants a chance to resprout between harvests.

A final type is cos or romaine lettuce. It supposedly came from the island of Cos in the Mediterranean Sea and was popular during Roman times. Cos lettuces generally are thick leaved and upright, with stiff leaf ribs and a crisp texture that is prized for certain salads. There are both red and green forms, and they range in size from about 8 to 24 inches tall.

Among the varieties considered intermediate between two types are some of the taller butterheads and a few looseleaf types that form a head rather than a rosette if left to mature. Celtuce is a type that differs radically from other types of lettuce. It bears single leaves up a swollen stalk, which is itself peeled and eaten. It is thought to be of Chinese origin.

Growing

The secret to growing good lettuce is to keep it growing fast; if it slows down, quality is going to suffer. It's that simple, but also that difficult.

As every gardener knows, the best-laid plans exist simply to give the weather something to play around with. No sooner do we water to relieve a two-week drought than a monsoon sets in. If we put shade over the lettuce bed to give it a respite from the hot July sun, that is a sure cue for the sun to leave. We do our best, and hope for the best in return.

Lettuce goes in the first part of our rotation, while the soil is at its richest. As soon as the ground is workable after tilling in the winter's cover crop, we lime (if necessary) and then plant out our first lettuce transplants. Depending on the weather, we might put a floating row cover over this crop to gain the week or so it will give us in a cold spring. If the spring seems to be moderate or warm, however, there is no advantage to a cover, as lettuce is a cool-weather crop anyway.

We don't direct seed lettuce for our production gardens. Instead, we maximize the use of our growing beds by using transplants and making sure that the young plants get special treatment. Trays of lettuce seedlings can be pampered in a cold frame or shade bed—depending on the season—to keep them growing fast, and then set out in the growing beds when needed. As each crop is harvested, the beds can be renovated before replanting, so the weeds never have a chance to get established.

We seed lettuce weekly in #162 plug trays, starting in mid-February. We use a sterile planting mix to prevent damping-off, because the cool, moist conditions that produce good, sturdy lettuce plants also favor this disease. It is worth the trouble to place just a single seed into each cell, because we save the time that would be spent thinning the trays if the seed was placed by the pinch. Once planted, the trays are watered and set on a germinating mat at 72°F. You could also put them on top of the refrigerator, in the furnace room, or some other warm place. Be sure to keep a close eye on the trays, though, because at 70°F or so the seed may germinate within 24 hours. Do not put your trays of lettuce in a spot where the temperature goes over 80°F or germination will be lowered drastically. Lettuce is a spring plant by nature, and the seed goes dormant at high, summerlike temperatures.

As soon as the seedlings emerge, move the trays to the lightest, coolest spot you have, along with things like onions, leeks, and parsley. The planting medium should be kept evenly moist, but not soggy enough to cause damping-off. Still air is a great enemy of seedlings, so whether you have the flats in the kitchen window or out in a greenhouse, try to keep the air moving, however slightly. Even if you don't feel it, the plants do, and it is very good for them. In a greenhouse, it also helps to keep the air mixed so the temperatures are even throughout, instead of cold on the floor and hot at the peak. If you use a fan, don't aim it directly at the plants.

The seedlings will need to be watered and fed regularly in bright weather. You can either mix a very weak fertilizer solution and use it with every watering, or feed them every week or so with a normal strength solution. The weak solution is an easier method in that you don't have to remember when you last fertilized the plants. For this kind of use, mix the fertilizer at a quarter or less of the usual strength. Keep an eye on the plants; if they begin to look pale, increase the strength of your solution slightly.

Our February-planted lettuce can take up to five weeks to reach transplant size under cloudy, cool conditions. Usually, though, lettuce in a #162 tray will be ready to transplant in three to four weeks. Left in the tray much longer, the seedlings may become plug bound. You can spot this problem by pulling a plug and looking at the roots; if they are beginning to circle the bottom of the plug, plant them out as soon as you can. By squeezing the plug's soil ball before placing it in the ground, you can wake up the roots and get the seedling actively growing again. This is not an ideal situation, but it works well enough. Transplants come out of plug trays more easily if they have just received a heavy watering.

We plant all our lettuce in a 3:2:3 layout. We straddle the bed and work backwards, pulling the tray of transplants along the prepared bed with us. It's easy to get a neat bed of lettuce without having to measure the distance between plants if you start at the end of the bed with a crosswise row of three plants; place one just far enough in from each corner that its leaves will reach the path at harvest time, then one in the center. Next, set a row of two, aligning them halfway between the first three plants, with the diagonal distance between all five approximately equal. Then repeat the process, alternating rows of two and three plants each, until you run out of plants or room in the bed. This makes it easy to keep the rows straight and the plants evenly spaced.

It's a good idea to give the transplants a shot of water when setting them out, unless the weather is perfectly cooperative. The best method I know is to put a trigger nozzle on the garden hose, and blast transplant holes with the stream. Set the plants in the holes immediately. As the mud settles in the hole, it will coat the roots and prevent drying out. Set the plants at the same depth they were in the flat; do not leave depressions around the transplants or they will catch rain and increase the chance of bottom rot in a wet season.

Give the plants a few days to settle themselves before cultivating. We cultivate with a hoe from the path, working diagonally along the bed and walking backwards. (See Part I for details.) By the time you have gone down one side of the bed and up the other, you have cultivated all sides of every plant. That is the real efficiency of bed planting: There is no in-row weeding or cultivating to be done. After we cultivate the plants, we run the hoe down both edges of the bed to keep them clear of weeds. For the first cultivation, we can use our widest stirrup hoe, which is 7 inches across. We then work our way down to a 3-inch hoe as the plants grow together.

Lettuce needs water, especially during hot weather. Unless there is regular rain, you should water at least once a week. We try to cultivate a day or so after watering. Since these both run on the same schedule, it's not too hard to organize even in a large garden—until the weather stops cooperating.

If the plants need an extra boost, we use a foliar feed. Fish emulsion and liquid seaweed—1 ounce of each—mixed with a gallon of water gives a consistent mix. Home gardeners can use weak manure tea. Though either can be watered into the soil, the plants will make quicker and better use of nutrients sprayed on the foliage.

Once we have cleared the bed of all the good heads, we yank the rest for our poultry and then rotortill in preparation for another crop. Keeping the beds cultivated, cleared, or cover-cropped is important to weed control; we try to move quickly from one stage to the next. To paraphrase an old saying, "Idle lands are a weed's playground."

By proper timing and choice of varieties, you can stretch the lettuce season. You may not succeed in harvesting lettuce year-round unless you have a greenhouse or shade house, but even with just a cold frame and cloches, you can more than double the effective length of a short growing season. For example, our frost-free period is generally the 90 days from Memorial Day to Labor Day, but we can harvest lettuce all the way from Easter to Thanksgiving.

Our first planting of lettuce—indoors—is in mid-February. For this planting we use fast-growing, short-day-tolerant butterhead lettuces. We try to set them out in a cold frame or under cloches by the end of the third week in March. They will be ready for harvest the second week in May, just as the last of the wintered-over lettuces are running out. We make a second planting a week or two later, and then switch to spring outdoor lettuces.

Lettuce is a spring plant by nature and just about all varieties do well then, though the short-day types will run to seed as soon as the days approach 14 hours in length. Young lettuce plants are quite hardy, and though they may freeze solid, they will survive temperatures well down into the twenties and recover quite nicely within a couple of weeks to yield a fine harvest. What they don't like is quickly alternating hot and cold, so if you are growing spring lettuce under cover, keep the plants well ventilated on bright days—the spring sun is quite strong, especially when plants are protected from the wind by frames or cloches.

From the first of April—the soonest we can ever work our garden—until the frost-free date at the end of May, we continue seeding new lettuce plants weekly. Figure how much you'll use each week and plant 20 percent more; that way you'll have enough plants for any eventuality. These plantings are likely to be your best, and the easiest.

Soon after the frost-free date, heat replaces cold as the enemy of quality salad lettuce, so we switch to seeding heat-tolerant summer varieties about the same time we put out our tomatoes. We keep

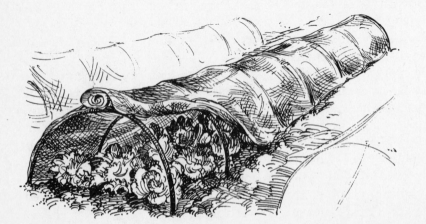

Lettuce shade tunnel

the seedling trays under a shade tunnel we made with metal hoops and commercial shade cloth (available at garden centers). This keeps the young plants from drying out on windy days, and stops the sun from baking their roots in the cells of the plug tray. We seed summer lettuces and grow them this way up until two weeks or so before the first fall frost.

During the hottest part of the summer —when the temperature is above 80°F— we let the flats sit in the cool back corner of our garage to germinate so they won't be sent into dormancy by the heat. As soon as the seedlings poke through, though, we put them out under the shade cloth. As August winds down and the days begin to shorten, we seed the first of our fall and winter lettuces. In areas where there is a long, gradual fall season, many of the same varieties that did well in the spring can be seeded again. Here, though, summer quickly turns to winter, at least as far as the average minimum temperature is concerned. We often get a killing frost in the low twenties by the end of September, and almost always have a night in the teens by Columbus Day. While young lettuces can survive those kinds of temperatures in the spring, when long days and strong sun give them the ingredients they need to recover, fall frost damage is much more severe.

Harvesting

Timing of the harvest is always a trade-off between size and tenderness. Lettuce is usable from the moment it shows above the ground, but we like to let it grow until its true form is evident. One of the most beautiful things about lettuce is its variation of leaf form and color on display in a salad bowl, so we wait to pick our lettuce until it is half to three-quarters full size. But we have visited farms that harvest their lettuce only slightly larger than the size at which we *transplant*—when the lettuce is at the six-to-eight-leaf stage and just beginning to round out, but not yet forming any kind of head.

To give you an idea of these sizes, consider that the standard commercial case of lettuce contains 18 heads. We fit 24 heads into the same carton, and that's *our* standard case. But 72 heads of the early harvested lettuce can be put into the typical lettuce box.

The first of the lettuces seeded in late summer will often be ready for harvest eight weeks or so from transplanting. The true winter types, which are adapted to cool, moist conditions and short days, will grow to half size, then stop, to begin growing again once the days lengthen in spring. These cold-hardy types may even die back to the ground over the course of the winter, only to resprout when conditions for growth are once again what the lettuce wants.

The Best Varieties

While the classification of lettuces by type provides a method for positively identifying any given variety, the gardener reading catalogs during the long winter night is more concerned with planning the bounteous season to come than a botany lesson. So we will try to note the seasonal adaptations of particular lettuce varieties in the discussion that follows. After all, some varieties are better adapted than others to long days and high temperatures, or to being buried in snow for months on end.

Butterhead Lettuces

A special class of butterheads is the forcing lettuces bred for greenhouse conditions. They differ from other types in that they will grow even during the short, gray days of winter as long as the temperature is kept above freezing. In addition, they have a lot of disease resistance bred in so they can stand the moist, stagnant air of the greenhouse. Most of the ones we're familiar with are from England and Holland, where light levels are quite low in the winter. Little heat is needed to "force" growth, unless they fall behind schedule. Because greenhouse culture is expensive, the lettuce must grow very fast to allow as many successions as possible within the limited space. If the greenhouse can be kept cooler than 80° to 85°F during the summer months by shading and ventilation, varieties such as CAPITAN and OSTINATA can be grown year-round. They are the most highly bred and expensive varieties we know, with seed running more than a penny a piece at retail prices. They are widely used for hydroponics.

(continued on page 109)

VARIETY SOURCE CHART

LETTUCE

Variety	When to Plant	When to Harvest	What to Harvest	Comments	Sources*
Butterhead					
BIBB	Early spring	8-10 weeks after seeding	Small, soft, green heads	Not heat resistant, but tops for texture in its season	Widely available
CAPITAN	Seed in flats	8-10 weeks after seeding	Pale green butterheads	For greenhouses; seed relatively expensive	ST/SS
CONTINUITY	Spring, summer	8-10 weeks after seeding	Deep red heads, 6″-8″ in diameter	Similar to FOUR SEASONS but with darker red coloring	NG/BG/ CG
DELTA	Seed in flats in late winter	4-6 weeks after transplanting	8″ green heads	Adapted to spring forcing under cover	CG

LETTUCE

Variety	When to Plant	When to Harvest	What to Harvest	Comments	Sources*
DIAMANTE	Seed in flats during winter	8–12 weeks after transplanting	8″–10″ deep green heads	For cold but frost-free greenhouses; a winter crop	JS
FOUR SEASONS (MERVIELLE DES QUATRE SAISONS, BESSON ROUGE)	Spring, fall (except in the far north)	6–8 weeks after seeding	Red heads, 6″–10″ in diameter	Very beautiful; red pales to cream color in heart	SS/PT/ LM/CG
MAGNET	Seed in flats in late winter	4–6 weeks after transplanting	8″–10″ green heads	Can also be wintered over, but growth will be much slower	CG
MAY KING	Early spring/early fall	8–10 weeks after seeding	Soft, pale green heads	Traditional early spring type, with red blush at leaf tips	SB/CG
OSTINATA	Seed in flats	8–10 weeks after seeding	Pale green butterheads	For the greenhouse; seed relatively expensive	ST/HP
PIRAT	Spring, fall (except in the far north)	8–10 weeks after seeding	Red- to bronze-tinged heads	Mottled with red; not as heat tolerant as CONTINUITY	CG/JS
PRADO	Early spring	8–10 weeks after seeding	Large green butterhead	Early butterhead for late spring harvest; very uniform	CG
VASCO	Very early spring, fall	8–16 weeks (seasonal)	Small, dark green heads	For greenhouse or outdoors (cool climate) "baby lettuce"	JS
VOLUMA	Spring, summer	8–10 weeks after seeding	Soft, shiny green heads	Very uniform and reliable; seed relatively expensive	CG
Crisphead					
ICEBERG	Spring/fall	8–12 weeks after seeding	Tight, green, blanched heads	Forerunner of today's "iceberg types"	CG/BP
ICE QUEEN, REINE DES GLACES	Spring/fall	8–12 weeks after seeding	Small, green, convoluted heads	Intricately toothed leaves, crisp texture, nutty flavor	LM/CG/ LJ

(continued)

LETTUCE

Variety	When to Plant	When to Harvest	What to Harvest	Comments	Sources*
Crisphead—*continued*					
ITHACA	Spring/fall	8-12 weeks after seeding	Small, tightly packed heads	Good variety for Northeast; withstands spring hot spells	Widely available
RED GRENOBLE	Spring/fall	6-12 weeks after seeding	Burgundy red leaves/ heads	Can be harvested young as looseleaf, or left to head up	LM/CG
ROSY	Spring/ fall	8-12 weeks after seeding	Tightly packed deep red heads	The first deep red crisp head type; heat tolerant	CG/PK
Intermediate					
AKCEL	Very early spring, fall	8-16 weeks (seasonal)	Small, deep green heads	Upright variety similar to VASCO	CG
BUTTERCRUNCH	Spring through summer	8-10 weeks after seeding	Compact, deep green heads	Thick juicy leaves; good heat tolerance; easy to grow	Widely available
CRAQUERELLE DU MIDI	Spring through fall	8-10 weeks after harvest	Small green romaine heads	Very heat tolerant	CG/LM
DEER TONGUE	Spring through summer	6-12 weeks after seeding	Leaves and/or firm heads	Also called MATCHLESS, if thinned and left to form pinnate heads	CG
LITTLE GEM	Spring through summer	8-10 weeks after seeding	Small, upright heads; 6″ in diameter	Very compact, firm heads; good taste; very heat resistant	SS/CG/ TM
WINTER DENSITY	Spring through fall (in north)	8-10 weeks after seeding	Upright, tightly folded heads	Good texture; tolerant of both heat and cold; compact	SB/CG/ JS
Looseleaf					
BIONDO A FOGLIE LISCE (BLONDIE)	Spring through fall	4-8 weeks after seeding	Pale green leaves, 4″-6″ long	Doesn't need thinning; harvest by cutting with scissors	CG

VARIETY SOURCE CHART

LETTUCE

Variety	When to Plant	When to Harvest	What to Harvest	Comments	Sources*
BLACK-SEEDED SIMPSON	Early spring	6-8 weeks after seeding	Loose, pale green rosettes	Heirloom variety known for early maturity and high quality	Widely available
CURLY OAKLEAF	ASAP in spring/in succession	4-8 weeks after seeding	Pale green, lobed 4″-6″ leaves	Deeply lobed leaves, good for cut-and-come-again harvest	CG
GREEN ICE	Spring through summer	6-12 weeks after seeding	Curly, medium green leaves/heads	Use early as a looseleaf or leave to head up; heat tolerant	PK/BP
LOLLO BIONDO	Spring through summer	6-8 weeks after seeding	Tiny, tightly curled heads	Pale green but similar in form to LOLLO ROSSA; 4″-6″ in diameter	LM/CG
LOLLO ROSSA	Spring through summer	6-8 weeks after seeding	Tiny, tightly curled heads	Pale green leaves with rose-colored tips; great for garnish	SS/VB/ CG/JS/ LM
OAKLEAF (BLONDE FEUILLE DE CHENE)	Spring through fall	6-10 weeks after seeding	Leaves and/or large rosettes	Pale green, oak-type leaves; good for cutting at 6″	Widely available
RED OAKLEAF	Spring through fall	6-10 weeks after seeding	Leaves and/or large rosettes	Oakleaf type with red coloring; names vary	JS/LM
RED SAILS	Spring through fall	8-10 weeks after seeding	Deep red leaves/ rosettes	Large, open-hearted, red looseleaf; good heat tolerance	Widely available
RED SALAD BOWL	Spring through fall	6-10 weeks after seeding	Leaves and/or large rosettes	Similar to SALAD BOWL, but deep red; both very heat tolerant	Widely available
ROSSA DI TRENTO	Spring through fall	4-8 weeks after seeding	Leaves at 4″-6″ or heads	Cut with scissors for mesclun; pale green and rose coloring	CG
ROYAL OAKLEAF	Spring through fall	6-10 weeks after seeding	Leaves and/or large rosettes	Improved OAKLEAF; dark green, shiny leaves; more pronounced	BP/CG

(continued)

LETTUCE

Variety	When to Plant	When to Harvest	What to Harvest	Comments	Sources*
Looseleaf—*continued*					
RUBY	Early spring	6–8 weeks after seeding	Deep red, open-hearted heads	Upright red looseleaf good for cutting	Widely available
SALAD BOWL	Spring through fall	6–10 weeks after seeding	Leaves and/or large rosettes	Deeply lobed, pale green leaves are good for cutting at 6"	Widely available
WINTER RED LEAF	Late summer	Late fall into winter	Leaves	Winter variety for mild climates or cold frame	CG
Romaine					
COSMO	Spring/fall	8–10 weeks after seeding	Tall, heavily savoyed heads	Bright green, crisp, and flavorful; not for midsummer	JS
ERTHEL (CRISP MINT)	Early spring	8–12 weeks after seeding	Savoyed, deep green heads	Crisp texture, good appearance with savoyed leaf tips	TM
LOBJOIT'S COS	Spring	8–12 weeks after seeding	Large, pale green heads	Early English variety	BG
PARIS ISLAND	Early spring	10–12 weeks after seeding	Large, tall, dark green heads	Traditional cos type; crisp, thick leaves; heat tolerant	Widely available
ROMANCE	Spring/fall	8–10 weeks after seeding	Tall, smooth, green cos heads	More tender than larger, supermarket-type cos lettuces	SS
ROUGE D'HIVER	Spring through fall	6–10 weeks after seeding	Leaves and/or tall red heads	Loosehead red romaine also used as a cutting lettuce	CG/LM/SS
VALMAINE	Early spring	6–12 weeks after seeding	Leaves; tall, deep green heads	Fine textured; also harvested young as a cutting lettuce	TM/PK/VB/ST/WD

*Listings correspond to seed companies included under Seed Source List at the back of the book.

Some varieties of forcing lettuce are worth growing for an early spring crop. MAGNET is a large, pale green butterhead with good heat resistance. DELTA is smaller but similar in habit. DIAMANTE is a good variety from midwinter into spring, with darker coloring. For a small but heavy head that allows closer planting, try AKCEL. And for greenhouse bibb lettuce, there is VASCO. These can be transplanted anytime after October, but should be kept cool; seeding around the first of September should provide good-size seedlings without the need for supplemental light, even in the North. If you plant in succession and keep them above freezing, it should be possible to have salads right through the winter. Keep in mind that soil temperature is a major factor in plant growth and is a lot harder to control than air temperature. Even if you keep the air temperature above freezing, you may find that your lettuce doesn't grow. Check the soil temperature—if it's below 40°F, you can't expect much in the way of growth because there just isn't sufficient chemical and biological activity around the roots to provide the engine needed for growth.

Because spring is the growth period for the species in nature, most varieties will do well if planted out as soon as the ground can be prepared. The ones that do not work well will fail only in the sense that they run to seed before forming a usable head or rosette. Within the broad range of types and varieties, I want to note particularly beautiful or otherwise exceptional varieties that are at their best in the spring, though they may grow well enough at other times as well.

Among butterheads, there are a number of varieties with beautiful coloring. FOUR SEASONS (MERVIELLE DES QUATRE SAISONS or BESSON ROUGE in French) is distinguished by a deep burgundy color that fades to green at the leaf edges and a deep creamy yellow in the blanched heart. It is considered the standard for beauty in red lettuces. While it is quite cold-hardy when young and therefore good for spring, FOUR SEASONS also withstands a certain amount of heat. It has a very smooth-textured leaf and is mild in flavor when grown quickly, without stress.

CONTINUITY is similar to FOUR SEASONS, but much deeper in color, with less tendency to green and cream at the extremities and in the heart; it is also somewhat more heat tolerant, giving solid, soft-hearted butterheads even in the middle of the Vermont summer.

PIRAT is a German summer butterhead that also does well in the spring. Its coloring is much more subtle than that of the two above, being pale green with bronze highlights that accent the shape of the softly folded head. All three of these have the soft texture that, with the pale yellow color of their hearts, gave rise to the type name, butterhead.

The classic green spring butterhead is BIBB, bred in the limestone lands of the mid-South, and often referred to as LIMESTONE lettuce. There are now many different descendants of the original bibb, and most breeding with this variety since that time has been for the purpose of slowing its race to seed, as it is one of the least heat-tolerant varieties and can be grown to perfection only in cool weather. Each seed house has a strain, so the best plan is to try a few and see what works best in your garden. If you must have the true BIBB lettuce, not just one of the many better-adapted butterheads of the Boston type that are larger and have many of the same fine, tender qualities of bibb, be sure to time your crop to mature before the onset of hot, dry weather, and provide plenty of water so its growth is not checked. Either of these stresses—heat or drought—will cause it to bolt.

Within the Boston types (now a generic term for butterheads in this country), there are many, many varieties that differ very little in taste, texture, or appearance. These are more or less disease resistant, and adapted to different climates and soil types. Your best bet, once again, is to try different varieties until you find one that works well in your garden. One of our favorites, PRADO, is a compact, fast-growing variety similar to the old favorite KAGRAN SOMMER, but that is even more resistant to bolting during that occasional spring heat wave. Another is VOLUMA, a Dutch variety that has shinier leaves than other butterheads and is particularly able to withstand poor drainage. An old heirloom that still has an honored place in the spring salad garden is MAY KING, a pale green variety tinged with pink at the margins; it is adapted to frames and cloches and is sometimes used for over-wintering in milder climates.

Looseleaf Lettuces

Many looseleaf lettuces are at their prime in the cool of spring. Old standbys like BLACK-SEEDED SIMPSON are still good for the early crop, and if grown fast—this variety is ready in only 45 days under good conditions—they are of fine quality. The best looseleaf lettuces include SALAD BOWL, its cousin RED SALAD BOWL, and OAKLEAF. These are heat-tolerant rosette lettuces—that is, they do not form heads as such, but grow from a crown in rosette form. They are very ornamental, with the deeply lobed leaves arranged in radial fashion around the center of the plant. The leaves get smaller as they approach the center, and the plants look like a sunburst of pale green (or deep burgundy in the case of the red). They are especially attractive when planted together. All are strongly resistant to bolting.

There are a few different variations on the traditional OAKLEAF lettuce. ROYAL OAKLEAF, a patented strain sold by Burpee, has a more angular leaf form and deep green color that makes it a fine counterpoint to the SALAD BOWL types. Several European OAKLEAF types have been selected for their ability to resprout quickly after the leaves have been cut or picked; BLONDE FEUILLE DE CHENE and FOGLIE DI QUERCIA (both translate simply as "leaf of oak") are a clear pale green, and will be very tender if picked young. RED OAKLEAF is similar to RED SALAD BOWL except that the red coloring does not extend to the leaf edges. WINTER RED LEAF also has this characteristic.

LOLLO ROSSA is a small, incredibly beautiful openhearted variety that combines a pale, clear green leaf with rose-red margins; LOLLO BIONDO is its green cousin.

An Italian lettuce that is well adapted to cut-and-come-again harvesting is the

DEER TONGUE lettuce

Italian variety BIONDO A FOGLIE LISCE. This true looseleaf is usually sown thick in the row and harvested with scissors. DEER TONGUE lettuce, also known as MATCHLESS, is an intermediate lettuce that is also cut as a looseleaf if sown thick; if thinned, it will head up into unusual pinwheel-shaped heads that have a fine, succulent leaf. This is also true of Burpee's GREEN ICE, the first lettuce to receive a plant patent, and ROSSA DI TRENTO, another Italian *lattuga di taglio,* or cutting lettuce. All of these, with the exception of BIONDO (BLONDIE), will head up if thinned out in the row and left to mature.

There are a number of other good looseleaf lettuces. RUBY, an All America Selections (AAS) bronze medal winner in 1958, is very fast growing and a beautiful deep burgundy color throughout. RED SAILS, a more recent AAS champion, is much larger and broader than RUBY, and is quite heat tolerant.

Crisphead Lettuces

Iceberg lettuce, and its European counterparts, the crispheads, are primarily adapted for spring conditions, and many varieties do not reliably form solid heads once the weather turns hot. The variety ICEBERG has a slight red tinge along the outer leaf margins, which was bred out when the variety was exploited as a shipping lettuce. Some of the American home garden types will head under less-than-ideal conditions and will provide a striking comparison with bland, store-bought iceberg-type lettuce. A few varieties that seem to be well adapted for home gardens are ITHACA, MONTELLO, and KING CROWN.

The true crispheads are more upright than the iceberg lettuces, and not so fully formed into heads. Among the most beautiful is REINE DES GLACES, or ICE QUEEN, a shiny spike-toothed heading lettuce whose finely cut and divided leaves resemble a crown of thorns. The leaves, used to line a salad bowl or simply added to a mix, hold dressing well and add a refreshing visual element to the salad bowl. This is a moderately heat-tolerant variety, and can be grown in all but the hottest months here in the cool mountains of the North. Southern gardeners may want to try it as a fall crop, as it is also fairly frost-hardy.

ICE QUEEN lettuce

Another of my favorite crispheads is RED GRENOBLE. This is a double-purpose lettuce: It can be harvested young as a looseleaf, at which time it closely resembles RED SAILS, the AAS-winning red looseleaf, or it can be left to form a fairly compact, deep burgundy-colored head. The shininess of the leaves makes it look fresh, cool, and crisp, even on sultry summer afternoons. Its heat and cold tolerance are equal to that of REINE DES GLACES.

Romaine Lettuces

Romaine lettuces are also best adapted to spring, but they are a bit easier to grow during hot weather than other types. Fans of romaine lettuce describe its texture as "substantial," but detractors insist the texture is nothing but coarse. Whichever your opinion, the firm structure of romaine is perfect for salads in which the texture and flavor of other ingredients might overpower the more refined butterhead.

It used to be that the only readily available variety was PARIS ISLAND. Then, a few years ago, new varieties began to show up in the seed lists of garden catalogs. First came VALMAINE, which is well adapted to the northern United States. LOBJOIT'S COS is an early romaine with good quality that can stand hot weather. ERTHEL, or CRISP MINT, lacks the flavor suggested by its name, but does produce a beautiful, savoyed head with ruffled leaf margins. We have had good luck here with COSMO, which has a certain amount of savoy in the outer leaves, and stands the heat of early summer relatively well.

More recently, a number of smaller, finer-textured romaines have been introduced to gardeners in this country from Europe, where some of them have been around for generations. ROMANCE has a fine, dark green leaf, a shiny complexion, and finer texture than most of the larger types.

LITTLE GEM, Shepherd's favorite lettuce, looks like a miniature romaine, sort of a tall BUTTERCRUNCH. This compact little lettuce is very heat tolerant, and grows well in spring, summer, and fall. It produces very heavy heads in a small space, because there are few loose outer leaves to take up room. LITTLE GEM is beyond a doubt the best sandwich lettuce we know.

The most heat-tolerant lettuce we've seen is an open-hearted intermediate called CRAQUERELLE DU MIDI. A step larger, but still of this tall intermediate type, is WINTER DENSITY. There have been good crops of WINTER DENSITY here in Vermont even in August, though it is also well adapted for growing through the winter in milder regions such as the Pacific Northwest. It holds up well under short-day conditions, but doesn't bolt so quickly when the days lengthen again in spring.

One last, interesting romaine is the old French heirloom ROUGE D'HIVER, or RED WINTER COS. Few American garden-ers have seen this fine variety, but it has been in existence for hundreds of years, and was highly recommended by the author of *The Vegetable Garden,* a book first published in 1853. The tall, spatulate leaves are colored a deep burgundy that fades as the plant reaches maturity; only in the heart is it green. While not all the plants in a bed will head up firmly, it is very slow to go to seed. Its color, combined with the simple cos leaf form, is striking in a garden salad or as a base for a plate of crudités. It does not seem to be winter-hardy in Vermont, but may stand through the dark season in milder climates. This variety is now widely grown by specialty producers in California for the restaurant trade.

MELONS

Melons differ from most other common garden vegetables in that taste has always been the primary goal of raising them, rather than economy or food value. This is important because it underscores some of the main concerns of this book. We don't grow melons for practical reasons, but because they taste good. Earliness and disease resistance matter to us only so far as they allow us to get a crop, and in this, choice of variety is important.

Growing

The melon grown in most American gardens may be called a cantaloupe, but in fact it is a muskmelon, a related plant known by its netted skin and "musky" odor when ripe. The smooth-skinned CHARENTAIS melon of France is a true cantaloupe. The honeydew-type melons—crenshaws, honeydews, and casaba—are members of a third, nonmusky branch of the family whose Latin name is, appropriately, *inodorous*. All three types require the same treatment in the garden as cucumbers, to which they are very closely related.

We prepare a high bed for melons, cover it with black plastic mulch to moderate moisture and raise the soil temperature, then cut crosswise slits every foot along the center of the bed. We hollow out a depression at each slit and fill it with compost mixed with a bit of phosphate.

We use calcium phosphate (available under the tradenames Lonfosco and Zo-Ra-Fos), which has a neutralizing effect on our acid soil. When planting (after the weather is thoroughly settled in early summer) we pour a half pint or so of transplant solution (see Part I) into the hole and set the plants directly in the mud, being careful not to injure the stem.

The best age for transplants is two or three weeks, so they should not be started until a week before the frost-free date. If they become potbound, development of the plant's taproot will be inhibited, and the plant will send out shallow, fibrous roots instead. During midsummer, these plants will require more water to sustain their growth because they will be less able to reach into the lower layers of the soil to draw up moisture. We use a #50 tray (about the size of a 2¼-inch peat pot). Melons require a high germination temperature, about 75° to 80°F.

If your frost-free growing season is 120 days or more, you may be able to get a crop from direct-seeded plants. In that case, put four to six seeds in each hole. Don't water them until the soil temperature is at least 60°F, or the seeds may rot. Once the plants are well up, thin back to only a couple of plants per hill at most.

Whichever way you start your plants, we recommend putting a floating row cover on them the moment they go in the ground to keep out striped and spotted cucumber beetles, the only pests that give us much trouble. They can completely wipe out young plants if they get to them at an early stage. Theoretically, the beetles can be controlled with a rotenone/pyrethrum spray, but we have not had much luck with this method. You might do better to plant just a few members of the cucumber family—leftovers from the seed flat—outside the cover, and use them as a trap for the beetles, which can then be caught and disposed of.

If you're going to trellis the plants to save space, you can put up the support when you remove the covers. In a short-season area like ours, it's enough to keep off the beetles until the plants have begun to run. Past that point, the insects can't physically harm the plants much, and any diseases they might pass on don't really have time to develop by the time plants are killed by frost.

Melons need plenty of water when they are young, but once the fruits have reached the size of a baseball, you should avoid watering them unless absolutely necessary. The flavor is concentrated by holding back on water for the last couple of weeks while the melons are ripening. If they get too much water at that point, the melons will taste bland.

Harvesting

Knowing when to harvest melons is one of the trickiest parts of growing them, and the right time differs for each type of melon. Many people have theories about how to tell when a melon is ripe: The stem detaches easily from the melon; the background color of the rind changes from green to yellow; the stem end exudes a sweet, "musky" odor; or the blossom end gives slightly when pressed with a finger. In fact, all of these are valuable signs of

VARIETY SOURCE CHART

MELONS

Variety	When to Plant	When to Harvest	What to Harvest	Comments	Sources*
AMBROSIA HYBRID	Frost-free date	When fruit slips from vine	6″-diameter 4–5-lb. fruits	The standard for taste in American muskmelons	PK/BP
CHACA HYBRID	Frost-free date	When skin turns yellow	3–3½-lb. smooth-skinned fruits	Hybrid between European and American types	NG
CHARENTAIS	Frost-free date	When skin turns yellow	2–3-lb. smooth-skinned fruits	Good for cool areas; very good flavor; doesn't slip from vine when ripe (see text)	LM/ST/ CG/BG/ NG
EARLISWEET	Frost-free date	When fruit slips from vine	5½″ round fruits	Good for northern climates	ST/NG/ VB
FLYER HYBRID	Frost-free date	When skin begins to turn yellow	2½–3-lb. smooth-skinned fruits	European-American type; very early; good for northern areas	JS/SB
JENNY LIND	Frost-free date	When fruit slips from vine	1–2″ turbaned fruit with netting	Variable heirloom type; does well in cool areas; good taste	PT/SB
NUTMEG (EDEN GEM)	Frost-free date	When fruit slips from vine	Up to 2 lb.; dark green netting	Very old heirloom type; early and hardy; also known as ROCKY FORD	SB/VB/ NG
PANCHA	Frost-free date	When skin turns a bit yellow	6″ diameter melons	Cross between American- and CHARENTAIS-type melons	SS

*Listings correspond to seed companies included under Seed Source List at the back of the book.

maturity in a melon, but some apply to one type of melon and some to others.

Muskmelons, which most of us call cantaloupes, are fully ripe when the melon separates easily from the vine and the stem cavity smells sweet. They can be picked a bit sooner, and texture and flavor may still improve some, but the sweetness will not increase. True cantaloupes do not slip from the stem, and should be cut, not pulled, from the vine when the melon begins to yellow and the blossom end softens, or even cracks. The same is true for the honeydew-type melons.

The Best Varieties

The most important consideration in choosing among the many varieties of the common American muskmelon is regional adaptation. There are some melons that you might want to try regardless of your climate, such as AMBROSIA, JENNY LIND, and CHARENTAIS. But in general, a well-grown melon of a variety suited to your area will taste better than one that, while regionally famous for flavor, may not grow well enough in your garden to live up to its reputation.

We've had good luck with early muskmelons like EARLISWEET and heirlooms like the turbaned little JENNY LIND melon that is renowned for its sweet flavor and productivity. We are also able to mature the French CHARENTAIS, its cousins VEDRANTAIS and IDO, and its hybrid relatives CHACA, PANCHA, and FLYER. These are all small, smooth-skinned, green melons that ripen in less than three months; this makes them feasible even in our short season, if started in peat pots or plugs a week or two before the frost-free date. One variety that's getting good notice is the NUTMEG melon, a small early sort of very old heritage, developed in this country and popular in Europe more than 100 years ago. It is a small, pear-shaped melon with sweet, juicy flesh and a strong, perfumed aroma.

ONIONS

Formerly, we didn't plant onions at all. "Dime a pound at the supermarket," we thought. "Why bother?" Well, there is a reason to bother. If all you've known is the supermarket onion, you haven't lived.

And if all you've grown for onions is the sets you bought at the store, you've lived, but only barely. That's because set onions are bred to make good sets, not good onions. The major reason is sulfur. Sulfur compounds give onions their pungency, and they're the ingredients that bring tears to your eyes. Sulfur is closely tied to the keeping quality of onions: Pungent onions keep well; mild onions don't. Since sets have to keep through the winter

to be usable, all are pungent varieties. So, if sets are all you've sown, strong onions are all you've grown.

Sulfurous onions taste strong and irritate the membranes of your eyes, nose, and throat. Your nose plays a very large part in the overall sense of taste, perhaps the dominant one, since the range of odors that can be recognized is nearly limitless, while taste is limited to the sensations of sweet, sour, bitter, and salty. The "sweetness" of onion varieties such as GRANEX 33 (known in the produce trade as Vidalias) and WALLA WALLA SWEET is caused by low sulfur, not high sugar. If you want to grow sweet onions, you'll need to watch soil sulfur in addition to choosing the right variety. So keep on growing your sets, and enjoy your winter onions, but also try some of the milder types for summer use.

Growing

Our first two crops of onions were total failures. One reason was that our land was poorly prepared and too acid. But we also made a conceptual mistake: We thought of them as root crops. The bulb of an onion (and its relatives) is actually a swollen bud that grows leaves from its top and roots from its underside. Once we shifted them into the part of our rotation that got more nutrients and more water to them—in with the lettuces, greens, squashes, and brassicas—we started getting good onions. This part is planted on land that was manured the previous fall, then planted to annual ryegrass. I have read that following ryegrass with onions leads to poor onions, but this has not been my experience.

Gardeners in parts of the country with acid soil will have a harder time growing sweet onions. The acidity of many soils in the Northeast is related to the presence of aluminum sulfate, from which onions will scavenge sulfur just like spinach goes for nitrates. Garden soil that is low in sulfur will grow sweeter onions because the plants pick up less of it. Adding enough lime to keep the pH up to 6.5 and adding plenty of organic matter is the best thing acid soil gardeners can do.

Onions are a great crop for organic growers because they like a lot of organic matter in a sandy loam soil. Excess nitrate can lead to double-centered bulbs and poor storage quality. But the slow release of nitrogen from rotted manure is just right for onions, and green manure crops break down into humus, which holds plenty of moisture without becoming waterlogged. To fertilize onions, add two bushels of rotted manure per 100 square feet and turn under before planting. If all you have is fresh manure, apply it in the fall before seeding your cover crop so it has time to rot by spring.

Some varieties of onions are more sensitive to day length (actually, night length). In the cooler latitudes of the United States, the onion prepares for a dormancy in winter by forming a bulb, and this is triggered by the changing day length (and to a lesser degree by temperature changes). In southern latitudes, the onions are dormant in the summer. So if you plant a variety adapted for the other area, you may end up with tiny cocktail-size onions come May up North or huge overgrown scallions with no bulb at all down South. North of a line running from Atlanta to San Francisco, you should plant "long-day" onions, and south of that line, "short-day" onions. If the person you get the seed from doesn't know which they are, you should be buying elsewhere. Onions are the only allium that shows this sensitivity to day length. Shallots, garlic, and potato onions are day-length neutral—that is, their bulbing reflex is not triggered by day length. Welsh onions and leeks don't form bulbs, so day length doesn't affect them.

We plant long-day onions. Around the second week in February, we start them from seed in 20-row trays filled with sterile potting mix. These inserts have 20 cavities running across the tray, each 1 inch deep, 1 inch wide, and 10 inches long. You can sow the seed randomly across an open planting tray or in hand-dibbled furrows, but onions in inserts are completely separate from one another, so diseases are confined to the individual rows. Because the roots can't become intertwined, this is a timesaver during transplanting. To sow seed in a way that reduces thinning later on, dribble a pinch of seed from between thumb and forefinger as you move along the row.

At 72°F, the seed should germinate in three or four days. We use a germinating mat with a thermostat, but the top of the refrigerator may do just as well if you have a few seeds to start and a kitchen that is warm. The first leaf to appear is called the "flag leaf." It is folded in half like a hairpin. Shortly after its emergence, the flag leaf unfolds (hence the name) and is soon standing straight and tall. Once this happens, thin the plants to ¼ inch or so apart along the row, and give them as much light as possible. If you want to grow really big transplants, use a #162 insert (9 rows by 18 rows of 1¼-inch-square cells) and sow a few seeds in each cell, thinning to leave the strongest shortly after they emerge.

Keep the seedlings trimmed to 3 or 4 inches—but not below the newest leaf—and fertilize weekly with seedling solution (see Part I) if the weather is bright. As soon as the danger of a hard freeze is past, put them out in an open cold frame, where they can be covered if necessary. You don't need to worry about frost when they are young, but the abrupt change from the summerlike conditions inside to spring conditions outside can cause plants to run to seed and form inferior bulbs; so keep onions in the coolest part of your seedling growing area or harden them off carefully before setting out.

Onions can be set out as soon as they have adjusted to the outside weather and the soil is dry enough to prepare. We might put some out as early as April 15, but our main crop doesn't go in until early May (three to four weeks before the frost-free date). Since temperature plays a part in triggering the bulbing reflex of onions, it can affect yields and storage quality. Even in the South, where onions continue to grow through the winter, they will not begin bulbing—though day length may be correct—until the average daily temperature reaches 60°F. This is because both the temperature *and* the day length must be right for bulbing to begin. Also, the higher the temperature after the start of bulbing, the sooner the plants will mature. This means that hot weather right after bulb initiation will decrease yields because the onions mature small; cool temperatures, on the other hand, will give them a chance to keep growing and increase yields by increasing average bulb size. All other factors being equal, there seems to be no connection between the size of the bulb and the keeping quality or flavor of the onion.

If you want big onions, set them out 6 inches on center—allowing 6 inches in all directions from the center of one plant to the next. In our garden, this is a 4:3:4 layout, alternating rows of three and four plants across the width of the bed. (See Part I for details.) If you're not so interested in big onions, but would like to have a substitute for scallions along the way, plant the seedlings 1 or 2 inches apart in rows 4 to 6 inches apart. By pulling alternate plants as they begin to crowd, you can have a summer-long supply of young onions and still have some to store for winter.

If your garden is bothered by the onion fly, which is closely related to the cabbage maggot fly, cover the newly sown or transplanted beds with a floating row cover. These pests are much less of a problem with onions grown from sets.

Most onion diseases are best prevented by crop rotation, though I have spoken with growers who think that some members of the family—garlic in particular—should be grown in the same place every year.

In a dry season or dry climate, you will need to irrigate. Although they will not tolerate poor drainage, all members of this family, from garlic to onions to leeks, appreciate ample water. Yields will suffer if they are deprived. Once the bulbs have formed and the tops start to die back, however, water should be withheld to encourage the bulbs to cure properly. Too much water shortly before harvest can reduce the storage quality of onions. This past summer we lost almost our entire crop because the month of August went by with no more than two clear days in a row. Half the bulbs rotted in the field, and even those we got into the barn wouldn't dry. If you mulch your onions with hay or straw, pull the mulch back when the tops begin to die back so the bulbs cure properly.

The biggest problem with growing onions is usually weeds. Because of its sparse foliage, this crop can't shade the ground enough to inhibit the growth of weeds, even when planted intensively. Keep the bed well cultivated as long as you can without harming the bulbs. We give the onion beds a thorough going-over every couple of weeks, using a narrower hoe with each cultivation. When the thinnest hoe (ours is only 2 inches wide) no longer fits, we stop cultivating and just patrol for weeds that threaten to set seed. Harvest onions according to your use for them. The leaves can be cut for salads or seasoning, but do this only on plants that you are planning to harvest early anyway or you'll reduce yields.

Harvesting

Once half the tops have fallen, it's time to harvest. We wait for the beginning of a dry spell, then pull an empty lawn roller down the beds to bend over the remaining tops. This convinces the slow learners among our class of onions that it's time to get on with things. A few days to a week later, depending on the weather, you can pull the plants and let them dry on the surface for another few days. When the dirt adhering to the "scales," or outer layers of skin, is dry, move them inside to

(continued on page 124)

ONIONS

Variety	When to Plant	When to Harvest	What to Harvest	Comments	Sources*
BERMUDA	Spring	When tops die down	Bulbs	Short-day type; non-hybrid; flattened globe onions for fresh use	VB/GY/PK
CARMEN HYBRID	Spring	When tops die down	Bulbs	Long-day type; better internal coloring than many reds	ST/TM/PT
FIESTA HYBRID	Spring	When tops dry down	Bulbs	Cross between SWEET SPANISH and storage types; best of both	ST/HM/SS
GRANEX 33 HYBRID	Fall for spring harvest	When tops die down	Bulbs	Short-day type; also known as Vidalia; very mild	BP
OWA 153	8–10 weeks before last frost	When tops die down	Long, cylindrical bulbs	Yellow bottle onion	GY
RED LUCCA (ROUGE DE FLORENCE)	Spring	When tops die down	Bulbs	Day-neutral type; spindle-shaped; for fresh use	CG/TM/LM/NG
RED, YELLOW, WHITE GLOBE	Spring	When tops die down	Bulbs	Long-day type, many sub-types; pungent storage onions	Widely available
RUBY	8–10 weeks before last frost	When tops die down	Red bulbs	SOUTHPORT RED GLOBE type good for a red onion	CG
SWEET SANDWICH HYBRID	Spring	When tops die down	Red bulbs	Long-day type; high yielding; milder after storage	ST/BP/TM/JS
SWEET SPANISH	Spring	When tops die down	Bulbs	Relatively mild long-day type; for fresh use or short storage	BP/VB/PT/NG

ONIONS

Variety	When to Plant	When to Harvest	What to Harvest	Comments	Sources*
TANGO	8–10 weeks before last frost	When tops die down	Red bulbs	Interior is red (as well as skin)	ST
TEXAS EARLY GRANO #502	Fall for spring harvest	When tops die down	Bulbs	Short-day type; nonhybrid alternative to GRANEX 33	PT
WALLA WALLA SWEET	Fall or early spring	When tops die down	Bulbs	Large, mild onion for long-day areas (north of 35th parallel)	SB/LM/ PT/JS/ NG/CG
Onion, Perennial					
EGYPTIAN (TREE ONION)	Spring or summer	Anytime	Any part of plant	Plant divided basal clump or bulbets on top of seed stalk	SB/TM/ NG/LJ/ SX
POTATO ONION	Fall or spring	When tops dry down	Bulbs and bulblets	"Multiplying" onion that makes large bulbs and small sets	KM/SX
Scallions					
CIBOULE ROUGE COMMUN (COMMON BUNCHING ONION)	Spring or summer	Anytime	Clumps of scallions	Perennial; harvest clump and replant 1 stem for next year	CG
EVERGREEN HARDY WHITE	Spring or summer	Anytime	Clumps of scallions; leaves	Very hardy; harvest clump and replant 1 stem for next year	JS/NG/ SX
ISHIKURA	Spring or summer	When stem is ¼"–½" in diameter	Clumps of scallions	Hardy to Zone 6	SB/ST/ TM/JS
KUJO GREEN MULTISTALK	Spring or summer	When stem is ¼"–½" in diameter	Clumps of scallions	—	SB/JS
LONG WHITE SUMMER	Spring	When stem is ¼"–½" in diameter	Individual plant stems	Best variety to blanch for Nebuka (see text)	ST/CG

*Listings correspond to seed companies included under Seed Source List at the back of the book.

cure. Spread the onions on screens that are supported at the corners so that air can circulate on all sides. We got our screens at the dump, and also use them for shading seedlings during the early summer.

When the outer skin layers become opaque and dry, put aside thick-necked onions for fresh use—they won't store well because their broad tops don't provide enough closure from the outside world to protect the bulbs. Of the rest, braid the ones with good dry tops for winter use. Even the sweet summer onions and spindle-shaped bottle onions will keep for a month or two if well cured.

This curing process is very important. Storage life is closely related to curing conditions, because the resistance of the onions to rot is a function of getting the scales and the top to dry without damage. Note that red onions will not color properly in the center of the bulbs unless they are allowed to mature fully and then are cured properly before storage.

The Best Varieties

The genetics of onions are relatively fluid, which is why we have so many kinds within one species. Onions are usually classified by shape and color. Onion shapes fall into four general types: flat, globular, top-shaped, and elongated (or bottle-shaped). Within each type the onions may be red, or yellow to golden brown, or white. Most set onions are flattish. This is because the bulb of the onion tends to flatten at maturity. The best shape for good storing onion sets is globular. Thus onions that are globule-shaped as sets will be flat at maturity.

You rarely see bottle onions of any kind in this country, even though they are one of the easiest types to grow. In the kitchen, they can be sliced much more easily than a flat or globular onion, but their shape suggests they may not keep well.

From a growing standpoint, the most important distinction is between long-day and short-day types. Short-day onions are planted in fall for a late spring harvest and do most of their growing during the winter months. Vidalia onions are grown on this schedule; these are simply the standard southern hybrid GRANEX 33, grown in the low-sulfur soils around Vidalia, Georgia. The same variety, grown elsewhere in the right kind of soil, will yield the same sweet onion as a "Vidalia," though it will be called a "Texas Sweetie" and a "Maui Sweet," or some other trade name that will excite the consumer. If you don't like hybrids, you might try TEXAS EARLY GRANO 502 or YELLOW, WHITE, or RED BERMUDA. These will give similar results, though without the high yields or consistency of the newer hybrids. All of these will produce a large, mild onion that is excellent for fresh use or stuffing but that does not store well.

For a large, mild onion in the north, try WALLA WALLA, an open-pollinated heirloom variety brought to Washington State by Corsican immigrants. After guarding the seed stocks for many years, they now sell the seed as a second crop. In a recent "taste off" sponsored by the Vidalia Chamber of Commerce, the WALLA WALLA lost to the hometown favorite by only 8 points out of a possible 4,000. In their home state

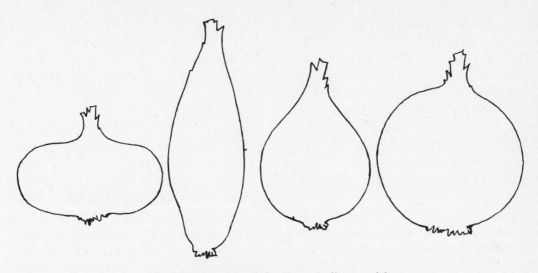

Onion shapes (from left): *flat, spindle, top, globe*

of Washington, they are sown in August for overwintering and a June harvest. This schedule and the soil conditions in Walla Walla are said to be responsible for the "sweetness" of the original. They are not fully hardy here in Vermont, but we have had some success wintering them in our cold frames, and the result is worth it.

You can also plant WALLA WALLA in spring if you start them very early—some growers sow them by the second week in January—so that they are good-sized by the time the garden is ready for planting. Aside from this difference, they can be grown just like regular onions. They may not grow as sweet and mild as they do in their hometown, but even so the WALLA WALLA is a large, high-yielding yellow onion that is milder than the storage types. If you want really big onions, start them early in plug flats and give them 8 inches apiece in the garden.

The bottle onions are among our favorites. These are tall, spindle-shaped onions with relatively thick necks. As far as I know, there are only two readily available varieties: OWA 153, a yellow-gold variety from Denmark, and RED LUCCA or ROUGE DE FLORENCE. We tracked this latter variety through an Italian seed house, which informed us that the variety sold in this country as ITALIAN RED TORPEDO was in fact the ROSSA DI LUCCA, which, he said, was sometime "incorrectly" referred to as ROUGE DE FLORENCE. When I checked my map of Italy, I found that the town of Lucca is only about 25 miles from Florence. Call them what you will, but try them out.

A hundred years ago there were many more varieties of spindle-shaped onions, including a French one called *Oignon Corne de Boeuf* or OX HORN onion. But it seems that breeding efforts have been for storage life and yield, and so they are no longer easy to find. The best keeper among the bottle onions—and it was said to keep very well—was a coppery-red, flat-topped little bulb of 2-inch length called the JAMES KEEPING onion. One American seed house still lists a variety by that name.

The shape of bottle onions has some advantages. Because of their shape, they can be spaced closer than regular onions. If allowed to cure thoroughly, they make a great braiding onion for short storage and they are ideal for slicing and for appetizers. At maturity they are about the size of a large pickling cucumber—1 to 1½ inches in diameter and 4 to 6 inches long. They are milder than storage onions, but not so mild as GRANEX 33 or WALLA WALLA. They also make good scallions when partly grown; just set them an inch apart in the row and thin to harvest.

The other type of long-day, short-storage, mild onion for fresh use is SWEET SPANISH, in both yellow and white forms. This type has been crossed with long-day YELLOW GLOBE storage types to get a variety that is mild and yet stores fairly well. FIESTA is a good choice; it is larger and milder than most storage onions, but will keep well into the winter if well grown and cured. The non-hybrid PECKHAM strain of YELLOW SWEET SPANISH is also relatively good for storage; it has been selected over the years for a thin neck, which, along with hard flesh, thick skin, and high sulfur content, is a requirement for good storage.

Most of the good storage onions are yellow, globe-shaped varieties, and in fact, the traditional storage variety is called YELLOW GLOBE. There are special strains called DOWNING YELLOW GLOBE, EARLY YELLOW GLOBE, and even SOUTHPORT YELLOW GLOBE. These are pungent, long-day onions. You can also find SOUTHPORT WHITE and SOUTHPORT RED GLOBE varieties. Any of these is a good bet for northern gardeners looking for a winter cooking onion, but the red and white varieties do not store as well as the yellow.

Now that color has become more important in vegetables, varieties have a renewed popularity. New red hybrids like CARMEN and TANGO have been developed that store much better than their predecessors. They also have a more uniform red coloring inside if properly cured. The red inside develops at maturity and while curing, as does the internal structure necessary for long storage. Don't harvest too soon if you want long-storing red onions. RUBY is an improved, open-pollinated red that matures in 105 days, has good interior color, and stores well.

The most interesting recent hybrid is SWEET SANDWICH, developed by Dr. Clint Peterson at the University of Wisconsin. This is a very high-yielding yellow storage type that, while pungent at harvest, mellows in storage to become unusually mild. Apparently this is because the sulfur compounds that cause pungency break down over time. This is not a cooking onion like the other storage types, though, because the flesh gets mushy when cooked. It will keep through April if well grown and cured. According to onion breeders I checked with, the mellowing trait may soon be transferred to other onions, including red varieties. Another good onion developed by Dr. Peterson is SPARTAN SLEEPER, the world champion of storage onions. With the SPARTAN SLEEPER, you can still be eating last year's onions while you harvest this year's crop!

Scallions

As noted above, you can harvest onions before they bulb, for use as scallions. White varieties traditionally have been used for this purpose, and now red varieties are popular as well, even though the red color does not extend through the flesh. Depending on your latitude, use either VIDALIA or WALLA WALLA for early harvest as mild scallions. You can simply plant your main crop at half the distance apart and harvest every other plant for scallions. Red bottle onions make good scallion substitutes because even as they start to bulb, their shape is like that of a scallion.

True scallions do not form a bulb, so you can usually have a continuous supply through the season. Sow on the same schedule as the other onions for the early crop, but then replant for a second crop one month later. A third planting of winter-hardy types will give you a harvest the following spring.

Here's a tip for growing scallions with a minimum of fuss: Put a pinch of seed (about a half-dozen) in each cell of a #162 flat insert. Grow them just like your other onion seedlings, but don't thin or trim them. At planting time put the whole plug in the ground, just like you would for big bulb onions, and in about two months you'll be able to harvest your scallions in bunches.

If you'd like to grow an American version of the tall, blanched Japanese Nebuka scallions, just plant a single row of plants or plug bunches (described above) down the center of a bed, then seed a fast-growing crop like arugula or cress on the edges. Once the greens have been harvested, use the extra soil in the beds to hill up the scallions as you would leeks so that they stretch for the light. Two good varieties for blanching—or for regular scallions—are LONG WHITE SUMMER and ISHIKURA. The blanched part of the stem on ISHIKURA—the part you want—can reach 12 inches.

For fall and winter plantings of scallions, use winter-hardy types, known as Welsh onions. You can grow them as a summer-sown fall crop, but they are actually perennial, and can be propagated by division, just like chives. Replant one stalk from each bunch you harvest, and by the following season, you will have another bunch. You can pick them at any time after the stems firm up in the spring. The previous season's growth will have partially decomposed, and the new growth will come from the center of the stalk. You can also cut the greens for soup or salad, and it doesn't seem to harm the plant, though it will slow down the growth of the clump.

Most of the good perennial varieties are Japanese; try EVERGREEN HARDY WHITE, and KUJO GREEN MULTISTALK. Both are completely hardy in our garden. There is a red variety from France that simply goes under the name CIBOULE ROUGE COMMUN, or COMMON BUNCHING onion. The red color is only skin deep, but they are just as hardy as the Japanese varieties.

Shallots and Garlic

Shallots are clumping onions, a sub-variety of the species *Allium cepa,* which includes onions. Their taste is similar to a regular onion, but more subtle, like a leek. Garlic is a separate species, and much more strongly flavored—to the delight of many cooks and the distaste of others.

Growing Shallots

Plant shallots just like onion sets. Break apart the clumps and plant individual bulbs with their tops just below the surface of the soil. Most varieties can be planted in spring or fall. If spring planting, we get them in as soon as the ground can be worked, but when fall planting, we wait until October 1 so they won't be tempted to put out any top growth. Otherwise they might be damaged by cold before the snow cover insulates them.

Give shallot sets at least 8 inches apiece, as each bulb will expand to become a whole clump. Except for the wider spacing, shallots have the same needs as onions, which we meet with a couple of bushels of rotted manure for each 100 square feet we will plant, good drainage, and regular, shallow cultivation. Use of a 3:2:3 layout makes the necessary cultivation quick and easy.

Harvesting

You can harvest shallots at any time, and many fanciers use them for scallions or cut the tops for salads. Doing so, however, will delay maturity of the bulb crop. Harvest your shallots when the tops die back to the ground. If you leave them much longer, storage quality will be hurt. Pull the soil away from the clumps so the

Onion braiding

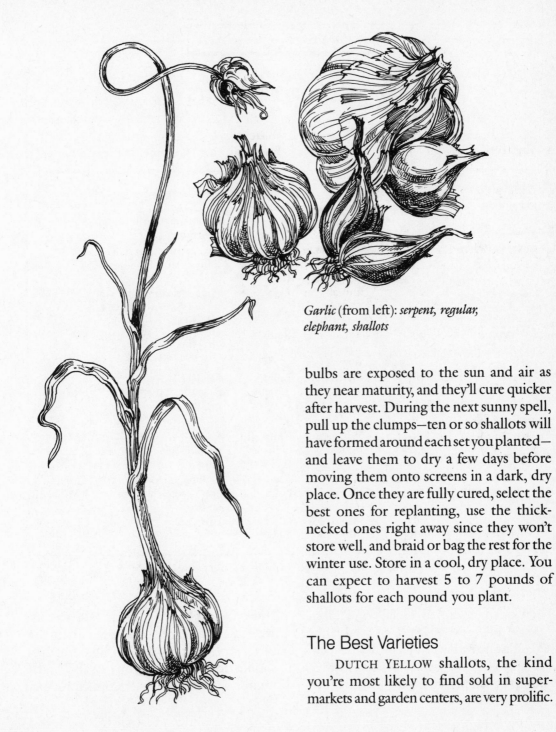

Garlic (from left): *serpent, regular, elephant, shallots*

bulbs are exposed to the sun and air as they near maturity, and they'll cure quicker after harvest. During the next sunny spell, pull up the clumps—ten or so shallots will have formed around each set you planted—and leave them to dry a few days before moving them onto screens in a dark, dry place. Once they are fully cured, select the best ones for replanting, use the thick-necked ones right away since they won't store well, and braid or bag the rest for the winter use. Store in a cool, dry place. You can expect to harvest 5 to 7 pounds of shallots for each pound you plant.

The Best Varieties

DUTCH YELLOW shallots, the kind you're most likely to find sold in supermarkets and garden centers, are very prolific.

VARIETY SOURCE CHART

GARLIC AND SHALLOTS

Variety	When to Plant	When to Harvest	What to Harvest	Comments	Sources*
Garlic					
ELEPHANT	Fall	1 week after tops die down	Bulbs	Much larger and milder than regular garlic (up to 1 lb. each)	SB/NG/ SX
GERMAN RED	Fall	1 week after tops die down	Bulbs	Strong flavor, but more difficult to grow; stores well	SH
ITALIAN PURPLE	Fall	1 week after tops die down	Bulbs	Higher yielding and milder flavored than GERMAN RED	SH
SILVERSKIN	Fall	1 week after tops die down	Bulbs	Standard type white garlic	SH
TOPSETTING (ROCAMBOLE)	Fall	When leaves wither	Bulbs, topsets	Milder flavor than regular garlic; topsets can be pickled	SB/NG/ SX/LJ
Shallot					
DUTCH YELLOW	Fall or spring	When tops die down	Clumps of bulbs	Can be harvested early as scallions; greens good for salad	TM/JS/ KM/SX/ SH/NG
FRENCH RED (FRENCH GRAY)	Fall	When tops die down	Clumps of bulbs	Oblong, up to 4″ long; good flavor, but poor keeper	TM/SX/ KM/SH
FROG'S LEG (PEAR, BRITTANY)	Fall or spring	When tops die down	Clumps of bulbs	Large bulbs; high yields	LJ

*Listings correspond to seed companies included under Seed Source List at the back of the book.

They can be planted in fall or spring. FRENCH RED and FRENCH GRAY shallots have a distinctive flavor, but are more expensive and not very good keepers, so they have to be fall planted. BRITTANY shallots, also known as PEAR, or FROG'S LEG, shallots, are large and more elongated than the other types, but not as high yielding; they should be fall planted. You can also find a number of heirloom varieties from specialty suppliers like Kalmia Farm or Southern Exposure Seeds. If you ask around, you may find you have a neighbor who has kept his or her own strain.

Growing Garlic

Garlic is a long season crop, which makes it difficult for gardeners in short season areas to get good yields. Two tricks can make the difference. The first is fall planting. Garlic is a very hardy plant and we've never lost a crop over the winter.

A second trick is to find a locally adapted strain of garlic. They exist. When the extension staff at Cornell University decided to do variety trials of garlic in 1983, they found 24 different strains being grown in their part of New York State, with radically different results. The variety LATE CALIFORNIA, which we can assume was adapted to a different climate, had an average bulb slightly greater than ¾ of an ounce, while 15 of the other strains had an average bulb weight of more than 2 ounces. One variety, listed only as GORTZIG— quite possibly the name of a farmer—had an average bulb weight of 3½ ounces!

Some strains send up a seed stalk crowned with what looks like a Mexican piñata. After a time this topset bursts open to reveal a twisted mass of bulblets that, if the weather is cool and wet, may sprout while still bound up with their brethren and dangling 2 feet in the air. If you're after large bulbs, you should break off this seed stalk as soon as it forms, but if you want to increase your stock quickly, you can let the bulblets mature and plant them

for the following year. Within 12 months they will have grown into a single clove, and in their second season they will divide into normal cloves (and quite likely send up a seed stalk of their own).

Garlic needs a fertile, well-drained soil. Divide a bulb of garlic into cloves, and set them 8 inches apart each way around the time of the first killing frost in fall. If you plant too early, they may start to grow and be hurt by winter cold. As with the other alliums, we put two bushels of compost or well-rotted manure on each 100-square-foot bed. Keep the bed well cultivated, as garlic does not compete well with weeds.

Harvesting

Garlic can be harvested anytime after it has shed its old bulb. Most garlic will be milder if harvested young, but it won't keep as well. Harvest the bulk of your crop when the tops have begun to yellow, then dry and cure in the same way as shallots; save the best for replanting and braid or bag the rest for winter use. Use the culls right away, as they won't keep.

The Best Varieties

Some good varieties to try include GERMAN RED, a hard, long storing variety with a strong flavor; ITALIAN PURPLE, a milder and softer bulb that is a bit less demanding; and SILVERSKIN, one of the standard California varieties that seems better adapted to Eastern conditions. SILVERSKIN did quite well in the Cornell trials, yielding bulbs with an average weight of 3 ounces.

Elephant Garlic

Elephant garlic is not as hardy as the regular types, though its huge size and mild taste make it worth growing. It's grown just like regular garlic, but it prefers a slightly higher soil pH. It should be planted deeper, too; 2 inches of loose soil over the tip of the bulb is ideal. Elephant garlic isn't harvested for fresh use, since it grows milder with maturity and storage—just the opposite of regular garlic. There are no named cultivars.

Topsetting Garlic

Also known as Rocambole, some sources list this as a separate species from regular garlic. But in our garden, it doesn't seem to differ from the regular types in any significant way. If you let the bulblets on top mature, the size of the underground bulb will be diminished. Rocambole is an interesting plant, and fun to see growing in the garden; the stalk curls around in a serpentine fashion that has led to its alternate name, "serpent garlic." There are no named varieties.

PEAS

*P*eas are the clock by which garden time is kept. The first question one gardener asks another around here is "Peas in yet?" The second, a week or two later, is apt to be, "Peas up yet?" In our garden these hardy legumes provide a backdrop for scheduling other crops. They are sown at the same time as the first spring salad crops, sprout with the first tentative shoots of early planted onion sets, bloom with the coming of the frost-free summer months, and bear from the solstice into the peak of the summer season, when the squashes, cucumbers, beans, and other heat-loving crops replace the peas' bounty with their own.

Homegrown peas, like homegrown sweet corn, are unmatched even at a garden stand. Just the drive home makes a difference in the flavor and texture of fresh peas, which, like sweet corn, begin to lose sweetness and increase in starchiness the moment they are picked.

Growing

Peas should be planted as early as the ground can be worked in spring. They like the cool weather and abundant moisture that precede the hot heart of the summer season. They fail to set pods once temperatures regularly exceed 80°F, and the vines can rapidly lose vigor. While the flowers cannot withstand more than a few degrees below freezing, the leaves are very hardy and take the last hard freezes of spring in stride. We plant six weeks before the frost-free date, and this is just time enough for the peas to grow to flowering size. After they flower, it takes another three or four weeks for the first small shell peas to form, just in time for our traditional Independence Day supper of salmon, peas, and new potatoes.

Rather than sowing the same variety of peas every two weeks to provide a continuous harvest, we do a single planting of three or four varieties with different growth rates. Early-maturing varieties are supplanted as the season progresses by higher-yielding main crop varieties. As the heat of summer builds, heat-tolerant strains like WANDO will continue the harvest. Although not up to the taste standard of the spring peas, these strains nevertheless yield a crop that is far superior to even the best commercially grown, mechanically harvested produce.

For those varieties that need support, we plant a double row lengthwise down the center of the bed, setting 6-foot poles every 8 feet or so. If you use wooden poles, drive 1½-inch roofing nails every 6 inches on the outer sides, starting a little more than 2 feet above the point. Set the poles 2 feet deep, so that the first nails are just a few inches above the ground. Loop untreated baling twine around the nails to make a fence for the vines to climb.

This quick and inexpensive trellis suits even the tall varieties of peas. It is also easy to take down after harvest. Unlike chicken wire, which has to be untangled from the vines, the twine can be simply tossed on the compost pile along with the plants. A "twining stick," composed of a short section of wood with an eye screw or fencing staple set in the end, will help make quick work of setting the twine on the nails. You simply feed the end of the twine through the eye screw and tie it to the first nail, then simply use the stick to run the rest of the twine, looping it around the nails as you come to them. The eye screw threads the twine off the roll without tangling.

Twining stick

Given enough stakes, we would trellis even the dwarf peas, but it seems that every spring, the wide expanse of newly tilled soil tempts me to plant many more peas than I really need. I just can't resist trying new kinds, and after the planter has been pushed down the length of the garden more times than it should have been, I find that I am forced to let some of the smaller, earlier peas fend for themselves.

Only the new bush-type peas should be left to stand on their own. The extra tendrils—which are actually just specialized leaves—intertwine between rows and hold up the peas. Bush peas should be planted in blocks to be able to support themselves. Three rows is just right for a 3-foot bed; put one row down the center of the bed and the others a foot to either side. You could also run the rows across the bed to make planting and cultivation from the path easier.

Sow peas 1 inch deep. Shepherd's grandfather always made a deep furrow for his peas, filled it to within an inch of the surface with well-rotted compost, then laid in the peas an inch or two apart as they fell from his hand, and pulled soil over the row with a hoe, tamping lightly to make sure the peas were well seated. For a fall crop, we plant during the first cool spell in midsummer, usually about 45 days before the first frost; this seed goes in 2 inches deep to ensure it will not dry out before it germinates. If the weather turns hot again before the seed emerges, you can put a board over the row to keep the sun from overheating the soil.

We almost always plant a quick-growing crop on the edges of the pea bed (except with bush peas planted in blocks). Spinach is a good choice in early spring; even when grown with the sprawling dwarf peas, it is up and gone before they need the space. As they cover the trellises, peas create a good, shady spot for cool-weather, shade-tolerant salad greens.

Cultivate as soon as the rows are up, and at least once more before the peas start to climb. After that, you should be able to get by with pulling the occasional invader that works its way up through the pea thicket. Any "catch crop" you've sown on the bed edges to make use of otherwise wasted space will need regular attention, but once it has been harvested, the bed edges can easily be kept free of weeds with a wide blade hoe or a narrow rake.

Harvesting

Start checking your peas regularly about three weeks after they begin to flower. Picking peas at their peak quality is something of an art, and it is best learned by experience paid for in empty pods. The size of the pod itself is not a sure indicator of the time to harvest, but there are other subtle changes that you'll learn to recognize at a glance. We tell the school kids who harvest our peas to look for pods whose seams have changed from convex to concave, but which still have a satiny sheen to them. Overripe pods lose that vibrant color, dulling as the peas stop growing and start converting their sucrose into starch. Once this metabolic milestone has passed, there is no going back. The peas might as well be picked (so they don't rob energy from new developing pods) and used for soup.

Snap peas can be harvested at any point after they emerge from the fertilized flowers. But do so before they become hard and starchy, which can be recognized by the same characteristics as for shelling peas. While snaps are a great treat for eating out of hand, most varieties still need to have the seams, or "strings," removed before use.

Snow peas, the small flat pods that are so good in stir-fry dishes, can also be harvested at any time from emergence until they lose the vibrant sheen described above. Most people will tell you that these edible-pod peas (also called Chinese peas) should be harvested before the peas begin to swell in the pod. They are good at that stage, but not as sweet as when the peas have begun to fill out. After all, the plant's leaves are sending their sugars to the peas, not to the pod, for storage.

The Best Varieties

Peas have been around the garden for a long time, and so, understandably, there are a great number of varieties within each of the four main types: shell peas, edible-pod peas, snap peas, and dry peas. *The Vegetable Garden,* the comprehensive encyclopedia of cultivated vegetable varieties published in France in the late 1800s, devoted more than 50 pages to peas. Some of the common varieties of that time have been lost, but some—or at least their direct descendants—are still in our gardens of today.

TALL TELEPHONE (or ALDERMAN) peas and their most recent derivatives, like MULTISTAR, have long been revered as high-yielding, full-flavored peas; their 5-foot

VARIETY SOURCE CHART

PEAS

Variety	When to Plant	When to Harvest	What to Harvest	Comments	Sources*
Edible-Pod Peas					
CAROUBY DE MAUSSANE	ASAP in spring	Just before peas swell in pod	Whole pea pods	Tall plants with beautiful, edible flowers and sweet pods	CG
CORNE DE BELIER	ASAP in spring	Just before peas swell in pod	Whole pea pods	Heirloom French variety	No current source

VARIETY SOURCE CHART

PEAS

Variety	When to Plant	When to Harvest	What to Harvest	Comments	Sources*
DE GRACE	ASAP in spring	Just before peas swell in pod	Whole pea pods	Early semidwarf similar to NORLI	HG
DWARF GREY SUGAR	ASAP in spring	Just before peas swell in pod	Whole pea pods	Harvest whole pods young for stir-fry; needs trellis	PK/WD/ VB
MAMMOTH MELTING SUGAR	ASAP in spring	Just before peas swell in pod	Whole pea pods	Tall vines; larger pods must be picked young	SB/HM/ LM/BP/ VB/PK
NORLI	ASAP in spring	Just before peas swell in pod	Whole pea pods	Early Dutch type; 2½″ pods are very sweet	WD/SS/ SB
Shell Peas					
GREEN ARROW	ASAP in spring	Just as peas fill the pod	Fresh green shelled peas	Long pods on short plants; easy to pick and tasty	Widely available
LINCOLN	ASAP in spring	Just as peas fill the pod	Fresh green shelled peas	Shorter than TALL TELE-PHONE; very high quality; good yields	Widely available
MAESTRO	ASAP in spring	Just as peas fill the pod	Fresh green shelled peas	Good disease resistance and high yields	BP/SX/JS
MULTISTAR	ASAP in spring	Just as peas fill the pod	Fresh green shelled peas	Improved form of TALL TELEPHONE; multiple pods per node	JS
PETIT PROVENÇAL	ASAP in spring	Just as peas fill the pod	Tiny fresh green shelled peas	Peas are small and sweeter than normal shell peas	CG
PRECOVIL	ASAP in spring	Just as peas fill the pod	Fresh green shelled peas	Semidwarf plants, but grow best on trellis	SS
TALL TELEPHONE (ALDERMAN)	ASAP in spring	Just as peas fill the pod	Fresh green shelled peas	Heirloom variety renowned for yields; 5′ vines	BG/SB/ HM/ST/ PT/VB
WAVEREX	ASAP in spring	Just as peas fill the pod	Tiny fresh green shelled peas	Small pods, small peas, good flavor	BG/LM

*Listings correspond to seed companies included under Seed Source List at the back of the book.

vines bear over a long period and produce a phenomenal number of peas for the amount of ground they occupy. Even so, most connoisseurs of shelling peas rate the old semidwarf varieties LINCOLN and GREEN ARROW as better tasting, while producing nearly as well. MAESTRO and other more recent versions of these old standbys have increased resistance to viruses and mildew; they are also easier to judge for readiness to harvest.

But if you really want a taste treat in shelling peas, try some of the French *petit pois* ("tiny pea") varieties. These are traditional shelling peas that mature when small on vigorous plants. Their overall production approaches that of the best large varieties, and their flavor and sweetness are especially beguiling. They are grown just like regular shelling peas, but remember that they ripen small and should be picked small for the best quality. Use the same visual tests for *petit pois* that you would for regular shelling peas. As far as our garden customers are concerned, one

of the better varieties is PETIT PROVENCAL, a heat-resistant variety from the south of France. The German baby pea WAVEREX produces lots of tiny ¼-inch peas in areas with cool summers, but in warmer areas it should only be grown as an early spring or late fall crop. PRECOVIL is a dwarf variety that is also adapted for spring planting. All *petit pois* should be steamed only briefly, as the delicate baby pea flavor is lost if they are overcooked.

Standard edible pod varieties that merit attention for productivity and taste include DWARF GREY SUGAR and MAMMOTH MELTING SUGAR. Among their lesser-known European varieties are NORLI, DE GRACE, and CORNE DE BELIER (or goat's horn). CAROUBY DE MAUSSANE is a 3-foot-high European variety that has lavender flowers beautiful enough to justify growing them purely for ornament; it produces a heavy crop of sweet, crispy pods for stir-frying, and yet it holds its sweetness until it reaches a large size.

PEPPERS

In parts of Europe, peppers are called capsicums, which is the botanical name of the genus to which they belong. Because the fruits are like a hollow box, some historians think the name came from the Latin word *capsa,* or box. But others feel that the name came from the Greek word *capto,* meaning "I bite," because of the pungency of hot peppers. The name "pepper" was attached to them when European explorers, returning home from their excursions to the New World, brought them along as a flavorful substitute for the black pepper berries of an east Asian shrub.

The only sweet pepper many gardeners have grown is the common green pepper, and in fact a lot of people think that red peppers are an entirely different plant. But sweet peppers that are green or purple when immature later ripen to red, yellow, gold, and even brown. Peppers are fruits that, like cucumbers, traditionally have been eaten in an immature state; but now more gardeners are letting multicolored varieties ripen fully before harvest. The difference in taste is dramatic. Green peppers are not sweet, but have a sour and bitter edge that, while subdued, is upsetting to some stomachs. When fully ripe, though—whatever the color—they are sweet and mild.

Hot peppers are a diverse lot and have many culinary uses, especially with the surge in popularity of Mexican and Thai cuisine. In the past, many of these heat-loving peppers didn't do well in northern gardens, but now breeders have developed new varieties of hot peppers that ripen less than three months after transplanting.

Growing

Like their cousins, the tomatoes and eggplants, peppers need to be started indoors in all but the warmest climates if you want to be sure of a harvest before frost. Since they get off to a slower start than tomatoes, seed them eight to ten weeks before the frost-free date. They like a higher germination temperature as well; 80°F is ideal. When they emerge, move them to a spot with plenty of sun and a lower temperature, in the neighborhood of 70°F.

If you started the plants in seedling trays or plugs, transplant them to peat pots or other individual containers as soon as the first true leaves show. We use a #50 plug for this stage, and then as the plants touch leaves again, move them up to 4-inch pots. Whatever container you use, the principles are the same as for tomatoes: Don't be in a hurry and plant too soon, and don't let the plants get leggy from too much heat and fertilizer. Young, vigorous plants that are as wide as they are tall will give you the earliest and the biggest yields.

Most pepper varieties positively resent cool weather, so wait until the garden is really warmed up before planting. Once the normal frost-free date arrives, harden the plants by setting them outside in the sun for increasingly long periods each day.

After a week or so of this treatment, they should be adjusted to outdoor conditions and the weather probably will be more moderate.

We set our peppers on 18-inch centers down the middle of a 3-foot-wide bed that has been covered with a black plastic mulch to warm the soil and to even out soil moisture. This, and a handful of colloidal phosphate mixed into the bottom of the planting hole and covered with compost, goes a long way toward preventing blossom end rot, which affects peppers as well as tomatoes. Peppers generally do not need staking. We also set basil plants along the edges of the bed equidistant from the peppers in the row. To get plants of the right size, seed the basil at the same time as the peppers.

Immediately after planting, we cover our peppers with a floating row cover. Some brands of covers are rough and can abrade the tender growing point of the plants. Either use a low abrasion cover, or make hoops from #9 fencing wire to keep the covers up off the plants. In either case, bury the edges of the fabric to keep crawling bugs from entering.

In a month or so, when the plants begin to flower, take off the covers to allow insects free access. You may need to spray or dust with a rotenone or pyrethrum mix to control aphids and tarnished plant bugs, which spread disease. In short-season areas, disease hardly has a chance to develop on vigorous plants before they are killed by frost.

If the flowers drop from the plants without forming fruit, the weather is probably too hot (above 85°F) or too cool (below 60°F). Don't worry; once the weather becomes moderate, the plants will come back into production. Even drought doesn't seem to do them any permanent damage—you may lose some fruit, but as soon as things get back to normal, the plants will begin producing again. If the end of the season is creeping up on your garden and you want those last few fruits to ripen quickly, you can stress the plants by pulling on them or cultivating close to the stem and cutting off some (not all!) of their roots. This will stimulate them into ripening as soon as possible.

Harvesting

Peppers can be harvested at any time, but the flavor doesn't develop much until maturity. Immature green peppers have a pleasant, cleansing astringency and a crunchy texture, but very little taste. What you notice most is a lack of pungency. But mature peppers are sweet, and the contrast between the taut, smooth skin and the flesh, which resembles watermelon rind in texture, is intriguing. Short-season gardeners will have a different set of criteria for deciding when to harvest, though. In milder climates, you can allow peppers to ripen fully before harvest and still expect a second crop, as the plants are stimulated to produce more flowers. But where the growing season is short, yields per plant will be reduced by leaving fruit on until full maturity. That's because the second flush of flowers probably won't mature before frost. Northern gardeners may have to trade off production for taste.

The Best Varieties

Most sweet peppers are members of the species *Capsicum annuum,* which covers a wide range of shapes, colors, and flavors. All of this genetic bounty is at its best in those last two weeks of August, and Ellen makes the most of it, filling bins and baskets to overflowing with the multicolored cornucopia. But some like it hot, and for those tough-tongued souls there is another whole range of peppers which, though closely related, are from the species *Capsicum frutescens.*

Sweet Peppers

Most green pepper varieties ripen to red, but how long they take to do so varies widely, as do the yields. Some varieties produce a green pepper that is large and firm enough for harvest very early, but do not ripen well. Others may be late to size up, but once they do, color rapidly.

These peppers vary widely in their regional adaption; for advice on a green pepper variety for your region, check with knowledgeable local gardeners or your extension agent. Two of the standard peppers for cold climates are ACE, and MERRIMACK WONDER; both grow and set fruit well under cool conditions. A good bet for color is SWEET CHOCOLATE, an open-pollinated strain developed by Dr. Elwyn Meader of the University of New Hampshire. This slightly tapered, blunt-ended pepper of 4 to 5 inches has very good cold tolerance. But most important is its taste. The thick flesh is very sweet (especially when grown in cool, relatively heavy soils) and the brick red interior is given a deep

(continued on page 144)

VARIETY SOURCE CHART

PEPPERS

Variety	When to Plant	When to Harvest	What to Harvest	Comments	Sources*
ACE HYBRID	8-12 weeks before last frost	When fruits are 2″-3″ in diameter	Tapered 3″-4″ lobed green fruit	Good for cold climates	Widely available
ACONCAGUA	8-12 weeks before last frost	When fruits turn red	8″-long tapered belled fruits	Large sweet frying type	HT
ANAHEIM CHILI	8-12 weeks before last frost	When fruits turn red	Tapered, 2-lobed, 8″-long fruits	Good pepper for chili dishes and other Mexican food	Widely available
CAYENNE	8-12 weeks before last frost	When fruits turn red	Tapered, thin, 6″-long fruits	Traditional hot pepper for drying; thread on string	PT/BP/ VB/WD/ SS/ST
CHOCOLATE BELL	8-12 weeks before last frost	When fruits turn dark brown	Blocky fruits, 3″-4″ across	Larger and later than SWEET CHOCOLATE	ST
CORNO DI TORO	8-12 weeks before last frost	When fruits turn red/ yellow	Tapered, twisted, 2″ × 8″ fruits	Relatively small, Italian frying type; Italian for "Bull's Horn pepper"	LM/CG
GOLDEN BELL	8-12 weeks before last frost	When fruits turn yellow/ gold	Blocky fruits, 3″-4″ across	Large nonhybrid, similar to GOLDEN SUMMER	PT/VB/ HM
GOLDEN SUMMER HYBRID	8-12 weeks before last frost	When fruits turn yellow/ gold	Blocky fruits 3″-5″ across	Large fruits; productive even in short-season areas	JS/CG
GYPSY HYBRID	8-12 weeks before last frost	When fruits turn yellow/ gold	Tapered fruits 3½″ long	High yielding; disease- and cool-weather tolerant	Widely available
ITALIA	8-12 weeks before last frost	When fruits turn red	2½-by-8″ tapered fruits	Similar to CORNO DI TORO	JS/PT
JALAPA/TAM JALAPENO HYBRIDS	8-12 weeks before last frost	When fruits begin to turn red	Tapered, blocky fruits, 1″ × 3″	New hybrid-jalapeno types, earlier and milder	PT/VB/ HM/ LM/NG

PEPPERS

Variety	When to Plant	When to Harvest	What to Harvest	Comments	Sources*
JALAPENO	8-12 weeks before last spring frost	When fruits begin to turn red	1″-by-3″ tapered, blunt fruits	Standard hot pepper for pickling and Mexican cuisine	Widely available
LAMUYO HYBRID (LA ROUGE ROYAL)	8-12 weeks before last frost	When fruits turn red	Tapered, blocky fruits, 6″-8″ long	European type; three-lobed bell; comes in other colors, too	LM
MARCONI	8-12 weeks before last frost	When fruits turn red/ yellow	Tapered, 3-lobed fruits, 3″ × 10″	Similar to CORNO DI TORO, but larger and sweeter	SB/CG
MERRIMACK WONDER	8-12 weeks before last spring frost	When fruits reach 3″-4″ diameter	Blocky bell-shaped green fruit	Early open pollinated variety for short season areas	SX
PAPRIKA (PIMENTO)	8-12 weeks before last frost	When fruits turn red	Flattened fruits, 2″ × 4″	Meat (not seeds) dried to make paprika; good for stuffing	SB/LM/ NG
PEPPEROCINI	8-12 weeks before last frost	When fruits are green/ yellow	Tapered, thin fruits, 4″-8″ long	Tall plant; ripens red, but used immature for pickling	SB/LM/ ST/NG
POBLANO (ANCHO)	8-12 weeks before last frost	When fruits turn dark brown	Heart-shaped fruits, 4″ long	Very late chili variety; best for hot climates	LM/SS
PURPLE BELL HYBRID	8-12 weeks before last frost	When fruits are purple or red	Blocky fruits, 3½″ across	Larger, later, and blockier than VIOLETTA	BP/ST
SERRANO	8-12 weeks before last frost	When fruits turn red	Tapered fruits, ½″ × 2″	Very hot pepper for drying and chili; unusual-looking plant	PT/SS/ LM/TM
SWEET BANANA	8-12 weeks before last frost	When fruits turn yellow/ red	Tapered fruits, 6″ long	Similar to GYPSY, but larger and sweeter	PT/BP/ WD/HM
SWEET CHOCOLATE	8-12 weeks before last frost	When fruits turn dark brown	Tapered, blocky fruits, 3″-4″ long	Very early, very sweet; tolerant of cool weather	SB/JS/ CG

(continued)

VARIETY SOURCE CHART—*Continued*

PEPPERS

Variety	When to Plant	When to Harvest	What to Harvest	Comments	Sources*
THAI HOT	8-12 weeks before last frost	When fruits turn red	Tiny fruits, 1"-1½" long	Very late, very hot; pot-up to mature fruit inside in the north	LM
TORITO HYBRID	8-12 weeks before last frost	When fruits turn red	Long, thin fruits, 1" × 8"	Hybrid CAYENNE type, though larger; high yields even in cool areas	CG
VIOLETTA HYBRID	8-12 weeks before last frost	When fruits turn purple	Slightly tapered, 3"-4" fruits	Similar in shape to SWEET CHOCOLATE, but tart, not sweet	LM/CG

*Listings correspond to seed companies included under Seed Source List at the back of the book.

brown cast by the greenish skin, so that the fruit looks like a large, shiny chocolate drop. It does not lose its color when cooked and makes a great combination on the crudité platter, along with GOLDEN SUMMER and VIOLETTA peppers. Another brown variety is CHOCOLATE BELL, about ten days later than SWEET CHOCOLATE, but a little larger.

GOLDEN SUMMER is a large, blocky pepper of the type that is flown in from Holland during the winter months for the gourmet trade. The fruits are very large and ripen from a pale green to deep gold. The flavor is very sweet and mild. It is widely adapted, but short-season gardeners might do better to try a variety like GOLD CREST, which matures a week or more ahead of GOLDEN SUMMER.

VIOLETTA is earlier, ripening from purple to red. The flavor is good, but if eaten at the purple stage, it is not as sweet as the chocolate peppers. It's a good performer in the north, and even a wet, cool summer won't stop it completely. Two other purple varieties are PURPLE BELL, which eventually turns from purple to blood red, and LORELEI.

One All-American winner, and a standard by which others are now judged, is the hybrid variety GYPSY. This 6-inch-long lime green pepper is a vigorous producer, even in the north, and it ripens to a bright yellow. An open-pollinated pepper of the same type is SWEET BANANA, of which there are several strains that range in maturity from 60 to 65 days (after transplanting).

Stuffing pepper

In the United States, these long, tapered peppers are called Italian peppers, but in Italy they are known as bull's horn peppers because of their long, twisted shape. The standard variety is CORNO DI TORO, which comes in both red and yellow maturing strains. This pepper is an inch or two across at the top and twisted over its 8-inch length. The flavor is sweet, but with just enough tang to let you know its cousins are hot. Similar to the bull's horn peppers, but specifically adapted for the north, is ITALIA, early at 55 days. It is similar in size and shape to the traditional types.

To American gardeners, probably the best known of this class of peppers is RED MARCONI, which has been listed in a number of American catalogs for years. It is a fine variety, similar in shape, texture, and taste to the simple cowhorn types, but much larger—10 to 12 inches in length and a good 3 inches across the shoulders. There is also a YELLOW MARCONI. Both ripen in patches; this oddity, combined with their convoluted surface, gives them an incredible appearance. Another large pepper of this type is the Argentinian variety ACONCAGUA, which is slightly broader than the marconi types and almost as long. It turns from yellow-green to red at maturity.

One family of European bell peppers, the LAMUYO hybrids, comes in a number of colors. They are now making their way into food shops under the name "La Rouge Royal." According to some sources, these varieties were bred from a number of eastern European strains. During the final phase of ripening, their color develops evenly rather than in streaks and blotches like the American bell types. We've seen both kinds of ripening in our garden, but always assumed that it was due to weather, not genetics. These Hungarian peppers are also said to be much sweeter at the green stage.

Of course the most famous Hungarian pepper is PAPRIKA, whose flesh (not seed) is ground to make the spice of that name. It is generally accepted that Hungarian paprika is the world's best, but this may be due to climate, not the variety.

PAPRIKA peppers are also excellent for stuffing. The squat fruits are very deeply lobed and have a thick, firm flesh that holds up well in the oven. Most people are used to using the traditional green pepper to make stuffed pepper dishes, but a mature PAPRIKA, or PIMENTO, pepper is less likely to rupture in the oven or to tip over and dump the stuffing. The flavor is sweet and mild, and the coloring of some varieties is especially beautiful if harvested just before they are fully ripe.

Hot Peppers

Hot peppers are in a class by themselves, and they take many shapes, colors, and forms. All they really share is the dominance of pungency over any sweetness the fruits may have. The strength ranges from the mild pickling and antipasto types through chilies to the super hot Thai and Asian varieties. The mildest of the hots are faintly sweet, and some of them have been mentioned above.

POBLANO, or ANCHO, chilies are 3-inch-long, heart-shaped peppers that are a staple of Mexican cooking. The green fruits ripen to reddish brown, and are used fresh for chilis rellenos or dried for sauce. This is a late variety that ripens in about 115 days. The fiery red PEPPEROCINI (65 days) is another relatively mild hot pepper. The Italians pickle them for antipasto, but they also dry quite well. If you want a larger mild-to-hot pepper, the ANAHEIM CHILI is similar to the cowhorn sweet peppers, but with a complex taste instead of a twisted physiognomy.

Then there are the *really* hot peppers: CAYENNE is a pencil-thin type that ripens in about 75 days, the practical maximum for cold climates. If your area is prone to cool spells in the summer, you might try a new hybrid called TORITO, which has done quite well for us, even in cool, wet summers. This is a moderately hot, thin red pepper that dries quite well; the peppers are attractive when braided and hung on the wall until you're ready to use them.

Further up the heat scale is the JALAPENO pepper, a stubby little thing that is often seen in its green stage, pickled and served as an appetizer with food that will probably be pretty hot itself. If you like JALAPENO, but it is still too much for you, there is now a slightly milder version called TAM JALAPENO, and a hybrid called JALAPA, which is well adapted to the northeast. Even hotter are SERRANO chilis, similar in appearance but smaller, and THAI HOT, a little bush with tiny, upright, red peppers, ½ inch to 1 inch long and hot as a bee sting.

POTATOES

Potatoes are a garden staple, but not all gardeners realize just how many different kinds of potatoes there are and how much they can differ in color, texture, and taste.

Have you ever tried LADYFINGER potatoes, the secret ingredient of German potato salad? Their moist texture and firm structure are unlike any of those starchy white potatoes you might have thought were the only kind around. How about ALL BLUE, a flavorful, highly nutritious variety with blue skin and lavender flesh? These are just two descendants of the thousands of varieties grown by the original domesticators of the potato, the Andean Indians of South America.

Growing

Raised beds are great for potatoes because of their good drainage and loose soil structure. After spring preparation of the garden, we create extra high beds that are 8 inches above the surrounding paths, and about 24 inches across at the top. You can do this by standing in the path and raking from the opposite side toward the center of the bed. Use a line stretched along the length of the bed to get the edges uniform.

Once the bed is formed, take out a shovelful of soil every foot along the center, and into the bottom of the resulting hole mix a shovelful of compost to supply a little extra phosphorus and potassium. If you're short of compost, use a handful each of phosphate rock and greensand—not manure, as it can increase the likelihood of scab. Mix this with the soil in the bottom of the hole, then plant the potato set, sprout (or eye) pointed up, and fill in the hole, leaving the top of the potato 4 to 6 inches below the surface of the bed.

Once the plants emerge, cultivate the bed. When the tops reach about 6 inches, cultivate again by raking the edges of the bed toward the center, hilling up soil around the growing plants as you go. Even if you almost cover the foliage, it will soon poke back through, and the plants will be much the better for it. Each time the foliage stretches 6 inches above the soil, cultivate and hill with the loose soil from the edges of the bed.

Potatoes are prone to a number of pests and diseases. The most common pest is the Colorado potato beetle, a humpbacked little beetle about ½ inch long with black stripes running along its back. The larvae are orange, soft bodied, and have two rows of black spots and a black head. The best control is to spend some time in the potato patch examining the undersides of leaves for the egg masses of this unlovable insect. The eggs are bright orange, ⅛ to ¼ inch in length, and stand on end in tight masses like bowling pins. Crush them with your fingers whenever you see them and you can keep the beetle population under control, although I doubt it's possible to get rid of them completely. If things get out of hand, you can dust with rotenone or pyrethrum powder, but that really shouldn't be necessary in a home planting.

Blight is another problem. If the foliage begins to turn yellow, then brown, then wither and disappear early in the season, yank up the affected plants and destroy them. You can eat the tubers if you want, but it's important to interrupt the life cycle of this fungus as quickly as you can so it doesn't spread to the other plants. Keep diseased plants off the compost pile—burning them is best, as this destroys the fungus spores before they can infect other plants.

Harvesting

You can harvest potatoes anytime after the tubers begin to form, though some varieties are better for this than others due to their moisture and starch content. A good sign that tubers are growing is the appearance of flowers on the plants, though there is no necessary connection between the two events. Since some plants never bloom, however, you can't just assume that if the plants haven't flowered there won't be any of those little tubers underneath. If you are careful and don't disturb the plants too much in the process of extracting a few new potatoes, the plants will keep on producing.

Ideally, potatoes that you intend to store should be left in the ground to cure for a week or so after the tops die down. This gives the skins a chance to toughen so that they can be handled without bruising. After harvest, another curing period of two to three weeks at 50° to 60°F with high humidity and good air circulation will help heal any minor cuts and bruises that do occur during harvest.

Potatoes store best at about 40°F, with high relative humidity but good air circulation. Absolute darkness is essential to prevent greening, which makes the tubers unfit for consumption. Lower temperatures may lead to the conversion of the potato's starch to sugars, and a consequent off flavor; higher temperatures will, in time, initiate sprouting, after which the potatoes will deteriorate. Bruised or poorly cured tubers will not store as well and can spread problems to the others, so store them in front where they'll be used first.

The Best Varieties

You might enjoy growing some of the standard potatoes you see in the market—traditional storing varieties for baking and boiling like RUSSET BURBANK, KENNEBEC, RED PONTIAC, and SUPERIOR. Each of these has its own character and climatic adap-

tions, and it is important that you pick a variety that does well under your conditions. But once you get the basics down and the larder filled, consider growing some potatoes for fresh use: the special salad potatoes, and the interesting—but fine-tasting—blue potatoes.

My favorite potatoes are the tiny ones I pull from underneath my still-growing RED NORLAND plants. This is a vigorous, early variety that produces lots of small, thin-skinned, round potatoes. They make the best boiled potatoes you ever had, and are one of the best white-fleshed varieties for making potato salad. If you leave some on the plant, they'll grow to a good size, but RED NORLAND is not a long-storage variety, so you've got to use them up fairly quickly.

IRISH COBBLER is a very early potato, first found as a sport of the variety EARLY ROSE in Massachusetts in the 1870s. It has

---

VARIETY SOURCE CHART

POTATOES

Variety	When to Plant	When to Harvest	What to Harvest	Comments	Sources*
ALL BLUE	2 weeks before last frost	After tops die down	Underground tubers	Flesh is lavender-blue, skin blue; high mineral content	GY/SB
BINTJE	2 weeks before last frost	After tops die down	Underground tubers	Small, moist, salad-type potato	SB/NG

(continued)

POTATOES

Variety	When to Plant	When to Harvest	What to Harvest	Comments	Sources*
CAROLE	2 weeks before last frost	After tops die down	Underground tubers	German potato salad variety	MT
GREEN MOUNTAIN	2 weeks before last frost	After tops die down	Underground tubers	Late variety good for cool areas; good taste	SB/MT
IRISH COBBLER	2 weeks before last frost	After tops die down	Underground tubers	White-fleshed early type; good picked young	GY/MT
KENNEBEC	2 weeks before last frost	When tops die down	Underground tubers	Standard for yield and disease resistance; good keeper	Widely available
LADYFINGER (FINGERLING, KIPFEL KARTOFEL)	2 weeks before last frost	After tops die down	Underground tubers	Small tubers; moist, pale yellow skin and flesh	GY
RED NORLAND	2 weeks before last frost	After tops die down	Underground tubers	Also very good harvested at 1″ diameter (just as tubers form)	Widely available
RED PONTIAC	2 weeks before last frost	When tops die down	Underground tubers	Standard variety	Widely available
RUBY CRESCENT	2 weeks before last frost	After tops die down	Underground tubers	Pink skin with yellow flesh; LADYFINGER type, but larger	SB
RUSSET BURBANK	2 weeks before last frost	When tops die down	Underground tubers	Good baking variety	Widely available
SUPERIOR	2 weeks before last frost	When tops die down	Underground tubers	Standard variety	Widely available
YELLOW FINN	2 weeks before last frost	After tops die down	Underground tubers	Most widely known of the yellow, waxy kinds	SB

*Listings correspond to seed companies included under Seed Source List at the back of the book.

LADYFINGER potatoes

and sandy soils, it yields well, but is not as disease resistant as some of the newer varieties.

LADYFINGER, also known as FINGER-LING or KIPFEL KARTOFEL, is a small, elongated, Austrian potato with a much firmer and moister texture than the starchy white potatoes we are familiar with in this country. They're great for salads and for frying because they can be sliced thinly without crumbling.

A recent import from Germany, where it is the most popular of the yellow varieties, CAROLE is medium early and shallow-eyed. Its creamy texture and almost sweet flavor make it good for baking or salads. These are high yielding plants.

One seed source, Seeds Blum, carries starter tubers of the LADYFINGER, plus some other fine new moist potatoes: BINTJE, YELLOW FINN, and RUBY CRESCENT. All of these share the moist texture of LADYFINGER, and can be used for the same purposes. They also sell sets for ALL BLUE, a highly nutritious variety whose deep lavender flesh may be unsettling to some, but whose good flavor has won it many converts.

a richer flavor than many newer varieties, and being early, is a good choice for new potatoes. However, its storage life is short. Another variety that is prized for flavor is GREEN MOUNTAIN, an heirloom from here in Vermont that has been around for more than 100 years and is still in demand for baking. A late variety that likes cool weather

SALAD CROPS

The latest thing in salad gardening is to mix a number of delicate and tender greens in the same growing bed and to harvest them very young. The French have been doing this for hundreds of years; they call the mix of plants "mesclun."

There are few things more beautiful on a glistening, dew-touched summer morning than a bed of mesclun, the short thick rows forming a tapestry of green and red. Deeply cut, feathery leaves of *frisée* interweave with the smooth red leaves of lettuce and the tiny fernlike fronds of baby chervil. The textures and colors of this ready-mixed salad stand out against a background of rich, dark soil in the growing bed. Snip a few feet with your garden scissors, wash the greens, add a simple dressing, and you've got a world-class salad that sells for $15 a pound at some New York City greenmarkets.

Growing

The most basic recipe for a mesclun bed calls for one packet each of two kinds of lettuce, a packet of chervil and a packet of curly endive; just dump them together in a bowl, mix the seeds, and plant them.

There are a number of other salad plants that can be added to the seed mix, among them *mâche,* mustard, orache, sorrel, parsley, basil, chives, fennel, cutting celery, and purslane. Wild and weedy ingredients that often find their way into mesclun are chickweed and miner's lettuce (*Claytonia*), two mild-flavored, easy-to-grow greens.

You can make your own mesclun mix if you like, and even give it your own name. The idea is to mix the seed of whatever plants you think might be good together in a salad, then plant the mix. Or consider growing each ingredient separately and combining them however you like at harvest time. Planting crossways on a 3-foot bed keeps the amounts of each ingredient manageable.

You can plant a bed of mesclun as soon as the ground can be worked in spring. A quarter of an inch is a good seeding depth. Since you'll be harvesting your greens when they're very young and less than 6 inches tall, the rows need only be far enough apart to allow for cultivation. Run a hoe between the rows each week (or after a rain), and in a month to six weeks your salads will be in prime shape, though you can harvest at any time.

Some gardeners grow their mesclun in broadcast beds. To use this method, spread the seed as evenly as you can over the entire surface of the bed, use a rake to settle the seeds, then water thoroughly. You may need to do some spot weeding before harvest, but if you started with a relatively weed-free bed, maintenance should be minimal.

Spring and fall are the natural seasons for good greens, but you can produce crops right through the summer in all but hot climates. During hot weather, cover newly seeded rows with a section of 2 × 4 lumber to keep the soil beneath cool until the seeds germinate, then shade the bed. We use two forms of shade in our garden. In early and late summer, when a little shade is enough, we plant our greens in beds between the rows of raspberries, which run north to south. That gives the greens some shade for most of the day. During the real dog days of midsummer, we put hoops made of #9 fencing wire over our bed, and cover it with nylon shade cloth (available by mail or at garden centers).

Fall crops should be started from late August until the first frost. In hot regions you may need to put a board over the rows until the seeds germinate (see above). For late fall or early winter harvest, plant shortly after the first fall frost. Harvest will probably be delayed by shortened day length. Mesclun sown in a cold frame can be overwintered for spring harvest. Remove mulch (if any) as soon as spring breaks and fertilize the plants; they should be ready for harvest in three to four weeks.

Harvesting

You can begin harvesting any time after the plants are up, but don't let the plants get taller than about 6 inches. One method of harvest is to cut along the row an inch above the ground with scissors, then water and fertilize the bed and wait for it to regrow. Under good conditions, you can get four harvests from a single planting, but don't expect equal vigor after each cutting. If you use this method, harvest just before use, because the greens may wilt within minutes if the weather is hot.

We prefer to plant in succession rather than wait for the greens to resprout. We seed just enough every week for a week's harvest later on; that way we always have sprightly, young greens coming along. A newly sown bed will be ready in almost the same amount of time as a bed that is cut and left to resprout, and we feel that the greens are more tender and flavorful when young. So instead of snipping off the greens, I run a knife along the row just beneath the surface, cutting off the roots just below the crown.

How to cut salad greens (golden purslane)

The Best Varieties

There are a number of traditional recipes for mesclun. Here are three from the Provence region of France and neigh-boring Piedmont in Italy. Each will appeal to a different palate and is adapted to a slightly different season. Each is a different mix of leaf shapes, textures, and colors.

Mesclun Niçoise

Nice is the market town for one of the most favored growing areas in Provence, a region of France famous for its produce. This is a mix for those who like their salads sharp, and it is guaranteed to wake up your taste buds. Most mesclun is served with just a simple vinaigrette dressing, but with this one, you might like to add a dollop of unflavored yogurt (there's a recipe in Part III).

The five ingredients of mesclun niçoise are curly endive, a very finely curled and slightly bitter plant; SPADONA, a broad-leaf, pale green cutting chicory that is more bitter tasting and is used sparingly; dandelion, a cultivated variety of the common weed that is also sharp on the tongue when unblanched and used in moderation; BROADLEAF, quick growing with a clear, peppery taste; and ARUGULA, the piquant Italian salad green with a mustardy overtone. We use equal parts of each ingredient, but you might like to experiment to find a proportion that suits you.

Mesclun Provençal

Similar to the niçoise, but not as tart, and a bit easier to keep in good condition during hot weather, this second recipe from Provence is grown just like the others. It is the most traditional of the mesclun recipes, and it has a standard proportion: two parts lettuce to one each of the other ingredients.

SALAD CROPS

Variety	When to Plant	When to Harvest	What to Harvest	Comments	Sources*
Arugula					
ARUGULA (ROCKET)	ASAP in spring/in succession	Anytime before plant bolts	Leaves at 4"–6" for salad	Piquant flavor; will reseed if left to seed	Widely available
Chard					
PERPETUAL SPINACH	ASAP in spring/in succession	Anytime before plant bolts	Leaves at 4"–6" for salad	A refined type of chard; can also be grown as a biennial	CG/TM
Chenopodium					
GOOD KING HENRY	ASAP in spring/in succession	Anytime before plant bolts	Leaves at 4"–6" for salad	Also known as "Mercury"; can be grown as a perennial; mild flavor	CG
Chervil					
BRUSSELS (BRUSSELS WINTER)	ASAP in spring/in succession	Anytime before plant bolts	Leaves at 4"–6" for salad	Slower bolting than other types of chervil; use for *mesclun*	CG/JS
CURLY	ASAP in spring/in succession	Anytime before plant bolts	Leaves at 4"–6" for salad	More decorative than BRUSSELS, but quicker bolting	CG/LM/ SS/NG
Claytonia					
CLAYTONIA	ASAP in spring/in succession	Anytime before plant bolts	Leaves at 4"–6" for salad	Also know as "miner's lettuce"; grows wild in waste places	CG
Cress					
BROADLEAF	ASAP in spring/in succession	Anytime before plant bolts	Leaves at 4"–6" for salad	Use BROADLEAF for salads, CURLY for garnish	CG/TM
CURLY	ASAP in spring/in succession	Anytime before plant bolts	Leaves at 4"–6" for salad	*Lepidium sativum*, also known as "peppergrass"	CG/JS/ NG/SS/ LM
UPLAND	ASAP in spring/in succession	Anytime before plant bolts	Leaves at 4"–6" for salad	*Barbarea praecox*, also known as "land cress"; for cool weather only	CG/SB

(continued)

SALAD CROPS

Variety	When to Plant	When to Harvest	What to Harvest	Comments	Sources*
Cress—*continued*					
WATERCRESS	Transplant into wet ground	Anytime	Leaves	*Nasturtium officianale,* peppery flavor; perennial; increase by division or seed	Widely available
Dandelion					
IMPROVED (FULL HEART, AMELIORE)	ASAP in spring/in succession	Anytime before plant bolts	Leaves at 4"-6" for salad	Selected for broader leaves; blanch to temper bitterness	CG
MAUSER'S TRESS	ASAP in spring/in succession	Anytime before plant bolts	Leaves at 4"-6" for salad	Selected for forcing, like Belgian endive	CG
Mâche					
COQUILLE DE LOUVIERS	ASAP in spring/in succession	Anytime before plant bolts	Leaves at 4"-6" for salad	Cupped leaves hold salad dressing well	CG/LM
D'ETAMPES	ASAP in spring/in succession	Anytime before plant bolts	Leaves at 4"-6" for salad	Very tender with mild, nutty flavor	CG
PIEDMONTE	ASAP in spring/in succession	Anytime before plant bolts	Leaves at 4"-6" for salad	Long, pale leaves; also known as "nussely," "fetticus," and corn salad	CG
VERT DE CAMBRAI	ASAP in spring/in succession	Anytime before plant bolts	Leaves at 4"-6" for salad	Productive round-leaved variety	SS/LM
VIT	ASAP in spring/in succession	Anytime before plant bolts	Leaves at 4"-6" for salad	Smaller, firmer leaves than other types	CG/JS
Mustard					
KYONA MIZUNA	ASAP in spring/in succession	Anytime before plant bolts	Leaves at 4"-6" for salad	Can also be grown as a biennial; milder flavor than others	CG/SB/ NG/JS
MIILKE PURPLE	ASAP in spring/in succession	Anytime before plant bolts	Leaves at 4"-6" for salad	Green leaves with purple veins; good for boiling greens	LM/JS/ CG

VARIETY SOURCE CHART

SALAD CROPS

Variety	When to Plant	When to Harvest	What to Harvest	Comments	Sources*
OSAKA	ASAP in spring/in succession	Anytime before plant bolts	Leaves at 4″-6″ for salad	Purple leaves with white veins, good for boiling greens	JS/CG
WHITE	ASAP in spring/in succession	Anytime before plant bolts	Leaves at 4″-6″ for salad	*Brassica alba;* fast growing (30 days); harvest young	TM/CG
Orache					
ORACHE (MOUNTAIN SPINACH)	ASAP in spring/in succession	Anytime before plant bolts	Leaves at 4″-6″ for salad	Red, yellow/white, and green forms available; mild flavor	CG/PT/ SB
Purslane					
GOLDEN	ASAP in spring/in succession	Anytime before plant bolts	Leaves at 4″-6″ for salad	Large golden leaves; thick, juicy, and mildly ascerbic	CG
GREEN	ASAP in spring/in succession	Anytime before plant bolts	Sprigs at 4″-6″ for salad	Selected from weedy purslane; larger leaves, upright habit	CG
Sorrel					
BLONDE LYON	Spring to summer	Anytime	4″-8″ leaves for salad and soup	Perennial; paler leaves than other varieties	LM
DE BELLEVILLE	Spring to summer	Anytime	4″-8″ leaves for salad and soup	Perennial; keep seed stalks picked off for increased yields	LM

*Listings correspond to seed companies included under Seed Source List at the back of the book.

Use any good cutting lettuce, keeping color and leaf form in mind, and mix it with ARUGULA, as in mesclun niçoise; BRUSSELS chervil, the parsleylike foliage which lends a slight anise flavor; and curly endive, the intricately cut leaves of which add both visual and culinary interest with their mild bitter taste.

Misticanza

This recipe is from the Piedmont region of northern Italy. It does not include arugula, but you may add arugula without changing the character of the salad. This is the only traditional mesclun recipe we've seen that includes radicchio.

The proportion for misticanza is five parts lettuce to four parts chicory. Here are some varieties to try:

Use any cutting lettuce, keeping texture, form, and color in mind, plus the same curly endive as other mesclun recipes; the spadona used in mesclun niçoise; radicchio TREVISO, a red chicory (though it isn't red during warm summer months) with leaves like Belgian endive; radicchio CASTELFRANCO, a round-leaf variegated red, green, and white chicory; radicchio GUILIO, a round-leaf red chicory that doesn't need cold weather to color up; and CERIOLO, a bitter green chicory that's very cold-hardy.

Mesclun Ingredients

Lettuce Mix

One of the most straightforward mesclun recipes—and a good one to start with—is a simple mix of lettuces with different leaf forms and colors. This is the mildest of the mesclun mixes, as all the young lettuces have a mild flavor. But be sure to keep the bed watered during hot, dry weather to avoid bitterness. If you will be harvesting on a cut-and-come-again basis, fertilize and water deeply after each cutting.

The Best Varieties

It's a good idea to use mostly loose-leaf varieties as they are the quickest to resprout after cutting. Some of our favorites for a bed of cutting lettuce include the following:

RED SALAD BOWL, a beautiful wine-red loose-leaf with undulant leaves; SALAD BOWL, which has the same good qualities, but with pale green coloring; ROYAL OAK LEAF, a variety displaying dark green leaves with deeply cut margins and a glossy sheen; ROUGE D'HIVER, a deep red romaine type, with a simple upright leaf form and great color that make it a great complement to the loose-leaf types; LOLLO BIONDO, a very tightly curled, frilly loose-leaf with pale green coloring; LOLLO ROSSA, a red-tipped cousin of LOLLO BIONDO; ROSSA DI TRENTO, an Italian cutting lettuce with the same coloring but a simpler leaf; BIONDO A FOGLIE LISCE, another Italian variety with pale, smooth, tender leaves; DEER TONGUE, with dark green, succulent leaves and a simple upright form; CURLY OAKLEAF, a particularly quick resprouter; ICE QUEEN (*Reine des Glaces*), a batavian type with incredibly convoluted, toothed green leaves; and FOUR SEASONS, a butterhead that has smooth red leaves with green and gold accents.

Other Ingredients

There are four basic flavors that characterize most of the salad greens you are likely to grow for mesclun: piquant, peppery, bitter, and bland (or mild). By combining these four flavor tones with a colorful lettuce mix, you can develop your own personal mesclun.

Arugula (Eruca sativa)

This piquant green is one of the most popular of the "new" salad greens. Like most of the other current favorites, it has been around for quite a long time, its use dating back through recorded history in

Europe. The first records of rocket—as it is also known—in this country are from 1631.

Mature plants are 2 to 3 feet tall, with coarse, slightly hairy and notched leaves that hug the ground in a rosette, and a sparsely branched main stem with insignificant leaves along it culminating in a widely spaced and somewhat uninteresting (at least from a distance) flowers. These flowers are sought for garnishes by dedicated salad gatherers, and some fans allow a patch to self-sow for a perpetual harvest.

Arugula is best grown quickly, with ample water and fertility, and without any kind of stress. Our best crops are grown in rich, moist parts of the garden early in the spring, protected by a floating row cover. The covers keep the wind off, protect the leaves from spattering soil, and block out the flea beetles. Harvest arugula while the leaves still have a juvenile look to them—relatively pale and smooth, with the edges of the leaves not yet fully defined, and no central stem growing up from the crown of the plant.

Cress (Lepidium sativum)

Cress is just about the easiest crop in the world to grow. It is the perfect child's garden plant, even more sure to succeed than radishes. But it is also quick to pass its prime. Cress, like arugula, is used when barely past the seedling stage. If you've ever seen one of those ceramic sheep on a friend's windowsill covered with the "woolly" green sprouts, you were probably looking at cress. Cress can also be grown in pots and window boxes, and it lends a nice, clean, peppery taste to the salad. In midwinter up

north it can be a real awakener from the culinary doldrums!

In the garden, we sow cress in the same bed as the arugula. It grows a bit faster. There are three common kinds of cress: plain, curly, and broad-leaf. The plain kind has mildly serrated leaves; the curly has very deeply serrated leaves, like curly parsley; and the broad-leaf cress has seedling leaves that are 1 inch across by 4 inches long. We prefer broad-leaf cress for green salads and sandwiches because the leaves are much more substantial. The delicate leaves of the curly type are excellent for garnishes or chopping up into spreads, dips, and prepared-meat salads. The plain tastes the same as the other two, but has no great qualities beyond that. We've heard tell of golden and even pink cresses, but have been unable to find a source for either.

As with arugula, you can harvest the flowers of plants that go by, or let the plants self-sow for a perpetual, semiwild salad garden, though I don't recommend it. The dried seedpods of cress make a very attractive winter decoration. For drying, cut the plants off at ground level just after the last of the flowers are finished and the little dishlike pods have begun to turn from green to tan. Hang the whole plant to air-dry in a dark, well-ventilated place.

Watercress (Nasturtium officinale)

This well-known perennial salad green is not really cress, but a member of the nasturtium family. Nonetheless, it shares the sharp, clean taste of the true cress. For it to grow well, you need lots of water, nonacid soil, and full sun. Its natural habitat is the eddies of clear running water in pastures or at the inlets and outlets of ponds. The best plantings of watercress are usually "established" in those places (they will spread on their own) rather than actually cultivated. You might be able to establish a bed of watercress next to the hose bib in your garden, where it will get plenty of splash and spray. Start the plants in sterile potting soil in early spring. The requisite water can be supplied by placing a capillary mat, which hangs into a reservoir of water, under the flat. This will "wick" water from the reservoir and keep the soil in the flat moist.

Upland Cress (Barbarea verna *or* B. praecox)

Upland cress, which is sometimes called American land cress, is also an entirely separate species from true cress. The plants resemble arugula more than cress, but the flavor is much clearer, lacking the spicy overtones of arugula. It is best harvested during the cool parts of the year because it, too, runs to seed quickly and becomes unpleasantly hot tasting in warm weather. As with the other cresses (and arugula) it should be harvested young, when less than 6 inches tall and before there is any elongation of the crown of the plant.

Mustard (Brassica *spp.*)

Mustard is the traditional companion to cress in a garden of small salad greens, and it is the second component of the classic English tea sandwich. Sow mustard a couple of days after the cress, if you can, because it grows faster. Plant one row of mustard for each two of cress.

White mustard is a traditional British type, but we prefer the Japanese purple mustards because of their color and the fact that the leaves hold their quality longer in the garden. Two good varieties are MIILKE PURPLE, which has a deep purple coloring and greenish veins, and OSAKA which has white veins. Both are frost-hardy and can be harvested any time they aren't actually frozen solid.

Finally, there is a biennial mustard known as KYONA MIZUNA. It has very finely cut leaves that look almost feathery, and a much milder flavor than other mustards, with only a hint of their peppery nature. Because it is a biennial, it does not run to seed as quickly as other mustards. In fact, a single planting can, with care, be kept in good cutting condition throughout the summer.

Mâche (Valerianella olitoria)

Also known as corn salad or lamb's lettuce, *mâche* has the mildest flavor and softest texture of any common salad green. It is a very small plant, and the rosettes are often served whole in salads with just the barest hint of a dressing. Although it is not fast growing, it is cold-hardy, relatively slow bolting, and bitter-free, even in hot dry weather.

Corn salad got its name from the fact that it used to be gathered wild from the grain fields in early fall. It succeeds well as a fall crop, seeded about two weeks before the first fall frost, just as our days begin to cool down. You can also start *mâche* as an early spring crop by seeding it in #162 plugs a month before the ground can be worked; as soon as the snow is gone and the garden dries, put out your first plants. We direct seed at the same time for our second, summer crop, setting the seed ¼ to ½ inch deep.

Mâche has a very subtle flavor, with a faint nuttiness that is easily overpowered by other, more strongly flavored greens. There are a number of varieties of *mâche*. The most beautiful is probably COQUILLE DE LOUVIERS, which has cupped leaves that hold dressing well. It is also one of the hardiest. Some other cold-tolerant varieties to try for overwintering are D'ETAMPES, VERT DE CAMBRAI and VIT. One other notable variety is PIEDMONTE, an Italian type that has long, pale leaves and is especially heat tolerant.

Chervil (Anthriscus cerefolium)

Chervil is a small plant with curly, pale green leaves and a slight anise flavor that, while rarely used alone, goes well with many other plants and is a major ingredient of the famous *fines herbes* of French cuisine. It resembles parsley, but the leaves are more delicate and fernlike.

We sow chervil as soon as the ground can be worked in short rows spaced 4 to 6 inches apart. The harvest begins when the plants reach about 6 inches in height, usually about six to eight weeks after planting.

The variety simply called CHERVIL is the original form, but CURLY chervil makes a better garnish because the leaves are more decorative; BRUSSELS WINTER is larger and slower to bolt in hot weather than the other two.

Purslane (Portulaca oleracea)

Yes, this is a relative of the tenacious, ground-hugging weed. A native of East India, it has a slight but refreshing acidity, a juicy, succulent texture, and a high vitamin content.

Cultivated forms of purslane are more upright than the common weed, having been selected over the years for easy harvest. Thick sowing within rows spaced 4 to 6 inches apart will force it into more upright growth. Harvest while the purslane is still small, before there are any signs of it going to flower. Replant regularly to have a succession of tender purslane for the salad bowl. In addition to GREEN purslane, there is also a GOLDEN purslane which is a bit thicker in all its parts and slower growing. The juicy leaves and stems of both types make a good complement to the thinner, softer leaves of most other salad plants.

Claytonia or Winter Purslane (Claytonia perfoliata)

You may know this plant in its wild form as miner's lettuce. When mature, the leaves form a funnel-shaped dish in which this small plant's white flowers are displayed, making it a very attractive addition to a salad. As with the other special salads we have been discussing, it can be direct seeded in succession or cut, fertilized, and allowed to regrow a few times through the season. The Germans call this plant *winterportulak,* and they grow it as a seedling crop in greenhouses, harvesting the plants just before they grow their first true leaves.

Orache (Atriplex hortensis)

Sometimes called "mountain spinach," orache closely resembles its cousin lamb's-quarters. It has been in our gardens for many years as a potherb. There are three varieties: GREEN orache, RED orache, and WHITE (or YELLOW) orache. The leaves are mild and tender if the plant has been grown quickly, as it should be. For salad use, sow thickly in short rows, as for other greens, and harvest at 4 to 6 inches tall. Succession plantings should be made, because once the weather is hot and dry, all three kinds will run quickly to seed. If you like, the plants can be allowed to mature and the seedpods used as a dried floral decoration. In this case, thin to 24 inches between plants.

Sorrel (Rumex acetosa)

This is a barely domesticated cousin of sheep sorrel, or sourgrass, a weed that inhabits the acid soils of many New England gardens. It is easily grown as a perennial. Sorrel leaves are sour, with a hint of lemon, and in the spring when they first green up, quite tender. As the summer progresses and the leaves get up to the size of your hand, they become tougher, but you can still use them for soups and for wrapping of chicken or fish before baking.

We start our sorrel plants in #98 plug trays and transplant them into a permanent bed at the edge of the herb garden, with the dandelion and a number of other perennial salad herbs. In rich soil you should be able to harvest the outer leaves in a month or so. As long as you keep the seed stalks picked off, you will force new growth and continue the harvest. After three or four years, divide the plants to keep the bed vigorous. Renew the soil with compost and manure at that time, or move the plants to a new section of the garden.

Sorrel is usually harvested leaf by leaf. The two major cultivated varieties are BLONDE LYON, and DE BELLEVILLE.

Dandelion (Taraxacum officinale)

This, too, is simply a cultivated form of a common garden weed, but the cultivated plants are much more productive, and they have a somewhat milder taste, especially when blanched.

You can grow dandelion just like sorrel, and you'll be glad for those spring greens that accompany the arrival of the daffodils. Once the plants are up and growing in the spring, gather the leaves loosely together with a rubber band and cover with a nursery pot for a week or so to blanch. This will moderate the otherwise strong taste. Cut off the plant an inch above ground level. Fertilize after blanching and harvest with fish emulsion or good compost. Stop them from spreading seed by keeping the seed stalks picked off.

There is a broad-leaf kind known simply as IMPROVED, AMELIORE or FULL HEART, and a second, forcing type called MAUSER'S TRESS.

Good King Henry (Chenopodium bonus-henricus)

A final inhabitant of the perennial salad bed, grown the same way as sorrel and dandelion, is the perennial cousin of spinach known as mercury, or Good King Henry. You can direct seed or start the plants in #98 plug trays to set out as soon as the weather is settled. Harvest the following and future springs at about the same time as the asparagus comes in. The young kalelike leaves will please those who do not care for the earthy taste of spinach.

Ornamental Kale
(Brassica oleracea, *Acephala Group*)

These colorful kale plants are equally at home in the vegetable or the ornamental garden. The taste will never match that of the best edible kale varieties, but then very few plants will ever be quite as beautiful as the new hybrid ornamental kales.

Both the color and the taste of ornamental kales improve with exposure to frost, so start them in #98 plug trays about 90 days before the fall frost date, then transplant them into their final locations once they fill the plug (lift the plant to check for root circling in the bottom of the cell). You will need to spray regularly with *Bacillus thuringiensis* (Bt) or pick off cabbageworms, because they find the plants as attractive as you do. You can harvest individual, tender leaves for salad use, or cut the entire plant off, pinch out the center, and use the head as a base on which to display crudités or a "composed" (that is, arranged) salad.

The ornamental border is a good spot for these kales because they are at their best when not much else is in bloom. The open-pollinated strains come in both smooth-leaf, heading "cabbage" forms and tightly curled, loose-leaf "kale" forms; both will grow up to 2 feet tall, and they range in color from white to pink, red, and violet.

Open-pollinated types are usually listed in catalogs simply as ornamental cabbage or ornamental kale. The seed for newer hybrids like the NAGOYA or OSAKA series comes in individual colors, but it is much more expensive. We think they are worth it because these plants are especially striking in groups, and uniformity is very important in mass plantings to make it look right. They are also less prone to stretching. The even newer hybrid PEACOCK strain is completely different. It has the same deeply cut, feathery appearance as MIZUNA mustard, but the leaves, laid atop one another in stark contrast, range from a mixture of white on a background of deep gray-green to outrageously bright pink, purple, and even coral.

SQUASH

D on't look now, but your average backyard summer squash or zucchini plant is the source of a great vegetable delicacy that is a snap to grow, yet rarely makes it to market in decent condition.

The French call them *courgettes* and the Italians *zuchette*. Both names have the "ette" in common and that means "small." European cooks, facing the yearly deluge of squash from the garden, discovered long ago that using them small is a sure cure for the zucchini blahs.

It's easy to grow these baby squashes—just take a knife out into the garden and cut loose those little zucchini when they're 3 inches long. That will solve any poten-

tial zucchini glut, and at the same time give you some of the best squash you've ever eaten. This technique works with all the summer squashes.

Growing

Squash is native to the Americas and will grow like a native if you give it the chance. It is endlessly productive; no matter how many babies you harvest, no matter how small or young, there will always be more.

We start our squashes in #50 plug trays two or three weeks before the frost-free date. The cells are the size of small peat pots, but easier to handle because they don't tip over or fall apart.

We start a few seedlings about a month earlier in case the weather is kind and we don't have a late frost. Most gardeners are loathe to start plants they may not be able to use. But it's no sin to have extra plants; it's foresight.

Before planting, we prepare a high bed and cover it with black plastic mulch. Raising the bed an extra 6 inches helps it drain faster after a cold spring rain, and high beds also catch more sun to warm the soil.

To build a high bed by hand, first stretch lines to mark the edges of the bed. Standing outside one of the lines, rake soil from outside the other line toward yourself. Work down the length of the bed this way, then back the other side. You can stand in the path created by your first pass to rake the second path. A final pass will smooth the surface of the bed and get it straight. Keep the bed regular in width, and you'll be able to fit in more plants.

Next, put down black plastic mulch, which comes in various widths for different size beds. After rolling out the mulch, cover the outer 2 or 3 inches of the edges with dirt. Work forward along the bed (I work on my knees) burying about 2 feet of running length at a time. First, form a furrow with your right hand, pushing away along the edge of the bed in front of you, then position the plastic with your left hand and pull the soil back with your right. Move forward a couple of feet and repeat the process. If your soil is too hard to do this job by hand, you can use a

shovel. In either case, be sure to get the mulch tight so the wind can't pick it up.

Every foot along the row, make a crisscross slit in the plastic. Mix a shovelful of compost with the soil at each slit. We've found that a 1-foot spacing gives plenty of room for the plants.

The flats of plants should be watered thoroughly before transplanting so the plants will lift easily from the trays. Pour a cup or so of transplant solution (see Part I) into each planting hole, place the transplant, and move on to the next. Things will go quicker with a helper, because one person can pour the water, while the other sets the plants. This is good work for a child, because the soupy soil is easy to firm around the plants without hurting them.

If you want to make the most of your garden space, poke holes with your finger along the edges of the bed between each squash plant and set basil plants in the holes. The basil will be ready to harvest before the squash begins to crowd in on it.

As soon as you've finished planting, put on a floating row cover of spunbonded fabric. If it's warm enough to put squashes out, then the cucumber beetles have already hatched, and they'll be out looking for dinner. Remember, they have nothing to do all day but look for food, and they are very persistent. Don't leave even an inch of cover open for those hungry beetles to enter the paradise underneath! If you anchor the sides properly, wind won't bother the covers because they are so porous the breeze can't pick them up.

Your attention won't be required for another month, unless the weather is very dry or cold. If there is no rain for a week after you transplant, give the squashes a good watering. Gardeners in arid climates would do well to put drip irrigation under the plastic mulch. Either buy a drip system with the emitters spaced every foot or make your own system (many suppliers sell the blank tube and emitters). Otherwise, you'll need to alter the spacing of plants in the row to make sure each plant gets watered.

If, like us, you like to rush the season, a cold snap could come along and give you some problems. The row covers will offer a degree or two of protection, but below 30°F, it would be wise to put on additional insulation in the form of blankets or sheets.

When you see the first signs of flowers, remove the covers so insects can get in to pollinate them. This means that the cucumber beetles will get in as well, but by then the plants will be big enough to withstand their appetite for squash leaves. Most squash fruits will rot if not fertilized within a few days after they form.

If you put in more than one bed of squash, don't put them right next to each other or you'll be short of room to work when they are full grown. One step on the terminal shoot of the plant, and that's it for the season, so be careful to leave enough room for harvesting. What we do is plant every other bed to another high-bed crop, like greens and leeks. The greens are harvested by the time the squashes crowd the path, and the soil from the greens rows can be used to hill the leeks, thus making the path for harvesting squashes even wider.

Harvesting

We don't leave any zucchini on the vines that are larger than 8 inches. If you don't have a use for them, throw the squashes on the compost pile, but keep them harvested. Leaving mature fruits on the plants will slow production.

Ideally, you should harvest at 6 inches or less. We pick half our crop at the flower stage, when it's still only finger-sized, and leave the other half of the fruits to develop. If the flower is in good shape, leave it on; if not, carefully cut it off. If you try to break it off, the end of the fruit may break, too.

Use a thin, sharp knife to cut squashes, and if you're cutting them in flower, lay only a single layer in the harvest basket. We alternate them left and right so that the stem end of one is next to the flower of its neighbor. That way they fit snugly together and won't roll around. If there are cucumber beetles in the flowers—likely if you harvest in the early morning—just swing the fruit in the air and they will be thrown loose. At this stage your squashes are very delicate and will bruise easily (which is why you don't see them in the market very often).

Harvest carefully; try not to poke the main stem when cutting the fruits from the vine. If squashes get damaged during harvest, remove them from the patch rather than leaving them to rot. Time taken cleaning up is well spent from both an aesthetic and a production standpoint.

The Best Varieties

Summer Squash

Variety and early harvest are your two best defenses against a zucchini glut. Even if you plant only one hill of summer squashes, mix the varieties in the hill so you don't get tired of the results. Early harvest will lower the daily take but not your enjoyment or, if you keep the plants in good shape, your total harvest. Most varieties can be used together or interchangeably in recipes, so it doesn't matter if you only get a few of each kind at every harvest.

We generally put in twice as many plants of regular green zucchini as we do the other varieties. Just about any variety will work for *courgettes,* though some will hold the flower better than others. Our choice is ELITE, a dark, straight hybrid. We've also tried SENECA GOURMET, ARLESA, and AURORA, all with good results. Breeders are now working on zucchini varieties bred especially to produce large male flowers for stuffing, but only time will tell if they make good home garden plants. The first of these is BUTTERBLOSSOM. One that has large blossoms on small zucchini is FLORINA. On both varieties, the blossoms tend to stay open longer, a boon to both cooks and specialty growers. With the standard types, there is only a short time each day when the blossoms are open and prime for harvest.

(continued on page 170)

VARIETY SOURCE CHART

SQUASH

Variety	When to Plant	When to Harvest	What to Harvest	Comments	Sources*
Summer Squashes					
ARLESA HYBRID	Frost-free date	Anytime after fruits form	Cylindrical green fruits	Good for *courgettes;* harvest small with flower still on	SS
AURORA HYBRID	Frost-free date	Anytime after fruits form	Dark green cylindrical fruits	Keep fruits on all varieties picked to increase yields	No current source

(continued)

SQUASH

Variety	When to Plant	When to Harvest	What to Harvest	Comments	Sources*
Summer Squashes—*continued*					
BIANCA DELLA VIRGINIA	Frost-free date	Anytime after fruits form	Pale green cylindrical fruits	Pale green skin with darker flecks of color	No current source
BUTTERBLOSSOM HYBRID	Frost-free date	As soon as male flowers open	Male flowers	Bred for male flower production (see text); blossoms may be stuffed	CG
COCOZELLE	Frost-free date	Anytime after fruits form	Cylindrical green fruits	Skin is dark green with lighter green stripes	JS/ST/ NG
ELITE HYBRID	Frost-free date	Anytime after fruits form	4"–8" long; cylindrical; green fruits	Cut when in flower for *courgettes,* or at 8" for slicing	HM/CG
FLORINA HYBRID	Frost-free date	Anytime after fruits form	4"–6" fruit with flower intact	Bred especially for *courgettes;* flower stays attached longer	CG
GOLD RUSH HYBRID	Frost-free date	Anytime after fruits form	4"–8" long; cylindrical gold fruits	True zucchini that is yellow/gold; good contrast with green	Widely available
GOURMET GLOBE HYBRID	Frost-free date	Anytime after fruits form	1"–4" diameter round fruits	Good flavor; vining plants	SS/TM
MULTIPIK HYBRID	Frost-free date	Anytime after fruits form	Bulbous, pale yellow fruits	Bush plants; very productive; fruit yellow right to the stem	HM/CG
RONDE DE NICE (TONDA DI NIZZA)	Frost-free date	Anytime after fruits form	1"–4" in diameter; spherical fruits	Cut at 1" (with blossom), or at 4" in diameter for stuffing	CG/ LM/TM
SCALLOPINI HYBRID	Frost-free date	Anytime after fruits form	Dark green, deep patty-pan-type fruits	Good taste and high yields; good color contrast with SUNBURST	CG/NG/ PT/LM/ ST
SENECA HYBRID	Frost-free date	Anytime after fruits form	Cylindrical dark green fruits	Standard variety for the Northeast	ST/NG

VARIETY SOURCE CHART

SQUASH

Variety	When to Plant	When to Harvest	What to Harvest	Comments	Sources*
STRIATA D' ITALIA	Frost-free date	Anytime after fruits form	Cylindrical green fruits	Skin is dark green with lighter green stripes	No current source
SUNBURST HYBRID	Frost-free date	Anytime after fruits form	Yellow/gold patty-pan-type fruits	Good for tempura at 1″ in diameter with blossom still attached	Widely available
TARA HYBRID	Frost-free date	Anytime after fruits form	Crookneck yellow fruits	High-yielding hybrid; disease resistant	HM
TROMBONCINO	Frost-free date	Anytime after fruits form	8″–18″ long, curved fruits	Vigorous vining plant; grows on trellis; good for slicing	CG/NG/ SB
WHITE BUSH MARROW	Frost-free date	Anytime after fruits form	Bulbous, creamy white fruits	English favorite	VB/ST/ NG

Winter Squashes

Variety	When to Plant	When to Harvest	What to Harvest	Comments	Sources*
DELICATA	Frost-free date	Before first frost (100 days)	3″ × 9″ cylindrical fruits	Outstanding flavor and texture; can be used without curing	CG/JS/ NG/ST
GOLDEN NUGGET	Frost-free date	Before first frost (85 days)	4″–6″ diameter globe; orange fruits	Good for short-season areas; good taste when well grown	JS/SB/ ST
JERSEY GOLDEN ACORN HYBRID	Frost-free date	Anytime after fruits form	4″–5″ diameter; acorn shaped; golden fruits	Tastes just like acorn squash, but can be used as summer squash, too	Widely available
SWEET DUMPLING	Frost-free date	Before first frost (100 days)	3″ in diameter; flattened, ridged globe	Small fruits great for single serving; can be used uncured	JS/CG/ LM/SS

*Listings correspond to seed companies included under Seed Source List at the back of the book.

Variation in appearance can be all it takes to make a basket of squashes interesting; try striped zucchini like COCOZELLE or STRIATA D'ITALIA along with the standard types. There are also round zucchini —TONDA DI NIZZA or RONDE DE NICE (both translate as "round niçoise"). WHITE BUSH MARROW is a bulbous, cream-colored English variety that has a mild taste and texture. BIANCA DELLA VIRGINIA, from Italy, is a very pale green with the mottling that is characteristic of green zucchini. Don't forget the new golden zucchini like GOLD RUSH, which make a great shape contrast with baby golden SUNBURST patty pan squash.

For yellow summer squash we use another hybrid called MULTIPIK, although I suspect most others would work just as well. Try your current favorite with early harvesting before switching. For a crookneck squash, we use TARA, another common American hybrid. One of the best varieties is the new yellow patty pan squash SUNBURST. This hybrid gets off to a slow start, compared to some of the other varieties we plant, but along with the round zucchini mentioned above, it makes the best *courgettes* for cooking whole with the flower on because its short body helps keep the overall length manageable. Also, the combined shapes of fruit and flower are particularly beautiful if sliced lengthwise. Another, deeper patty pan is SCALLOPINI, with a dark gray-green color that provides a nice contrast to SUNBURST.

One last variety of summer squash we grow is called TROMBONCINO, or "Italian

Patty-pan squash

trombone squash." This variety does best if grown on a trellis like cucumbers. The fruits are long and thin, curving over their length to a small bulbous end like the tip of a question mark. Babies are 8 inches long, but TROMBONCINO are sweet and tender all the way to 18 inches or so. If left to mature, they will harden and become a 3-foot-long ornamental winter gourd. The plants are extremely vigorous; one row down the center of a bed will turn the place into a jungle by mid-August. As long as you keep the fruits picked, they'll keep on producing.

Winter Squash

Our favorite winter squash is JERSEY GOLDEN ACORN, which can either be cut young for summer squash or left on the plant to harden up enough to store for the winter. Some other exceptional varieties for kitchen use are DELICATA and SWEET DUMPLING, two small, cream-colored fruits with dark green, longitudinal stripes. SWEET DUMPLING is about 4 inches in diameter and perfect for a single serving. The size, along with the sweet golden flesh, and the fact that it needs no curing before storage, recommend it. DELICATA is very similar, but it is longer and thinner. The fruits are 3 inches across at the top and up to 9 inches long. Both are long-season squashes, requiring 90 to 100 days to mature. One other favorite of Shepherd's and his grandfather's is GOLDEN NUGGET. This is a very early, small golden squash borne on compact plants. They're about 5 inches in diameter and weigh 1½ to 2 pounds each. Well grown, the flavor is great, and it is just about the earliest winter squash available.

TOMATOES

*T*omatoes are the single most popular garden vegetable, grown in more gardens than any other crop. It takes only one trip to the market to learn that the modern supermarket tomato might just as well be manufactured out of textured soy protein for all it has in common with a garden-ripened tomato.

Because of their popularity, there are literally hundreds of varieties, ranging from tiny, marble-sized currant tomatoes up to beefsteak types that regularly reach 2 pounds apiece. The range of taste, texture, and color is just as broad.

Growing

We start our tomatoes in #162 plug trays a full two months before the frost-free date, using a sterile, soilless potting mix. Sow two seeds in each cell or pot, and once the seedlings have grown their first true leaves (the ones with serrated edges) get rid of the weaker one. Cut the reject off at the soil line instead of pulling it up so you don't disturb the roots of the seedling you're keeping.

Give the plants as much light as possible. If you're growing plants in the house, you may have to settle for whatever temperature the house is, but you can increase the number of early fruits with a "cold treatment." To do this, allow the temperature to fall to 50° to 55°F at night for the first three weeks after thinning. Then return to a normal household temperature of 60°F nights and 70°F days. This will increase the number of flowers (and therefore tomatoes) in the first few clusters of fruit.

Fertilize weekly in sunny weather, using seedling-strength liquid fertilizer (we use a liquid seaweed/fish emulsion mix at 1 ounce of each to 1 gallon of water). As your tomato seedlings start crowding one another, transplant them into larger and larger containers (we go into the #50 plug trays and then 3½-inch pots that fit 18 plants per tray). Each time you transplant your tomatoes, bury the whole stem below the first set of leaves—tomatoes will send out roots from the buried stem—and by the time you set out your plants, they'll have a strong root system.

A good tomato plant should be at least as wide as it is high. Plants get leggy when the temperature is too high and the light levels too low, whether due to cloudy weather, crowding, or just a lack of someplace sunny to put the plants. Leggy plants will need more attention until they have established themselves in the garden, so try to keep your tomato plants as stocky as you can by growing them in bright, dry conditions.

Harden off your plants before setting them out. The simplest way is just to put them outside for increasingly long periods each nice day and cut back some on watering so they get used to going without.

Tomatoes should go into the second or third part of a rotation plan, so that any manure applied to the garden will have had time to break down. Recently manured beds are likely to be high in nitrogen, and too much nitrogen leads to lush vegetative growth, but not much fruit. Before planting, we mix a handful of colloidal (calcium) phosphate into the bottom of the hole; this helps fight blossom end rot and increases fruit set.

Immediately after planting we water in the plants with transplant mix and cover the beds with floating row covers. The covers provide a little respite from wind and rain and keep flying bugs at bay. If you're planning to stake or cage the plants, wait until they are established, then remove the covers and carefully put up the cages or stakes. In any case, the covers will have to be removed once the plants flower to allow insects in to pollinate them.

There are two basic types of tomato plants: bush varieties and vining types. Bush tomatoes are called determinate because their size is largely determined from the beginning. Indeterminate, or vining, tomatoes continue to grow unless the growing point (the very tip of the main stem) is removed or the plants are killed by frost. In general, determinate varieties are earlier, but less disease resistant than the indeterminate. Either type can be grown sprawled on the ground or trellised.

We trellis all our tomatoes. The short determinates can be tied loosely to a short stake with strips of fabric, or a cage of wood or wire can be placed around them so that the plants grow intertwined with it. The aim is to keep the fruit up off the ground. Tall varieties can also be staked, or better, braided up a string tied loosely to an overhead support. Number 9 fence wire stretched between 4 × 4 posts spaced 8 to 12 feet apart is sufficient for the overhead support. Tie the strings around the base of the plants with a loose, nonslip knot and then loosely to the top wire with a bow knot, leaving an extra foot or so of string in the knot.

As the plants grow, intertwine the main stem of the plant with the string, allowing at least one wrap of string for each flower (later fruit) cluster, taking slack out of the top knot as needed. Keep suckers (the new shoots that grow out of the leaf joints) pruned; if you want a second stem to bear (two is the practical maximum), the sucker that grows from beneath the first flower cluster is your best choice. If you don't want to prune the plants, you should space them 4 feet apart in the row and get more string. The first year we used this method I thought that pinching back the SWEET 100 cherry tomatoes was too much trouble, but when mid-August arrived I had to go in with a machete just to clear a path for harvesting!

Our biggest problem in growing tomatoes is early blight (*Alternaria*), which causes irregular brown spots and a targetlike pattern on the lower leaves of the plants. The bacteria are splashed from the soil onto the leaves by rain or irrigation. Eventually the disease will work its way up the plant, leading to severe defoliation and (usually)

Tomatoes braided up a string trellis

other, more serious diseases. Many of the early determinate-type tomatoes on which northern growers depend lack resistance to early blight.

Blights are more severe in wet weather, but they can be nearly eliminated if the foliage of the plants is kept dry and soil spattering of the leaves prevented. For complete protection, grow them under cover and water with drip irrigation. Though the plants get plenty of water, the foliage never gets wet, and these diseases never spread past the first few leaves. Mulches also help stop the spread of these bacteria, so we mulch our tomato beds. Burning any diseased plants at the end of the season will help control the disease.

Blossom end rot is a disorder that starts as a brown discoloration on the bottom of the fruit, which over time becomes sunken and leathery. A soft rot usually invades the damaged spot, and eventually the entire tomato rots. This can be prevented by making sure there is adequate soil calcium (colloidal phosphate helps with this) and by keeping soil moisture consistent. Alternating dry and wet conditions can lead to serious outbreaks of blossom end rot, and once the problem has begun to affect a particular fruit, there is no going back; you might as well remove it from the plant. Blossom end rot is more prevalent on very early crops and on tomatoes trained to a single stem.

Another disorder caused by irregular water supply is cracking. If a dry spell slows growth of the plants, the skins of the fruit will harden. And then, when an abundance of water is available, the growth rate increases dramatically and the skin splits. Regular watering during dry spells is the best preventive measure.

Flea beetles can be kept off by covering the plants with a floating row cover until they are big enough to fend for themselves. Potato beetles and the tomato hornworm are easily handpicked unless you have a large number of plants, in which case you can spray with rotenone mixes or *Bacillus thuringiensis* (Bt).

Harvesting

I don't see any point in harvesting tomatoes until they are dead ripe: fully colored and easily depressed by the touch of a finger. The packers and the shippers are after shipping quality, but we go for the full, rich flavor that develops in those extra few days on the vine. The few exceptions to this rule are noted in the descriptions below.

The Best Varieties

The unique taste of tomatoes is a delicate balance between sweet and sour. The vegetable sugars that develop at maturity shouldn't be overpowered by the acidity of the juice, but many gardeners feel that tomatoes without the bite of acidity (this includes many of the golden, yellow, and "white" types) are practically a different vegetable. Low-acid varieties of tomato have opened up a whole new range of taste treats for those who find the acidity of standard tomatoes too much for them. Whichever your preference, keep in mind that red tomatoes are highest in acidity, and as the color (at maturity) pales toward white, the variety will probably be less acidic and sweetness will dominate.

Salad Tomatoes

Pink tomatoes, orange tomatoes, yellow tomatoes, and even white tomatoes—what will they think of next? Actually, none of these is new, though some of the specific varieties may be.

Any tomato for fresh use is a salad tomato. MARMANDE and its descendants are the classic red "beefsteak" type garden tomatoes in France and in much of the rest of Europe. MARMANDE is an early, indeterminate type that is well suited for short-season and cool-summer areas. Over the years, European breeders have succeeded in improving MARMANDE's disease resistance as well. Another flavor favorite, recommended by Kent Whealy of the Seed Saver's Exchange, is BRANDYWINE.

In addition to the beautiful effect they have in a salad or sliced onto a plate, orange, yellow, and white tomatoes have their own unique flavor. Most of the lighter colored tomatoes we have grown are relatively slow-maturing indeterminates, which means that they are not sure performers in the north. Nevertheless, some have done quite well here, including SUNRAY and VALENCIA. MANDARIN CROSS is a new hybrid yellow from Japan. Another good bet is LEMON BOY, a yellow indeterminate. TAXI, which is yellow and the only determinate type in the bunch, is also much earlier.

Red tomatoes have pink flesh, but the yellow-orange skins make the whole fruit look red. Pink tomatoes have clear skins, so the interior color shows right through. Some of the standard beefsteak types come in a pink version, like PINK PONDEROSA, but there are also some new hybrid pinks, like FIREBIRD, that are early enough for the north and have resistance to many diseases bred in. These gain a purplish cast at full ripeness as the flesh darkens.

PRUDEN'S PURPLE, an heirloom tomato, isn't really purple, but it's too dark to be called a simple red. These indeterminate plants bear moderately well, and while the fruits are subject to cat-facing and other minor defects, this is an early variety with good, full tomato taste and an outstanding meaty texture. WHITE BEAUTY is a mild, cream-colored indeterminate that bears meaty, ½-pound fruits with few seeds and a high sugar content. At 85 days it's too late for northern gardens, but southerners looking for a really mild tomato might want to give it a try.

Cooking Tomatoes

Fried tomatoes are a favorite in our family. We eat them for breakfast, coated with bread crumbs. A firm tomato is best, and many people use green tomatoes. The English, who may be the inventors of the dish, have a variety, ALICANTE, that remains firm even as it nears full maturity. It's an early, indeterminate variety that, like MARMANDE, grows well in cool, short-season climates. It also makes an excellent side dish for a poultry dinner and works very well for salsa.

Of course, you can also stuff tomatoes. You can use whatever variety you currently grow for stuffing, but certain types have an extra firm shell and a minimum of meat. This makes them ideal for stuffing, as they are less likely to go limp during cooking. In fact, some of these varieties, like the MEXICAN RIBBED or STRIPED CAVERN, are nearly empty, like a green pepper.

Cherry Tomatoes

Cherry tomatoes are one of the perfect crudités: bite-size, with an interesting textural change as you bite into them, the smooth exterior giving way to a mass of astringent, jellylike pulp, and soft, moist, fuzzy meat. There are some exceptional cherry tomatoes, and one of the best is the SWEET 100. This vigorous indeterminate hybrid ranks among the sweetest we have ever tried, and it is no more trouble to grow than a regular tomato, except for a tendency to crack as it reaches maturity.

Another good cherry type for home gardeners is GARDENER'S DELIGHT, also known as SUGAR LUMP. This nonhybrid has a bit more tomato flavor than SWEET 100, but is not quite as sweet. Both will be a lot easier to harvest if staked, because the fruit is borne in large clusters like grapes. Both of these varieties have fruit about 1 inch in diameter; if you'd like to grow really small tomatoes, try the indeterminate variety called RED CURRANT.

(continued on page 180)

VARIETY SOURCE CHART

TOMATOES

Variety	When to Plant	When to Harvest	What to Harvest	Comments	Sources*
Cherry Tomatoes					
GOLD NUGGET	6–8 weeks before last frost	When fruits are deep yellow	1"–1½" golden fruits	Parthenocarpic—sets well in cold, wet weather	JS/NG
GOLDEN PYGMY	6–8 weeks before last frost	When fruits turn golden-yellow	1" round, golden fruits	Potato-leaf type needs no support; good for containers	LM
IDA GOLD	6–8 weeks before last frost	When fruits turn golden-yellow	1" round golden fruits	Very early; good for northern gardens; not disease resistant	JS
RED CURRANT	6–8 weeks before last frost	When fruits turn red	Tiny red fruits, ½" diameter	Very small fruits	SB

(continued)

TOMATOES

Variety	When to Plant	When to Harvest	What to Harvest	Comments	Sources*
Cherry Tomatoes—*continued*					
RED PEAR/ YELLOW PEAR	6-8 weeks before last frost	When fruits are fully colored	Pear-shaped fruits, 1″ × 2½″	Unusual shape, meaty flesh; for salad, crudités, and preserves	Widely available
SUGAR LUMP (GARDENER'S DELIGHT)	6-8 weeks before last frost	When fruits are fully colored	Round, red fruits, 1″ in diameter	Indeterminate; very sweet	JS/TM/ SB/BG/ BP
SWEET 100 HYBRID	6-8 weeks before last frost	When fruits are fully colored	Round, red fruits, 1″ in diameter	Indeterminate; very sweet; pick promptly to avoid cracking	ST/CG/ HM/ WD/ VB/BP/ PT
Tomatoes					
ALICANTE	6-8 weeks before last frost	When fruits are fully colored	Red fruits, 6-8 oz.	Early, firm variety used for frying and stuffing	CG/TM
BELLSTAR	6-8 weeks before last frost	When fruits are deep red	1″-by-3″ plum-shaped fruits	High-yielding bush paste type	JS/ST/ TG
BRANDYWINE	6-8 weeks before last frost	When fruits are fully colored	Dark pink-red 10-12 oz. fruits	Potato leaf foliage; exceptional taste; Amish heirloom	SX/SB
FIREBIRD HYBRID	6-8 weeks before last frost	When fruits are fully colored	8-10 oz. pink globe fruits	Disease-resistant pink hybrid; main crop variety	JS
GARDEN PEACH	6-8 weeks before last frost	When fruits are fully colored	Solid blemish-free fruits	Blemish-free fruits will store for 2-3 months without refrigeration	SB
GOLDEN SUNRISE	6-8 weeks before last frost	When fruits are fully colored	Golden fruits, 6-8 oz.	Nonhybrid golden; mild, sweet flavor	BG
LEMON BOY	6-8 weeks before last frost	When fruits are fully colored	Light yellow fruits, 8-10 oz.	Lighter color than other yellows; mild flavor	JS/NG/ ST/VB

TOMATOES

Variety	When to Plant	When to Harvest	What to Harvest	Comments	Sources*
LONG KEEPER	6-8 weeks before last frost	When fruits are fully colored	Orange-red fruits, 8 oz.	Blemish- and disease-free fruits; will store 6-12 weeks	WD/BP/PT
MANDARIN CROSS HYBRID	6-8 weeks before last frost	When fruits are fully colored	Yellow-gold fruits, 6-10 oz.	Heavy foliage cover; good for sunny, warm area	LM
MARMANDE	6-8 weeks before last frost	When fruits are fully colored	Flattened red globes, 8 oz.	Semi-determinate plants; French heirloom main-crop type	SS/WD/CG
MEXICAN RIBBED	6-8 weeks before last frost	When fruits are almost colored	Ribbed, hollow red fruits	Stuffing tomato; harvest young for firmer fruits	SB
MORETON HYBRID	6-8 weeks before last frost	When fruits are fully colored	Slightly flattened, red fruits, 8-12 oz.	Good taste; small plants good for cage growing	HM
PINK PONDEROSA	6-8 weeks before last frost	When fruits are fully colored	Large beefsteak-type fruits	Pink fruits are large and flavorful, but too late for North	VB/TG
PRINCIPE BORGHESE	6-8 weeks before last frost	When all fruits are fully ripe	Clusters of small, red fruits	Fruit holds onto plant after ripening; hang whole plant to dry	CG/PT
PRUDEN'S PURPLE	6-8 weeks before last frost	When fruits are pink-purple	Top-shaped pink-purple fruits	Good taste, but prone to disease and cracking at maturity	PT
ROMA II	6-8 weeks before last frost	When fruits are fully colored	Plum-shaped, red fruits, 1″ × 3″	Determinate plants; meaty fruits good for sauce and paste	Widely available
SAN MARZANO	6-8 weeks before last frost	When fruits are fully ripened	Long, blocky fruits, 2″ × 2″ × 4″	Best taste for sauce and paste; good for oven drying	Widely available
STRIPED CAVERN	6-8 weeks before last frost	When fruits are almost colored	Ribbed, pepperlike fruits	Thick walls hold up for stuffing and cooking	TM

(continued)

VARIETY SOURCE CHART—*Continued*

TOMATOES

Variety	When to Plant	When to Harvest	What to Harvest	Comments	Sources*
Tomatoes—*continued*					
SUNRAY	6–8 weeks before last frost	When fruits are fully colored	Deep, globular, golden fruits	Nonhybrid main-crop variety; indeterminate	VB
TAXI	6–8 weeks before last frost	When fruits turn deep yellow	Medium-size, round yellow fruits	Good yellow variety for northern climates; determinate	JS
VALENCIA	6–8 weeks before last frost	When fruits turn deep orange	8–10 oz. orange fruits	Maine heirloom variety good for northern climates	JS

*Listings correspond to seed companies included under Seed Source List at the back of the book.

A golden tomato that is only slightly larger than these is IDA GOLD, an early determinate type bred in Idaho for short-season areas. IDA GOLD is not blight resistant, but the small golden fruits taste good and their color makes a nice addition to salads and the crudité platter or sliced on tea sandwiches and canapés. Also worth trying is the dwarf variety GOLDEN PYGMY, which has larger leaves and an upright habit that makes it good for containers and baskets. Plants grow 18 inches high and bear yellow-gold fruits about 1 inch in diameter and sweet enough to make a kid forget candy. Just released by Oregon State University and ideal for northern gardens is GOLD NUGGET, which will set fruit even during a cold spell, as it does not need fertilization to bear. The flowers must still be pollinated, but this occurs naturally as wind rustles the plants.

Pear tomatoes are closely related to cherry tomatoes, differing mostly in shape. Pear tomatoes are meatier and less astringent than the cherry types, and they have an intense tomato flavor. For an interesting display, slice pear tomatoes and arrange them around the edge of the crudité platter, slightly overlapping like the fronds of a fan. The varieties we grow, called simply RED PEAR and YELLOW PEAR, are vigorous indeterminate plants that respond well to the pruning and trellising we give them.

Tomatoes for Storing

For use in making tomato paste, we grow SAN MARZANO, an old indeterminate tomato that is not as early nor as disease resistant as ROMA II or BELLSTAR, but has a deep, tomato flavor and a smooth, creamy texture like well-made mashed potatoes. It requires much less boiling to get good paste because when fully ripe, the fruits are practically juiceless and the seeds retract from the wall of the tomato and can be easily "shucked" out by hand, leaving only pulp and skin. SAN MARZANO tomatoes are also good for drying, which is another, increasingly popular way to preserve tomatoes for winter.

Just as any tomato can be made into sauce or paste, any tomato can be dried. The Italians, who are tomato-lovers supreme, have developed special varieties just for drying. One in particular, called PRINCIPE BORGHESE, is a small cherry type, the fruits of which stay on the plant at maturity so you can hang the whole plant on a sunny wall to dry. While the flavor is not especially strong at harvest time, it is dramatically improved after drying and storage. We don't know the reason for this, but we've observed it in our own garden.

Even if you have to remove the tomatoes from the plant and dry them individually, the process is simple. When the fruits reach full maturity, split them, spoon out the seeds, and lay them flat on screens in the sun. You can cover the tomatoes with cheesecloth to keep off insects and windblown debris. In cooler climates, you can dry them inside a greenhouse or sunspace. If the weather won't cooperate, we dry our tomatoes in the oven, using just the heat from the gas pilot light. A solar or electric dryer would work just as well.

Gardeners store tomatoes for one very good reason: the horrendous state of supermarket tomatoes during the winter. Some seed houses have recently brought back an old tomato type that will store well fresh, without refrigeration. Tomatoes with this storage characteristic have been around for a long time, but taste has always been a problem. One of the old-fashioned fresh-storage tomatoes, available through seed suppliers that sell heirloom varieties, is the GARDEN PEACH. Burpee has gotten in on the act, too, with a variety called the LONG KEEPER.

These storage tomatoes should be started a bit later than other varieties so that they mature as the weather begins to cool in the early fall. Don't wait for LONG KEEPER to turn full red: These tomatoes mature to a deep orange color that is the result of a light skin and a deep red interior. Harvest only perfect, unblemished specimens, and store them, not touching each other, in ventilated boxes or on shelves in a spot that stays between 40° and 60°F. Under these conditions, storage tomatoes will keep until early January at least, and some people claim to have stored them until April. Using your own fresh tomatoes for a Christmas salad here in Vermont is a miracle surpassed only by the main event of the season.

TURNIPS, RADISHES, AND OTHER ROOT CROPS

Turnips

Turnips will perhaps never be a "best seller" among vegetables, but there will always be a loyal band of devotees. We grew them for sale three whole seasons before we actually began eating them ourselves. One night, Ellen made a mashed potato substitute for dinner that was half carrots and half turnips. The combination was better than either vegetable alone, and now turnips are a regular part of our menu, and a more important part of the garden.

Growing

Sow turnips in succession with the kohlrabi and salad beets, and they'll be just the right size for fresh use when you are finishing off the other crops in that bed and ready to renovate it. They need the same treatment as the other two crops: not-too-rich soil and even watering. When you thin, save the greens; they are quite tasty when young.

Harvesting

For fresh use, harvest your turnips as soon as the root reaches the size of a spool of thread. For storage, the roots can be left until the first frost, and then trimmed an inch above the crown and stored in damp sand or sawdust at temperatures just above freezing.

The Best Variety

We only grow one turnip in any quantity, DES VERTUS MARTEAU from France. It's a half-long variety whose roots will grow to be 1 pound or so each at full maturity. If harvested at that stage, they will keep well in the root cellar.

Radishes

We don't plant spring radishes as a separate crop. We grow them right in the carrot rows. The quick-germinating radishes mark the rows, and they are harvested long before the carrots need the space.

VARIETY SOURCE CHART

TURNIPS, RADISHES, AND OTHER ROOT CROPS

Variety	When to Plant	When to Harvest	What to Harvest	Comments	Sources*
Celeriac					
ALABASTER	ASAP in spring	When swollen stem is 2″–3″ in diameter at ground level	Swollen stems	Very slow growing; quality is best after light frost	SB/BP
JOSE	ASAP in spring	When swollen stem is 2″–3″ in diameter	Swollen stems	Resistant to internal discoloration	JS
PRAGUE	ASAP in spring	When swollen stem is 2″–3″ in diameter at ground level	Swollen stems	Similar to ALABASTER; many variants of this type are available	SB/ST/ WD/PK
Parsnips					
COBHAM IMPROVED MARROW	ASAP in spring	After fall frost	Tapered white roots	New English variety sweeter than older types	JS
HARRIS MODEL (AND VARIATIONS)	ASAP in spring	After fall frost	Tapered white roots	Slow growing; can be overwintered	SB/HM/ VB/JS/ ST
HOLLOW CROWN	ASAP in spring	After fall frost	Tapered white roots	Slow growing; can be overwintered	SB/LM/ BP/ST/ WD/VB

(continued)

TURNIPS, RADISHES, AND OTHER ROOT CROPS

Variety	When to Plant	When to Harvest	What to Harvest	Comments	Sources*
Radishes					
AOKOMARUSHIN	60 days before first fall frost	When roots push up out of soil	Large green and white roots	Unusual oriental fall type; makes very decorative crudités	No current source
CHAMPION	ASAP in spring	When roots reach 1″ in diameter	Round red roots	Standard variety	HM/ VB/ST
CHERRY BELLE	ASAP in spring/in succession	When roots reach 1″ in diameter	Globed-shaped red roots	Reliable, standard-type radish	Widely available
CHINA ROSE	60 days before first frost	After first fall frost	Bulbous pink roots, 1″–2″ × 6″	Storage type; milder than most fall types if well watered	SB/PT/ ST/VB
EASTER EGG HYBRID	ASAP in spring/in succession	When roots reach ½″ in diameter	Multi-colored roots ½″–2″ in diameter	Holds well; provides nice mix of colors for salad; beautiful	Widely available
EIGHTEEN DAY	ASAP in spring/in succession	When roots reach ½″ in diameter	White-tipped, cylindrical red roots	Very early FRENCH BREAKFAST type; harvest promptly	CG
FRENCH BREAKFAST	ASAP in spring	When roots reach 2″ in length	White-tipped, cylindrical red roots	Improved types available: FLAMVIL, FLAMBO, FLAMBOYANT	Widely available
GOLDEN BALL (FRENCH GOLDEN)	60 days before first frost	When roots reach 1″ in diameter	Round yellow/gold roots	Mildest flavor if harvested during cool fall weather	NG
MUNICH BEER	60 days before first frost	When roots reach 1″–2″ in diameter	Globular to bulbous white roots	Slice for crudités, or let run to seed and harvest seedpods	TM
RAT TAIL	Midspring	When seedpods form	Fleshy seedpods	Variety MUNICH BEER can also be used for fleshy seedpods	SB
VALENTINE	ASAP in spring/in succession	When interiors turn red	1″–2″ globe-shaped to top-shaped roots	Red-colored flesh makes these good for crudités	ST/SB/ CG

TURNIPS, RADISHES, AND OTHER ROOT CROPS

Variety	When to Plant	When to Harvest	What to Harvest	Comments	Sources*
VIOLET GOURNAY	60 days before first frost	After first frost	Tapered, dark violet roots	Variant of LONG BLACK WINTER; storage type; white flesh	CG
Salsify MAMMOTH SANDWICH ISLAND	ASAP in spring	After fall frost	Long, thin, white-skinned roots	Slow growing; can be overwintered; slight oyster taste	Widely available
Scorzonera DUPLEX	ASAP in spring	After fall frost	Long, thin, black-skinned roots	Mix radish seed in row to aid in seedling emergence	No current source
GIANT BLACK RUSSIAN	ASAP in spring	After fall frost	Long, thin, black-skinned roots	Heirloom variety	LM
GIGANTIA	ASAP in spring	After fall frost	Long, thin, black-skinned roots	Also (incorrectly) known as black salsify; a perennial	JS
Turnips DES VERTUS MARTEAU	ASAP in spring/in succession	After roots are 1″ in diameter	Globe-shaped to enlongated white roots	Good for fresh use at 1″ in diameter, or storage at 1 lb. or more	CG/HG
GILFEATHER	Early spring/ midsummer	When roots are 2″–3″ in diameter	Green-topped white roots	Old Vermont heirloom type; good flavor; good storage quality	TM/VB
GOLDEN BALL (JUANE BOULE D'OR, ORANGE JELLY)	60–80 days before first frost	When roots reach 3″–4″ in diameter	Globe-shaped golden roots, 1″–4″ in diameter	Storage type turnip; can also be planted for spring crop	WD/ NG/SB
MILAN (DE MILAN, MILAN EARLY RED TOP)	Early spring	When roots are 1″–2″ in diameter	Rose-purple topped, white roots	Early variety for fresh use	SS/LM

(continued)

VARIETY SOURCE CHART—*Continued*

TURNIPS, RADISHES, AND OTHER ROOT CROPS

Variety	When to Plant	When to Harvest	What to Harvest	Comments	Sources*
Turnips—*continued*					
PRESTO	Early spring	When roots are 1″–2″ in diameter	Flattened, globe-shaped white roots	Slower bolting than TOKYO CROSS, so better for early crop	NG/ HM/SB
TOKYO CROSS HYBRID	Midspring (4 weeks before last frost)	When roots are 1″–2″ in diameter	Flattened, globe-shaped white roots	Very early variety for fresh use and pickling	ST/WD/ BP/PK

*Listings correspond to seed companies included under Seed Source List at the back of the book.

Growing

For a complete discussion of how we grow spring radishes, see the section on carrots.

We sow fall radishes about 60 days before the first fall frost so they will mature during cool weather. The pungency of fall radishes is increased by hot, dry weather just before harvest. Watering during any late-summer hot spells will help temper their bite.

Harvesting

For the best flavor and texture, pull spring radishes while they are small (less than 1 inch in diameter). Fall varieties can be left to grow much larger, and their flavor is improved by a light touch of frost. Harvest before hard frost, though, because roots whose crowns have been frozen will not keep. Layer them in damp sand or sawdust with your other root crops.

The Best Varieties

Spring Radishes

Our favorite spring radish is EASTER EGG, a multi-line type that yields large, fine-textured crops in four colors: white, red, lavender, and violet. We consider violet the most beautiful color and would grow them just for the color, but they are also excellent radishes of the CHAMPION type.

We also grow one called EIGHTEEN DAY, though it rarely lives up to its name. It is, however, a good variety of the FRENCH BREAKFAST type, with a long red shaft and a white tip. It is really not suitable for summer plantings, so we mix it up separately with our earliest carrot seedings. Two other interesting varieties are VAL-ENTINE and AOKOMARUSHIN. These two are Asian varieties that have a green skin and red and white interiors. They are an interesting novelty, and look quite nice on the crudité platter, but they are not for the faint-hearted. One last novelty radish is the GOLDEN BALL or FRENCH GOLDEN radish.

Fall Radishes

We've had good luck with MUNICH BEER radish, a large white radish that has a relatively mild flavor. We serve this variety sliced and salted, with a mug of cold beer at hand. It seems closely related to the RAT TAIL radish, which is grown for its fleshy, pealike seedpods that are tasty steamed or sautéed. The MUNICH BEER radish, planted in spring, will produce a large number of pods of good size.

Another old favorite is the CHINA ROSE, different from most other radishes in that it is larger at the root end than at the crown. It's thought by some to be the closest garden radish to the original wild forms. We've heard of white and violet strains as well, but have never seen them. CHINA ROSE is mild and crisp even when large, and is a good keeper.

The third type we like is the VIOLET GOURNAY. Although its pungency may limit its use to radish fanciers like us, it makes a beautiful display on the plate and as a shredded condiment, either pickled or straight.

Celeriac

This is a type of celery bred for its swollen root, and if you've never tried it, you are missing a great vegetable with a minty celery flavor and the crisp, juicy texture of kohlrabi.

Growing

Celeriac is much easier to grow than stalk celery, and although it's a long-season crop, it's not bothered by pests or disease. It needs the same conditions as leeks, so we plant a bed with a row of celeriac in the center and a pair of late leek rows just in from the edges of the bed. After frost, we pull the celeriac, and then use the loosened soil in the center of the bed to hill the leeks for blanching.

In short-season areas, you'll have to start celeriac indoors. We start ours at the

Celeriac

same time as the leeks, 8 to 12 weeks before the frost-free date, using a #162 plug tray. The seedlings should be grown cool to keep the plants stocky, but if they are exposed to frost, their biennial clock may tell them it's time to set seed, and they will bolt without forming a decent root.

Set the plants out 8 to 12 inches apart, and make sure they get plenty of water throughout the season. If you want a smoother root, pull the soil back from the crown of the plant after a couple of months and rub off the little side roots on the topside of the knob that forms at the surface of the soil.

Harvesting

Harvest any time after the roots have reached the size of a golf ball. For fresh use, you can trim the small roots and wash the knobs, but for storage, just cut the foliage off an inch above the top of the knob and store in damp sand or sawdust with the other root crops.

The Best Varieties

The two traditional varieties are PRAGUE (and a number of its descendants with slightly different names) and ALA-BASTER. There is also a new Dutch variety called JOSE, which is good for intensive plantings because it is a more compact plant and tolerates close planting well.

Parsnips

Although not widely grown, parsnips are worth a try if you like root vegetables. Parsnips have a sweet, nutty flavor that lends itself well to soups and stews.

Growing

Parsnips are a long-season crop and should be direct seeded in the bed as soon as the ground can be worked in spring. If you are tight for space in the garden—and who isn't?—interplant them with another, quicker-growing crop that can share space while they are still young.

Unless your soil is deep and mellow, build a high bed to get the best roots. The seed should be sown ½ inch deep; we mix in a bit of radish seed to break the soil and make emergence of these slow sprouters easier. After the seedlings emerge, thin to 4 to 6 inches apart in the row. A sprinkling of wood ash and an occasional side dressing with a weak fish emulsion/seaweed mix are all the care they'll need, beyond keeping the weeds down.

Harvesting

Parsnips develop their best flavor after the first frosts of fall, and if left until spring, the flavor improves still further. If you do overwinter the plants, mulch them after the first hard frost to prevent heaving and to protect the crown of the plants. Come spring, pull back the mulch and dig the roots for a real treat! Be sure to harvest the roots before they sprout; once they do, the texture becomes woody and sweetness declines.

The Best Varieties

The two most frequently planted parsnip varieties are HARRIS MODEL and HOLLOW CROWN, of which there are a number of variant selections. There is also a new English variety called COBHAM IMPROVED MARROW.

Salsify

Salsify is a long-season biennial similar to the parsnip, but with smaller roots. The attraction of salsify is its taste, which is hauntingly like oysters.

Growing

If your soil is shallow and you can't make up high beds, another method for getting good roots is to take a digging bar or stake and drive it 1 foot or so into the ground, then rotate it with a stirring action to make a conical hole that is 3 or 4 inches across at the top. Fill the hole with mellow compost and plant your seed ¼ to ½ inch deep in the compost. Thin to a single plant per hole once the seedlings are well up. The roots will grow easily within the soft confines of this little paradise, regardless of how unforgiving the soil might be just outside.

Harvesting

If a hard freeze threatens, the plants should either be dug or covered with mulch. In mild climates or where there is good snow cover, 3 or 4 inches of mulch should be enough; in some areas you might need as much as 1 foot of insulating material. If the ground can be kept from freezing, you can harvest roots as desired through the winter months. As with parsnips, be sure to harvest before the plants begin to regrow in spring.

For storage in the root cellar, cut the tops off 1 inch above the crown, and store as close to freezing as possible in some moisture-retentive material, such as damp sand or sawdust. Roots will not store well if their crowns have frozen.

The Best Varieties

Salsify has not received a lot of attention from breeders, and the only widely available variety is MAMMOTH SANDWICH ISLAND.

Scorzonera

Scorzonera is sometimes incorrectly called black salsify. It is quite similar in habit and appearance, but has black roots. The leaves of scorzonera are broader than those of true salsify, and its flowers are yellow instead of violet. The flowers and leaves of both can be used in salads, but scorzonera roots have the advantage of not losing their quality when the plant runs to seed in their second spring.

Growing

Follow the guidelines for growing salsify.

Harvesting

You can harvest scorzonera roots at any stage, but they taste best in cool weather. Since this plant is a perennial, the roots can be left in the ground and do not need to be protected from frost.

The Best Varieties

GIANT BLACK RUSSIAN is an older variety, joined more recently by two new varieties from Holland and Denmark called GIGANTIA and DUPLEX. Since these are perennial plants, you might want to put them in the herb garden with other plants, like sorrel, rhubarb, and asparagus.

PART III

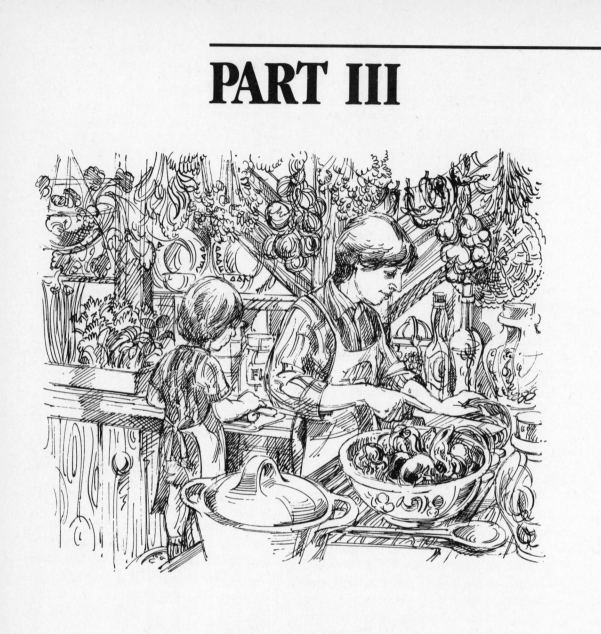

IN THE KITCHEN

*I*n this section, you'll find some of Ellen's favorite recipes for using the vegetables and varieties we've written about in this book. We've organized them according to the type of dish, rather than the vegetables used, to facilitate menu preparation.

As you'll see, we're fans of simple food that is well prepared and nicely presented. If we're having carrots, we want to taste the carrots themselves, not what is poured over them at the last minute. We feel that sauces and seasonings should be used to augment the dishes they are added to, not dominate them.

APPETIZERS AND CONDIMENTS

Roasted Red Peppers

Sweet red peppers packed in oil are a treat for antipasto or in winter salads.

4 servings

4   sweet red peppers, roasted*
⅓   cup olive oil (approximately)
¼   teaspoon dried oregano

Cut peppers into thirds and arrange on a lightly oiled baking sheet. Set oven on warm. Dry peppers in oven for 5 to 8 hours, then cut each piece into 1-inch wedges. Pack into a sterilized ½-pint jar and pour oil on to cover. Sprinkle with oregano. Place lid on jar and store in refrigerator.

Herbed Red Peppers with Feta Cheese

This appetizer has an unusual combination of flavors. For a variation, use radicchio leaves in place of the red peppers. Serve with slices of warm French bread.

4 servings

2   tablespoons olive oil, divided
4   sweet red peppers, roasted*
½   pound feta cheese, cut into 8 slices
1   tablespoon each fresh or dried thyme, oregano, and basil
    freshly ground black pepper, to taste

Preheat oven to 400°F.
Spread 2 teaspoons oil on 4 gratin baking dishes.
Cut peppers in half.
Fold each pepper half around a slice of cheese. Place 2 pepper halves in each dish.
Mix remaining oil with herbs and divide evenly over peppers. Add ground pepper, to taste.
Bake for 15 to 20 minutes.

*To make roasted peppers, broil until skin is charred, then put peppers in a paper bag for a few minutes. Peppers will steam in their own heat, and skins will loosen. When cool, peel and remove seeds.

Compound Butter

Compound butter is made by stirring herbs or edible flowers into softened butter. The butter is then shaped in waxed paper and chilled. When hot food comes off the grill or out of the oven, the chilled butter is sliced and placed on top. The advantage of a compound butter is that it replaces the need for a heavy cream sauce while adding an extra depth of flavor. Compound butter is, of course, delicious on cooked vegetables. Keep it in the freezer, and you will be rewarded with fresh herb butter year-round.

This traditional recipe from the south of France is particularly good on fish and vegetables.

Makes about ½ cup

¼   cup butter, softened
2   tablespoons finely chopped sweet red peppers
2   tablespoons finely chopped fresh oregano
2   tablespoons finely chopped black olives
2   teaspoons finely chopped red onions
    freshly ground black pepper, to taste

In a small bowl combine all ingredients and stir until completely blended.
Spoon onto a sheet of waxed paper, and shape into roll about 1 inch in diameter. Refrigerate for at least 2 hours to allow flavors to blend.

Pear Tomatoes and Snow Peas Stuffed with Boursin

For most of us, a favorite hors d'oeuvre is a platter of raw vegetables with a tasty dip. I like to use a more original variation, a vegetable stuffed with a dip. My favorite dip is a forcefully flavored boursin. Boursin can be made at home to great advantage—to save money and to get stronger herb flavorings than most commercial brands offer. There are multiple variations of boursin, but it is basically a bland cheese, such as cream cheese, mixed with herbs (preferably chopped fresh) and crushed garlic. The following recipe can be considered a basic version, but the cook's imagination should fly free. Sorrel, chervil, and even chopped arugula could be substitutes for the listed herbs.

6 to 8 servings

BOURSIN

  8   ounces cream cheese
  2   cloves garlic, chopped
  1   tablespoon chopped fresh basil
  1   tablespoon minced fresh dill
  1   tablespoon chopped fresh chives
  6   pitted black olives (optional)

VEGETABLES

  1   pint yellow pear tomatoes
  1   pint red pear tomatoes
  ½   pound snow peas, stems removed and strings discarded
      Nasturtiums or basil flowers for garnish (optional)

To make the boursin:
Blend cream cheese, garlic, and herbs in a food processor or blender until smooth, scraping down sides as necessary. Add olives, if used, and blend again briefly until combined.

To prepare the vegetables:
Remove a third off the top of each tomato. Carefully scoop out seeds and invert tomatoes on a paper towel.

Steam snow peas briefly to tenderize, if desired. Split peas down the string side, keeping the two parts connected by the other seam.

Fill tomatoes and snow peas with boursin. Arrange on a decorative plate so that the peas overlap around the edge. Alternate the red and yellow tomatoes in the center.

Add garnish if desired.

Green Sauce

"In the markets of Hesse," writes a friend, "the market ladies sell paper twists with a bunch of the properly mixed herbs inside. This was Goethe's favorite salad fixing. It is traditional to use any seven of the following herbs, since seven is a lucky number: borage, chervil, chives, dill, lovage, parsley, pimpernel (salad burnet), sorrel, or tarragon."

Green sauce has been made for centuries by crushing seasonal herbs and greens with a mortar and pestle, or, these days, by blending in a food processor. The sauce can be a dip, a spread, or even a creamy sauce for hot vegetables. The following is a recipe for a green sauce for vegetable dip.

Makes about 3 cups

  1½ cup mixed greens and herbs of your liking (such as spinach, orache, *mâche,* purslane, nasturtium leaves, dandelion, sorrel, chives, etc.)
  4   shallots, peeled
  ½   cup lite mayonnaise
  1   cup plain yogurt
  ½   cup sour cream
  ¼   cup lemon juice

Combine the above in a blender or food processor and mix to the consistency desired.

SOUPS

Hot Sorrel Soup

Sorrel is a perennial, emerging early in the spring with tender, green leaves that are wonderful in salads. The flavor is tart, with lemony overtones. The leaves should be harvested for soups when they are about 6 inches long. Though this soup may be served chilled or hot, once made, it shouldn't be reheated because the cream and sorrel will curdle if boiled.

This recipe can also be used to make watercress or arugula soup.

4 servings

2	tablespoons butter
½	cup chopped onions
3	cups chicken or vegetable stock, heated
3	cups coarsely chopped fresh sorrel leaves, firmly packed
1	cup heavy cream
2	egg yolks

Melt butter in a large saucepan. Add onions and sauté for 3 minutes, or until golden brown. Add stock and sorrel and simmer for 10 minutes, stirring frequently.

Pour stock mixture into a food processor or blender and blend until smooth. Return stock to saucepan.

Beat together cream and egg yolks. Pour 1 cup hot stock into egg mixture, whisking constantly. Slowly add second cup hot stock and continue to whisk.

Add egg and stock mixture to remaining stock in saucepan. Continue to cook and stir, just until soup reaches a simmer. Serve immediately.

Cold Sorrel Soup

4 to 6 servings

¼	cup butter
½	cup chopped onions
3	cups coarsely chopped fresh sorrel leaves, firmly packed
2	large potatoes, scrubbed and thinly sliced
3	cups chicken or vegetable stock
1	cup milk or half-and-half

Melt butter in a large saucepan. Add onions and sauté for 3 minutes. Add sorrel and cook for 2 minutes. Add potatoes and stock. Bring to a boil and simmer until potatoes are tender, about 20 to 30 minutes.

Pour mixture into a food processor or blender and process until smooth. Return to original saucepan and stir in milk or half-and-half. Heat almost to a boil. Remove from heat, allow to cool, then chill before serving.

Onion Soup

6 servings

¼	cup butter
1	tablespoon olive oil
4	onions, thinly sliced
3	large leeks, sliced and well rinsed
5	scallions, sliced
2	cloves garlic, minced
¼	cup chopped shallots
¼	cup minced fresh chives
2	tablespoons flour
5	cups chicken or vegetable stock
1	teaspoon fresh thyme or ½ teaspoon dried thyme
6	toasted rounds of French bread
3	cups grated Gruyère or mozzarella cheese

Melt butter with oil in a large saucepan over medium heat. Add onions, leeks, scallions, garlic, shallots, and chives. Sauté, stirring, until onions are soft. Cover and cook over low heat for 30 minutes, stirring occasionally.

Increase heat to medium. Add flour and mix well. Cook, stirring, for 2 minutes. Add 2 cups stock, bring to a boil, stirring and scraping bottom of saucepan. Add remaining stock and thyme. Stir to blend and cook over low heat for 45 minutes.

Preheat oven to 375°F.

Divide soup evenly into 6 ovenproof bowls. Place a round of bread on top of each and sprinkle with ½ cup cheese.

Place bowls on baking sheet in oven. Bake for 15 minutes or until cheese is bubbly and brown.

Chilled Zucchini Soup with Stuffed Squash Blossoms

Chilled soups make a refreshingly light meal in the summer. The creamy consistency of the zucchini soup makes a wonderful base for the stuffed squash blossoms or for any number of unusual garnishes.

6 servings

SOUP

2   tablespoons butter or olive oil
2   scallions, including green stalks, chopped
3   cups chopped zucchini
6   squash blossoms, washed and chopped
2   cups chicken stock
½   teaspoon fresh summer savory
1   cup half-and-half

GARNISH

½   cup mozzarella cheese
¼   cup grated Parmesan cheese
2   teaspoons chopped fresh basil
6   whole squash blossoms
1   teaspoon butter, melted

To make the soup:

Heat butter or oil in a medium-size saucepan. Add scallions, zucchini, and chopped squash blossoms and cook over medium heat for 5 minutes. Add stock and savory. Bring to a boil and simmer over low heat for 10 minutes, or until zucchini is very tender.

Pour stock mixture into a food processor or blender and puree. Add half-and-half and blend briefly. Chill in refrigerator.

To make the garnish:

Preheat oven to 350°F.

Combine cheeses and basil in a small bowl. Stuff whole squash blossoms with cheese mixture. Place stuffed blossoms in baking dish, drizzle with melted butter and bake for 10 minutes, or until cheese is melted.

Divide soup among 6 serving bowls. Slice stuffed squash blossoms and garnish each serving with blossom slices.

Gazpacho Soup with Arugula and Watercress

There are many variations of gazpacho; all of them are good, and all taste still better with garden-fresh produce. Arugula and tomatoes are generally too acid for each other's company, but in this soup they combine nicely.

6 servings

6   large tomatoes, cut into wedges
1   large cucumber, peeled and seeded
1   small onion, chopped
1   sweet red pepper, chopped
1   clove garlic, chopped
½   cup coarsely chopped watercress
½   cup coarsely chopped arugula
2   tablespoons olive oil
2   tablespoons red wine vinegar
    French-bread croutons

Blend tomatoes, cucumber, onions, peppers, and garlic in a food processor or blender for 2 or 3 minutes, stopping to scrape down the sides of container as necessary. Add watercress and arugula, then blend until smooth and greens are finely chopped, about 30 seconds.

Pour mixture into a large bowl and add oil and vinegar. Stir, then chill until ready to serve.

Garnish with croutons.

Leek, Potato, and Celeriac Soup

4 to 6 servings

¼   cup butter
4   leeks, roots and tops removed
3   medium potatoes, scrubbed and cut
       into ½-inch slices
1   celeriac knob, peeled and cut into
       1-inch chunks
4   cups chicken or vegetable stock
       fresh thyme, basil, and/or sweet
       marjoram, to taste

Melt butter in stockpot.

Slice leeks into ¼-inch slices and add to stockpot.

Sauté for 5 minutes or until golden. Add potatoes and celeriac and sauté for 5 minutes. Cover and cook for 3 minutes. Stir in 1 cup stock, cover, and continue to cook until potatoes are tender, about 25 minutes. Remove from heat.

Pour vegetables and stock into a food processor or blender and puree. Return puree to stockpot and add remaining stock and herbs. Cover and simmer for 15 to 20 minutes. Serve hot.

SALADS AND DRESSINGS

The best salads combine a mixture of textures and flavors that appeal to both the eye and the palate. For a good balance of flavors, go heavy on the mild-flavored greens and add the ones with a stronger taste sparingly.

Among the greens with a mild flavor are purslane, spinach, *mâche,* cabbage, claytonia, and orache.

Salad greens with a stronger flavor include endive, chicory, sorrel, dandelion, arugula, cress, and mustard.

After washing your salad greens, care should be taken to remove the excess moisture left on the surface because the dressing oil will not coat the leaves if they still have moisture clinging to them. Dry in a salad spinner or let them drip in a colander. Salad spinners are helpful, although many

of the delicate greens such as *mâche* and butterhead lettuce might be bruised from the rough ride. Wrap greens lightly in soft, absorbent cloth or paper towels and chill them in the refrigerator.

To store washed greens, place them loosely in a plastic bag and add a few single sheets of paper towel to absorb extra moisture. Loosely tie the end of the plastic bag.

Just as the ingredients in your salads will change with the seasons, your dressing should vary according to the greens. Milder greens such as *mâche* are at their best with a light coating of olive oil and lemon or vinegar. Though the best dressing is one that highlights the greens, not itself, you may want to tame some of the sharper greens by adding a tablespoon of plain yogurt to the basic vinaigrette. Before you add any dressing, mix the greens in the salad bowl with 1 tablespoon of olive oil to coat the surface of each leaf thoroughly. This conditions them against wilting, a reaction caused by the vinegar and salt of the dressing releasing natural juices in the leaves.

Salads

Mesclun Salad

Traditionally, a mesclun salad includes whatever greens are available wild or in the garden.

4 servings

- 1   clove garlic, halved
- 1   shallot, chopped
- 2   tablespoons red wine vinegar
- 1   tablespoon balsamic vinegar
- ½   cup olive oil
- 3   cups mesclun or 1 handful each of whole, young salad greens

Rub inside of a large salad bowl with garlic halves. Mix shallots and vinegars in bowl and let stand for 5 minutes. Pour oil into bowl in a slow, steady stream, whisking until well blended. Add mesclun or greens and toss with dressing. Serve immediately.

NOTE: If bitter greens are used for this salad, stir 1 tablespoon plain yogurt into dressing.

Mâche and Orache Salad with Warm Vinaigrette

Mâche and orache are very mild and require a subtle dressing.

4 servings

- 3   tablespoons sherry vinegar
- 3   tablespoons olive oil
- 3   tablespoons walnut oil

- 1   shallot, chopped
- 2   cups fresh orache
- 1   cup *mâche*
     sliced mushrooms, hard-boiled eggs, croutons, and walnuts for garnish

Combine vinegar, 2 tablespoons olive oil, all of walnut oil, and shallots in a small saucepan and heat over low heat until just simmering. Mix greens in a large salad bowl and toss lightly with remaining olive oil. Pour hot dressing over greens and toss to coat. Garnish with mushrooms, eggs, croutons, and walnuts. Serve immediately.

LITTLE GEM Lettuce with Orange and Dill Vinaigrette

4 servings

- ¼   cup fresh orange juice
- 1   egg yolk
- 2   teaspoons balsamic vinegar
- 1   teaspoon finely chopped orange rind
- 1   teaspoon fresh dill
- 2   tablespoons olive oil
- 4   heads LITTLE GEM romaine or small lettuce, sliced in half lengthwise watercress and coarsely broken toasted walnuts for garnish*

In a small saucepan simmer orange juice until reduced to ⅛ cup, approximately 3 minutes. Whisk egg yolk, vinegar, orange rind, and dill in a small bowl. Whisk in orange juice. Slowly add oil in a slow, steady stream, whisking until well blended.

Arrange lettuce halves with cut sides up on 4 salad plates. Drizzle dressing over each half and garnish with watercress and walnuts. Serve immediately.

*To toast walnuts, coat lightly with olive oil, place on baking sheet, and roast in a 250°F oven for 20 minutes, tossing every 5 minutes.

Radicchio and Greens with Hot Dressing

4 servings

1   small head butterhead lettuce
1   cup arugula
1   medium-size head radicchio
¼   cup olive oil
3   tablespoons balsamic vinegar
1   tablespoon red wine vinegar
1   shallot, minced
1   teaspoon chopped fresh basil

Tear lettuce into bite-size pieces and place in a large salad bowl along with arugula. Tear radicchio into slightly larger pieces and add to bowl.

Heat oil, vinegars, and shallots in a small saucepan, stirring occasionally. Pour hot dressing over greens and toss gently. Sprinkle salad with basil and toss again. Serve immediately.

CERIOLO Chicory with Yogurt Dressing

CERIOLO grows in a small round rosette and has a thick, chewy leaf. Yogurt is added to this basic oil and vinegar dressing to tame the bitterness of this spring chicory.

4 servings

1   clove garlic, halved
1   tablespoon red wine vinegar
1   tablespoon chopped fresh chives
2   tablespoons chopped sorrel
2   or 3 fresh basil leaves, chopped
2   tablespoons olive oil
1   tablespoon plain yogurt
2   cups CERIOLO chicory
3   tablespoons sun-dried tomatoes, drained and chopped*
3   coarsely grated baby carrots

Rub inside of a medium-size salad bowl with garlic halves. Add vinegar, chives, sorrel, and basil and mix lightly. Pour oil into bowl in a slow, steady stream, whisking until well blended. Stir in yogurt. Add chicory, tomatoes, and carrots. Toss to coat and serve immediately.

*For a less expensive alternative to store-bought sun-dried tomatoes, try the recipe Oven-Dried Tomatoes found in the box on page 205.

Arugula Salad

Italian restaurants often serve arugula on its own with a strong garlic-flavored oil and vinegar dressing. Mixed with milder greens and a good dressing, though, arugula is less dominating. Sweet red peppers add color.

4 servings

2   tablespoons balsamic vinegar
1   teaspoon Dijon mustard
1   clove garlic, minced
⅓   cup olive oil
2   cups mixed lettuce: romaine, iceberg, and red-leaf (or your choice)
1   cup arugula, stems removed
½   pound mushrooms, sliced
1   sweet red pepper, cut into thin strips

In a small bowl whisk together vinegar, mustard, and garlic. Add oil in a slow, steady stream, whisking until well blended. Let mixture stand in bowl for 5 to 10 minutes to allow flavors to meld.

Tear lettuce into bite-size pieces and arrange on 4 salad plates. Distribute arugula among plates. Arrange sliced mushrooms and peppers on top. Drizzle salad dressing over each salad just before serving.

Belgian Endive and Apples

4 servings

2   apples
     lemon juice
2   heads Belgian endive
     coarsely broken toasted walnuts*

⅓   cup walnut oil
3   tablespoons raspberry vinegar

Peel, core, and slice apples into ¼-inch slices. Sprinkle with lemon juice to prevent browning.

Arrange endive and apple slices in circular pattern with overlapping edges on individual salad plates and sprinkle with walnuts. In a small bowl whisk oil and vinegar together and drizzle over salads before serving.

*To toast walnuts, coat lightly with olive oil, place on baking sheet, and roast in a 250°F oven for 20 minutes, tossing every 5 minutes.

Mâche and Beet Salad

Mâche *is a tender green with a mild, nutty flavor that goes well with the beets in this recipe.*

4 servings

4   to 6 red, golden, or white salad beets, or any combination
1   teaspoon fresh lovage or parsley, finely chopped
2   tablespoons balsamic vinegar
5   tablespoons olive oil
2   cups *mâche*
2   hard-boiled eggs, chopped
½   cup whole-wheat croutons

Wash and trim beets, leaving 1 inch of stem attached. In a medium-size saucepan steam beets for approximately 25 minutes or until tender. Remove tops, peel, and slice.

In a medium-size bowl mix lovage or parsley, vinegar, and oil. Add cooked beets and toss to coat. Cover and marinate beet slices for at least 1 hour.

In a medium-size salad bowl toss beets with *mâche*. Sprinkle with eggs and croutons.

NOTE: Golden or white salad beets will not bleed onto the other ingredients.

Potato Salad with Chervil

4 servings

2   pounds new red potatoes, quartered
⅔   cup plain yogurt
1   tablespoon tarragon or dill vinegar
½   teaspoon fresh lemon juice
2   tablespoons chopped fresh chervil
2   sweet pickles, chopped

Boil potatoes for approximately 15 minutes or until tender. Drain and cool slightly.

In a large bowl whisk together yogurt, vinegar, lemon juice, chervil, and sweet pickles. Add potatoes, toss gently, and chill until ready to serve.

Celeriac Remoulade

This classic recipe is similar to American coleslaw.

4 servings

½   cup mayonnaise
1   tablespoon Dijon mustard
2   tablespoons finely minced fresh parsley
2   tablespoons finely minced fresh tarragon or 2 teaspoons dried tarragon
1   clove garlic, minced
2   sweet pickles, finely chopped (optional)
2   celeriac knobs, peeled and coarsely grated (2 to 2½ cups)

In a medium-size bowl mix together mayonnaise, mustard, parsley, tarragon, garlic, and sweet pickles, if used. Add celeriac and toss until completely coated. Cover and chill until ready to serve.

NOTE: Celeriac may be grated and dropped into boiling water briefly if it is a large and tough knob.

Fennel and Pepper Slaw

Roasted peppers add a special flavor to this salad.

4 servings

2 tablespoons fresh lemon juice
1 tablespoon finely chopped fresh
  coriander leaves
¼ cup olive oil
2 sweet red peppers, roasted and cut
  into strips*
2 sweet yellow or golden peppers,
  roasted and cut into strips*
1 fennel bulb, trimmed and sliced into
  thin strips

Combine lemon juice and coriander in a medium-size bowl. Add oil in a slow, steady stream, whisking until well blended. Add peppers and fennel and toss together. Cover and chill before serving.

*To make roasted peppers, broil until skin is charred, then put peppers in a paper bag for a few minutes. Peppers will steam in their own heat, and skins will loosen. When cool, peel and remove seeds.

Red and Yellow Pepper Slaw

Serve this salad in a clear glass bowl to enjoy the wonderful color of the peppers.

4 servings

¼ cup fresh lemon juice
1 tablespoon finely chopped fresh mint
1 tablespoon finely chopped fresh
  coriander leaves
⅓ cup olive oil
2 large sweet red peppers, sliced into
  thin strips
2 large sweet yellow peppers, sliced into
  thin strips

Combine lemon juice and herbs in a medium-size bowl. Add oil in a slow, steady stream, whisking until well blended. Add peppers and toss until coated. Cover and chill for at least 1 hour before serving.

Dressings

Horseradish Vinaigrette

This vinaigrette is good with any salad combination.

Makes about ¾ cup

¼ cup red wine vinegar
1 to 2 teaspoons fresh lemon juice
½ teaspoon dry mustard
½ teaspoon low-sodium soy sauce
¼ teaspoon freshly grated horseradish
  (rinsed and drained prepared horseradish may be substituted)
1 clove garlic, minced
2 to 3 teaspoons fresh herbs: equal parts
  basil, dill, parsley, and chervil
½ cup olive oil

Place all ingredients in a jar. Cover and shake jar vigorously until mixed.

Cheddar and Onion Dressing

This dressing is good served on fresh spinach or beet greens.

Makes 1¼ cups

2 egg yolks, at room temperature
1 teaspoon water
½ cup olive oil
2 tablespoons sour cream or plain
  yogurt, at room temperature
2 tablespoons butter
⅓ cup finely chopped onions
¼ cup white wine vinegar
½ cup grated sharp cheddar cheese
freshly ground black pepper (optional)

Whisk egg yolks with water in a medium-size bowl until smooth. Add oil in a slow, steady stream, whisking until smooth. Stir in sour cream or yogurt. (Don't worry if this mixture appears to separate after standing. A few turns with a whisk will mix it again.)

Melt butter in a small saucepan over medium heat. Add onions and cook until soft. Stir vinegar into onion and butter mixture and bring to a simmer. Remove from heat. Add cheese to onion mixture and stir until cheese is melted and mixture is smooth. Cool to lukewarm.

Slowly whisk onion-cheese mixture into egg yolk mixture and season with pepper, if desired.

Dressing may be stored in a covered jar in refrigerator for up to 2 weeks.

MAIN DISHES

Swiss Chard Enchiladas

Vegetable gardening demands creative cooking. This is a basic recipe for you to adapt to what is available, at the moment, in your garden. The simple combination of red and green swiss chard is appetizing, and with luck, the other ingredients will be ready to harvest at the same time—probably in the early fall.

4 servings

2   tablespoons butter
2   tablespoons flour
1   cup milk
1   tablespoon olive oil
1   sweet red marconi pepper, seeded and diced
1   clove garlic, chopped
½   cup leeks, chopped
½   cup fresh flageolet beans
4   cups red and green swiss chard, or beet greens, chopped
1   tablespoon tarragon vinegar
8   corn or flour tortillas

To prepare the white sauce:
Melt butter in a small saucepan.

Whisk in flour, stirring until smooth. Heat the butter and flour mixture for 1 minute.

Slowly add milk, stirring constantly. Cook over medium heat until sauce is thickened.

To prepare the enchiladas:
Preheat oven to 350°F.

Heat olive oil in a skillet over moderate heat. Add pepper, garlic, and leeks, and cook for 3 minutes.

Add beans to this mixture. Cook, stirring, for 2 minutes.

Bring ¼ cup water to boil in a saucepan. Add chard or beet greens, cover, and cook until soft, 2 to 3 minutes. Drain.

Add bean and leek mixture to chard or beet greens in the saucepan. Add tarragon vinegar and stir.

Combine white sauce with mixture, stirring to mix well. Cover the saucepan and remove from heat.

Steam tortillas or soften in a microwave. Put about ½ cup of mixture on half of each tortilla and fold over the other side. Place tortillas in an open baking dish, each overlapping another. Bake for 20 minutes.

Grilled Bluefish Wrapped in Basil Leaves

*This recipe calls for two types of basil—*MAMMOTH *basil and* LEMON *basil.* MAMMOTH *basil leaves grow large enough to be used for wrapping, and* LEMON *basil adds a subtle, refreshing flavor to any fish or chicken dish.*

Wrapping a vegetable or meat in a leaf is one way of keeping the cooked ingredients tender and moist. The leaves should be soaked in water prior to wrapping to keep them from turning black during the cooking process. Moisture from the leaves gently steams the ingredients and lends a subtle flavor.

4 servings

8	to 10 mature fresh MAMMOTH basil leaves
2	tablespoons butter, at room temperature
2	teaspoons fresh lemon juice
2	tablespoons chopped fresh LEMON basil
1½	pounds bluefish fillets

Heat your outdoor grill as you would normally.

Soak MAMMOTH basil leaves in water.

In a small bowl cream butter with lemon juice and LEMON basil.

Cut fish fillets into strips crosswise about 2 inches wide (8 to 10 slices). Spread each slice with butter mixture.

Wrap MAMMOTH basil leaf around each slice of fish and secure closure with toothpick.

Place wrapped fish pieces on hot grill over glowing coals, 6 inches from heat. Cover and steam for 5 minutes on each side.

VARIATION: To prepare this recipe in a microwave oven, place wrapped fish slices in microwave-proof dish and cover loosely with waxed paper. Microwave on high power for 6 minutes or until fish flakes.

Ratatouille with CINNAMON Basil

The eggplant shells in this recipe are used as serving bowls for the ratatouille. A roundish variety like VIOLETTE DI FIRENZE *can be stuffed from the top and will stand up on its own. Parboil eggplant shells and then quickly put under the broiler to crisp before stuffing.*

4 servings

4	small eggplants, about ½ pound each
6	tablespoons fresh lemon juice
1	medium onion, sliced
1	clove garlic, minced
¼	cup olive oil
1	medium zucchini, coarsely chopped
2	tablespoons chopped fresh CINNAMON basil
2	tablespoons chopped sweet basil
5	plum tomatoes, seeded and chopped
1	red pepper, chopped, or ½ cup prepared roasted red peppers, drained and chopped
¼	cup chopped fresh parsley

Cut ½-inch slice along length of each eggplant. If using round variety, remove about 1 inch of top. Carefully scoop out flesh, leaving ½-inch-thick walls.

Chop eggplant flesh, place in a medium-size bowl, and toss with 1 tablespoon lemon juice. Set aside.

Using another tablespoon of lemon juice, brush inside of each eggplant shell. Invert shells on paper towels.

In a large skillet over medium heat, sauté onions and garlic in oil. Add chopped eggplants, zucchini, and basils. Cook, stirring, until eggplants are tender. Add tomatoes and peppers to mixture and cook for 2 or 3 minutes. Remove from heat. Stir in parsley and remaining lemon juice.

Divide ratatouille among eggplant shells. Cool and serve at room temperature.

Sweet Onions Stuffed with Broccoli

The sweet WALLA WALLA onions are best for this recipe, which was given to us by a customer who prepares the onions in the morning, then bakes them for dinner after a long day in the garden.

4 servings

- 2 WALLA WALLA onions or any variety of sweet onion, halved
- 1 pound fresh broccoli, stems removed, and florets coarsely chopped
- ½ cup grated Parmesan or Asiago cheese
- ⅓ cup mayonnaise
- 2 teaspoons fresh lemon juice

Steam onion halves in a vegetable steamer for 10 minutes. Drain and cool.

Using a sharp knife, remove centers of onions, leaving ¾-inch walls. Set onion shells in buttered, ovenproof serving dish. Chop reserved onion centers.

Preheat oven to 375°F.

Steam broccoli in a medium-size covered saucepan for 5 minutes. Drain.

In a large bowl combine broccoli, chopped onions, cheese, mayonnaise, and lemon juice.

Fill each onion half with stuffing.

Onions may be covered and refrigerated for baking later or baked immediately for 20 minutes.

Stuffed Round Zucchini

Round zucchini are perfect for stuffing when harvested at about the size of a tennis ball. You can stuff this versatile vegetable with something as simple as bread crumbs and herbs or with a combination of vegetables, ground meats, and cheeses.

4 servings

- 2 small RONDE DE NICE or GOURMET GLOBE zucchini
- ¼ cup olive oil
- 2 tablespoons minced onions
- 1 clove garlic, minced
- 2 tablespoons chopped green peppers
- 1 cup chopped tomatoes
- ½ cup dry bread crumbs
- ½ cup grated Parmesan cheese

Trim off stem end of squashes and drop squashes into a medium-size pot of boiling water. Cook for 5 minutes. Drain and cool.

Cut squashes in half from top to bottom and scoop out insides, leaving a ¾-inch-thick shell. Place shells in baking pan.

Preheat oven to 400°F.

Heat oil in a skillet over medium heat. Add onions, garlic, and peppers. Cook, stirring, until vegetables are tender. Remove from heat and stir in tomatoes and bread crumbs.

Fill each squash half with stuffing and top with cheese. Fill pan with 1 inch of water and bake for 25 minutes.

Fish and Vegetable Kabobs

4 servings

8   small yellow squashes
8   small green round zucchini
8   small eggplants
8   small onions
4   round carrots
2   large red, green, or yellow peppers, cut
    into 1-inch chunks
¼   cup fresh lemon juice
2   tablespoons red wine vinegar
1   tablespoon each minced fresh basil,
    thyme, and sweet marjoram, or 1
    teaspoon each dried basil, thyme,
    and sweet marjoram
2   tablespoons minced fresh parsley
2   cloves garlic, minced
¾   cup olive oil
8   wooden 12-inch skewers
¾   pound fresh tuna or swordfish, cut
    into 1½-inch chunks

Place squashes, zucchini, eggplants, onions, carrots, and peppers in a steamer with small amount of water. Steam, covered, for 2 or 3 minutes. Remove vegetables immediately and plunge into ice water. Drain.

In a small bowl combine lemon juice, vinegar, herbs, and garlic. Add oil in a slow, steady stream, whisking until well blended.

Place vegetables in a large bowl. Pour in enough of marinade to cover each vegetable lightly, and stir gently. Cover and refrigerate for at least 2 hours, or overnight.

Soak wooden skewers in water. Arrange vegetables and fish chunks on skewers, alternating vegetables with fish.

Grill kabobs over glowing coals, turning and basting with remainder of marinade, for 8 to 10 minutes, or just until vegetables are tender and fish is cooked.

Tortellini with Sun-Dried Tomatoes

Sun-dried tomatoes* have many uses. They add a special flavor to this traditional pasta dish.

4 servings

1   pound spinach or egg tortellini, or a
    combination
½   cup coarsely chopped sun-dried
    tomatoes
1   tablespoon nasturtium buds or capers
1   tablespoon Dijon mustard
2   cloves garlic, chopped
2   teaspoons fresh lemon juice
½   teaspoon red pepper flakes
3   tablespoons minced onions
⅔   cup olive oil
    fresh basil or nasturtium leaves, for
    garnish (optional)

Cook tortellini in a large pot of boiling water for 8 minutes. Drain and cool.

Combine remaining ingredients in a large bowl and mix well. Pour mixture over tortellini and toss until coated. Garnish with basil or nasturtium leaves, if using, and serve at room temperature.

*For a less expensive alternative to store-bought sun-dried tomatoes, try the recipe Oven-Dried Tomatoes found in the box on page 205.

Pizza with Sun-Dried Tomatoes

Each week during the summer, Ellen makes a pizza for Friday night. It uses the same basic crust and tomato base but has a different vegetable topping depending on what is in season. Mid-July brings sliced zucchini with chopped squash blossoms; during August we take advantage of the red, yellow, and chocolate peppers; and in September we enjoy pizza topped with broccoli and roasted walnuts.

2 medium-size pizzas

DOUGH

1	tablespoon dry yeast
1¼	cups warm water
1½	cups unbleached white flour
1½	cups whole wheat flour
1	teaspoon salt
1	tablespoon olive or safflower oil

SAUCE

3	cups thick tomato sauce
1	tablespoon finely chopped fresh oregano, basil, sweet marjoram, or Italian parsley, or 1 tablespoon of a combination of these herbs
2	cloves garlic

TOPPINGS

1	pound mozzarella cheese or part cheddar/part mozzarella cheese, grated
1	small sweet red onion, thinly sliced
1	green or red pepper, thinly sliced
⅛	cup coarsely chopped sun-dried tomatoes*
¼	cup grated Parmesan or Asiago cheese

To make the dough:

In a large bowl, dissolve yeast in warm water and allow to proof, about 10 minutes.

Sift flours and salt together.

Add oil and enough flour to yeast to make a firm dough. Continue adding flour until dough can be turned out of bowl onto floured surface. Knead until smooth, about 5 minutes.

Place dough in an oiled bowl and turn to coat both sides with oil. Cover with a warm, damp cloth. Allow to rise in a warm place or until double in size, about 1 hour.

To make the sauce:

Combine all of sauce ingredients. Set aside.

Preheat oven to 475°F.

To assemble the pizza:

Lightly oil 2 round pizza pans.

Punch down dough, knead briefly, and divide into 2 balls. Roll out each circle to fit each pan and turn edges to form raised ridge.

Spoon tomato sauce evenly over each crust. Sprinkle with mozzarella or mozzarella/cheddar cheese, onions, peppers, and tomatoes. Top with grated Parmesan or Asiago cheese.

Bake for 15 to 20 minutes or until outer crust is crisp and cheese is melted.

NOTE: If using food processor to make dough, start with flour and salt, then add oil. Mix in combined yeast and water and stir until it forms ball. Turn out onto floured surface and knead until smooth, about 3 minutes.

*For a less expensive alternative to store-bought sun-dried tomatoes, try the recipe Oven-Dried Tomatoes found in the box on page 205.

Oven-Dried Tomatoes

You've probably seen sun-dried tomatoes in specialty shops either hanging in a large bunch from the ceiling or packed in olive oil in decorative jars. Homemade oven-dried tomatoes are as good as anything you'll find in the store, and they are simple to prepare. These tomatoes take between 12 and 24 hours to dry.

Makes 2 pints

4	pints PRINCIPE BORGHESE or SAN MARZANO tomatoes
12	fresh basil leaves
	olive oil

Slice tomatoes in half lengthwise and remove seeds. Place halves in single layer on cookie sheets, flat side down. Set oven to warm (150°F) and place cookie sheets in oven.

When tomatoes are fully dry, after 12 to 24 hours, they look and feel like fruit leather. Pack in 2 sterilized 1-pint jars, alternating with layers of basil. Cover with olive oil, place lid tightly on jars, and store in refrigerator.

Spaghetti Primavera

Every gardener who likes to cook has his or her own unwritten recipe for primavera—pasta with fresh seasonal vegetables. "Primavera" means spring, and this recipe is the first celebration of the harvest. In the spring and early summer, asparagus and fresh peas can be the special attractions of this dish; in midsummer, it's a great way to use up extra zucchini. When fall comes, we add cauliflower, broccoli, brussels sprouts, and sweet red peppers.

4 servings

2	tablespoons olive oil
2	tablespoons butter
1	medium onion, coarsely chopped
1	clove garlic, minced
	handful of chive blossoms
½	cup sliced whole round carrots
½	cup fresh peas
6	spears asparagus, cut into 1-inch pieces
½	cup chopped sorrel
5	tablespoons drained and chopped sun-dried tomatoes* (optional)
1	pound thin spaghetti
2	cups grated cheddar cheese
1	cup fresh parsley, chopped

Heat oil and butter in a skillet over medium heat. Add onions, garlic, and chive blossoms, and sauté for 2 or 3 minutes. Add carrots, peas, and asparagus to skillet, and sauté for 5 minutes. Add sorrel and tomatoes, if used, and cook, stirring, for another 5 minutes. Reduce heat to low and keep warm.

In a large pot, bring 1 quart of water to a rapid boil. Add spaghetti and cook for 8 minutes or until al dente. Drain and place in a large serving bowl.

Toss sautéed vegetables, cheese, and parsley with spaghetti. Serve.

*For a less expensive alternative to store-bought sun-dried tomatoes, try the recipe Oven-Dried Tomatoes found in the box on page 205.

SUNBURST Squash with Ricotta

4 servings

4	SUNBURST patty-pan squashes, 4 inches or less in diameter
1	cup ricotta cheese
½	cup coarsely grated cheddar cheese
1	cup cooked corn kernels
2	tablespoons minced scallions or fresh chives
2	tablespoons minced radishes
	chopped fresh parsley, for garnish

Preheat oven to 400°F.

Bring water to a boil in a large saucepan. Add squashes, cover, and steam for 5 minutes. Drain.

Remove center core of squash and scoop out a 1- to 2-inch circular opening through center of squash.

In a medium-size bowl mix cheeses, corn, scallions or chives, radishes, and parsley.

Fill center of each squash with cheese mixture. Place in a casserole, cover, and bake for 10 minutes. Uncover and bake for another 20 minutes, or until squashes are tender and browned. Garnish with parsley before serving.

Vegetable Tempura

The stars of this tempura are tiny summer squashes with their blossoms still attached. Suggested vegetables to use: small RONDE DE NICE and SUNBURST squashes (1 inch in diameter); small eggplants or SLIM JIMs; filet green and yellow beans; small or round PLANET carrots; wedges of either golden, green, red, or chocolate peppers; slices of WALLA WALLA onions; small potatoes; beets; broccoli cut into florets; wedges of LEMON cucumbers; SUGAR SNAP peas; and EASTER EGG radishes.

The batter is prepared ahead of time to break down any rubberiness.

6 servings

DIPPING SAUCE

- ¼ cup safflower oil
- ¼ pound tofu
- ⅛ cup fresh lemon juice
- ⅛ cup tahini
- 1 garlic clove, peeled
- ¼ cup water

BATTER

- ½ cup unbleached white flour, sifted
- ¾ cup whole-wheat pastry flour, sifted
- ½ teaspoon grated lemon rind
- 1 cup water
- 1 egg white, whipped until stiff
- 2 cups vegetable oil
  mixture of small vegetables, trimmed and washed
- 1 large cabbage or radicchio leaf

To make the dipping sauce:

Place oil, tofu, lemon juice, tahini, garlic, and water in a food processor or blender and process until smooth. Set aside.

To make the batter:

In a large bowl, mix flours, lemon rind, and water and beat until smooth. Store in a covered container in refrigerator for 3 to 12 hours.

Just before frying, remove batter from refrigerator and fold in whipped egg white.

Add oil to a wok or deep fryer and heat to 350°F. Maintain this heat level throughout cooking.

Dip vegetables one by one into batter.

Drop a few vegetables at a time into hot oil and cook for 2 or 3 minutes on each side, or until golden brown. Remove, drain on paper towels, and keep warm.

Place dipping sauce in a cabbage or radicchio leaf.

When all vegetables are cooked, serve immediately with brown rice and dipping sauce.

Chicken with Sorrel Sauce

Sorrel has many culinary uses. The flavor is pleasantly sour, hence the common name of sourgrass. It is said that the Romans ate a great deal of sorrel to offset the richness of their daily diet. The young leaves are refreshingly tart in a spring salad, and as the plant grows larger, the leaves may be chopped into a sauce. Sorrel sauce is quite versatile: Pour it over poached fish or steamed vegetables, or try this chicken dish.

4 servings

- 3 tablespoons butter
- 1 shallot, finely chopped
- 2 cups chopped fresh sorrel
- ½ cup heavy cream
- ⅛ teaspoon freshly grated nutmeg (optional)
- 4 boneless chicken breasts, with skin removed

Heat 1 tablespoon butter in a medium-size saucepan over medium-low heat. Sauté shallots until translucent. Add sorrel and sauté, stirring, for 2 or 3 minutes or until sorrel wilts. Add cream and the nutmeg, if using. Cook for 2 minutes and set aside.

Heat remaining butter in a large skillet over medium heat. Add chicken breasts and cook for about 20 minutes or until cooked through, turning occasionally.

Reheat sorrel sauce just to a boil. Arrange chicken breasts on serving plate. Spoon sauce over chicken and serve.

Stir-Fried Beef Strips with Hot Pepper Jelly

4 servings

2   tablespoons butter or oil
1   pound tender beef, cut into 2-inch
       strips
½   onion, chopped
1   shallot, chopped
1   green pepper, cut into strips
¼   pound whole snow peas
1   cucumber, peeled and coarsely
       chopped
2   teaspoons hot red pepper jelly
¼   cup medium cream
       freshly ground black pepper

Heat butter or oil in a 10-inch pan on medium heat. Sauté beef strips for 3 minutes. Remove beef from pan with slotted spoon and reserve.

In remaining butter or oil, sauté onions and shallots until golden brown. Add green peppers, peas, and cucumber, and continue cooking for 3 minutes. Then stir in hot pepper jelly.

Return meat to pan and reheat. Add cream and cook over medium-high heat, stirring occasionally, for 3 to 5 minutes. Sprinkle with pepper and serve with hot rice or pasta.

Dandelion-Green Fettuccine with Alfredo Sauce

The following is a basic pasta recipe that will also work with many greens, including kale, cress, sorrel, basil, or spinach.

In this recipe, the pasta should be undercooked, because it will receive additional cooking when reheated with the sauce.

4 servings

DOUGH
2   cups finely chopped dandelion greens
2   eggs
½   to 1 cup flour

SAUCE
1   cup heavy cream
3   tablespoons butter
       freshly ground black pepper
1   tablespoon vegetable oil
⅔   cup grated Parmesan or Asiago cheese

To make the dough:

Place greens and eggs in a food processor or blender and blend until smooth. Spoon into bowl. Gradually add flour, stirring with wooden spoon. Continue stirring until stiff dough is formed. Turn dough out onto floured surface and knead for 5 minutes. Form dough into a ball, then roll out with a floured rolling pin until ⅛ inch thick. Let rest in a warm place for 1 hour.

To make the fettucine noodles:

Loosely roll sheet of dough like a jellyroll, then cut into ¼-inch slices with a large knife. Carefully unroll strips and set aside.

To make the sauce:

Place ⅔ cup cream and the butter in a large saucepan. Heat over medium heat until butter is melted, then simmer until thickened, about 2 minutes. Add pepper to taste. Turn off heat.

In a large kettle, bring 4 quarts water to a boil, then add oil to water. Carefully add fettuccine. Return water to a boil and shut off heat. Pasta should be undercooked. Drain.

Transfer fettuccine to a pan with cream and butter and turn heat to low. Add remaining cream and grated cheese and toss briefly until cream has thickened and fettuccine is coated. Serve immediately.

Ratatouille with TROMBONCINO Squash

We discovered these long "trombone squashes" quite by accident. A picture in an Italian seed catalog caught our attention, and we ordered some seed to try. The plants grew rapidly, reaching the top of their trellis within weeks. Tubular fruit the shape of a question mark began to appear, reaching 3 feet in length practically overnight. We bravely took one into the kitchen for Ellen to experiment with, and she made a big batch of ratatouille. It was delicious. This squash is unusually sweet and tender.

6 servings

⅓ cup olive oil
2 cloves garlic, chopped
1 large onion, chopped
3 tablespoons flour
1 18-inch TROMBONCINO squash, cut into ¼-inch slices
1 small eggplant, peeled and cubed
2 green peppers, cut into strips
5 tomatoes, coarsely chopped
1 tablespoon each chopped fresh basil and oregano
1 tablespoon capers or nasturtium buds

Heat oil in a large skillet. Add garlic and onions and sauté until transparent.

Place flour in a plastic bag. Add squash and eggplant, close bag, and shake gently to coat pieces. Add squash, eggplant, and peppers to skillet. Cook, uncovered, over low heat for 1 hour, stirring occasionally. Add tomatoes and herbs and simmer, uncovered, until mixture is thick. Add capers or nasturtium buds during last 15 minutes of cooking. Serve hot or cold.

Baked Stuffed Fennel

4 servings

4 tablespoons butter
1 shallot, chopped
2 cups seafood: 1 cup boned whitefish, cut into 1-inch chunks; ½ cup scallops; and ½ cup tiny shrimp pieces (or your choice)
1 tablespoon chopped fresh fennel leaves
2 tablespoons chopped sweet red peppers
2 tablespoons flour
1 cup warm milk
2 large fennel bulbs
   bread crumbs

Preheat oven to 350°F.

Melt 2 tablespoons butter in a medium-size skillet. Add shallots and sauté. Add seafood and cook, stirring, over medium heat for 3 minutes. Transfer to a bowl. Add fennel and peppers and toss.

Melt remaining butter in a medium-size saucepan over low heat. Add flour and stir for 2 minutes. Slowly add milk and cook until thickened, stirring constantly. Pour over seafood mixture, and gently stir until combined thoroughly.

Remove all but 4 inches of fennel stalks. (Reserve remainder for adding to a salad.) Parboil bulbs in boiling water for 2 minutes. Drain.

Place in a buttered baking dish. Scoop out center of each bulb, leaving ½- to ¾-inch walls. Fill each bulb with seafood mixture. Sprinkle with bread crumbs and bake for 30 minutes.

SIDE DISHES

Haricots Verts Vinaigrette

Haricots verts, also called filet beans, are so tender they need only be steamed for a few minutes. When harvested young, they're stringless, so simply trim the ends, steam, and drain them. You can marinate the beans for immediate use or freeze them for later. Marinated vegetables will keep for up to a week in the refrigerator, so you may want to steam a mixture of bite-size pieces, store them in the vinaigrette, and add to salads as you wish.

Other, more colorful beans, such as the yellow BUERRE DE ROCQUENFORT and the purple ROYAL BURGUNDY, can be combined with the green beans for a rich contrast. Cooking time should be kept to a minimum because purple beans, for example, will turn green when cooked for more than 2 minutes.

4 servings

- 1 pound filet beans, ends trimmed (2 cups)
- 2 tablespoons minced shallots
- 1½ tablespoons fresh lemon juice
- 1 tablespoon chopped fresh dill, tarragon, savory, or thyme
- ⅓ cup olive oil

Steam beans until just tender, about 2 minutes. Drain and plunge into ice water until cool. Pat dry between towels and place in a medium-size bowl.

In a small bowl mix shallots, lemon juice, and herbs. Add oil in a slow, steady stream, whisking until well blended.

Pour mixture over beans and toss until completely coated. Cover and chill in refrigerator before serving.

Leeks Vinaigrette

Leeks are often added to soups and stocks, but they are also tasty on their own, coated with a light vinaigrette. They have the subtlest taste of all the onion relatives and look as beautiful on the plate as they do in the garden.

4 servings

- 12 small leeks, roots and tops removed
- 1 cup chicken or vegetable stock
- ⅓ cup fresh lemon juice

- ⅛ cup chopped fresh chives
- 1 tablespoon finely minced shallots
- 1 tablespoon Dijon mustard
- ½ cup olive oil

Place 4 salad plates in refrigerator to chill.

Cut leeks in half lengthwise to within ½ inch of root end. Wash thoroughly under cold running water.

Put stock in a medium-size saucepan, add leeks, and simmer over low heat for 15 to 20 minutes, or until tender, adding additional stock or water if necessary during cooking. Drain thoroughly.

Combine lemon juice, chives, shallots, and mustard in a medium-size bowl. Add oil in a slow, steady stream, whisking until well blended.

Arrange 3 leeks on each chilled plate. Drizzle about ¼ cup dressing over each serving. Chill before serving.

Leeks Mornay

3 or 4 servings

- 6 to 8 leeks, but 1 to 2 inches of tops removed
- 2 cups chicken or vegetable stock
- 2 tablespoons butter
- 2 tablespoons flour
- ½ cup grated Swiss cheese
- ¼ cup finely chopped scallion tops or fresh chives
- ½ teaspoon Dijon mustard
- 2 tablespoons grated Parmesan cheese

Cut halfway through each leek lengthwise and rinse well under running water. Place leeks and stock in a large saucepan and simmer over low heat for 15 to 20 minutes, or until tender. Drain, reserving 1 cup of stock (add water to make 1 cup if necessary).

Preheat broiler. Arrange leeks in a flat ovenproof casserole.

Melt butter in a medium-size saucepan and whisk in flour, stirring to form a smooth paste. Cook over low heat, stirring constantly, about 2 or 3 minutes. Add reserved stock and continue cooking and stirring until sauce has thickened. Stir Swiss cheese, scallions or chives, and mustard into sauce, mixing well. Cook, stirring constantly, until cheese is melted and sauce is smooth.

Pour sauce over leeks and sprinkle Parmesan over top. Place casserole under broiler briefly until top is lightly browned.

Serve immediately.

Gingered Carrots

6 servings

2   tablespoons butter
⅓   cup fresh orange juice
2   tablespoons honey
½   cup water
1   tablespoon grated orange rind
1   teaspoon ground ginger
1   2-inch piece gingerroot, sliced
12 small whole carrots, washed and
       trimmed

Melt butter in a small saucepan over medium heat. Add orange juice, honey, water, orange rind, and ground ginger. Cover and simmer for 6 to 8 minutes. Add sliced ginger and cook, uncovered, over medium heat until liquid is reduced by half. Turn heat down to low.

Steam carrots until tender. Drain and place in a serving dish.

Remove sliced ginger from glaze and pour glaze over carrots.

Baby Carrots in Herb Vinegar

Round carrots are so sweet and tender that no cooking is really necessary, but it helps to bring out the flavor. Serve as a side dish or alongside a roast with potatoes and small onions.

4 servings

20 small round carrots, washed and
       trimmed
¾   cup water
1   tablespoon fresh lemon juice
1   tablespoon butter
2   tablespoons tarragon or raspberry
       vinegar

Place carrots, water, and lemon juice in a small saucepan. Cover and simmer over low heat for 5 minutes. Remove cover, increase heat to high, and cook, stirring occasionally, until liquid is nearly gone (about 5 minutes).

Turn heat down to medium, add butter and vinegar, and gently stir until carrots are coated. Serve immediately.

Flageolets with Garlic and Thyme

Fresh flageolet shell beans are hard to come by unless you grow them. Fresh are better than dried because they don't need to be cooked as long. Baked flageolets are a traditional French accompaniment to lamb.

4 servings

2   cloves garlic
1   medium onion, chopped
⅓   cup olive oil
3   tomatoes, peeled, seeded, and
       chopped
2   tablespoons chopped fresh parsley
1   tablespoon chopped fresh thyme
1   pound shelled flageolet beans (about
       1½ cups)
4   sprigs thyme flowers, for garnish

Preheat oven to 350°F.

In a small skillet, sauté garlic and onions in oil until transparent.

Place tomatoes in a medium-size saucepan, cover, and simmer for 5 minutes. Add onion mixture, herbs, and beans to tomatoes and continue simmering for 10 minutes. Transfer to a casserole, cover, and bake for 30 minutes.

Garnish each serving with sprig of thyme.

Sautéed Pear Tomatoes

The tiniest bit of cooking enhances the natural sweetness of tomatoes. Try not to overcook them or they will become mushy.

6 to 8 servings

¼ cup butter
½ pint yellow pear tomatoes
½ pint red pear tomatoes

Melt butter in a medium-size skillet. Add tomatoes and cook, uncovered, over medium heat, tossing gently while cooking. Cook until tomatoes are shiny and heated through, about 5 minutes. Serve immediately.

ROMANESCO Broccoli with Lemon and Garlic

This recipe was created to take advantage of the unusual shape of the florets of ROMANESCO broccoli. A lemon butter drizzled on the cooked florets also works nicely.

6 servings

1 lemon
2 cloves garlic, crushed
1 tablespoon oriental sesame oil (optional)
¼ cup olive oil
½ head ROMANESCO broccoli, broken or cut into florets (about 1 pound)

Remove rind from lemon in long, thin strips and drop rind into boiling water for 30 seconds. Drain, pat dry with towel, and chop finely.

Squeeze juice from ½ lemon. Combine lemon juice, lemon rind, garlic, and the sesame oil, if using, in a medium-size bowl. Add olive oil in a slow, steady stream, whisking until well blended.

Steam broccoli for 5 minutes, or until just tender. Drain and transfer to a serving dish.

Pour lemon sauce over broccoli. Toss gently and serve.

Baby Beets with Horseradish-Dill Butter

For this dish, harvest the beets when they're about 1 inch in diameter and use them whole. If they're larger, slice them first. You might want to use red and green salad-bowl lettuce as a base for each serving.

4 servings

12 small beets, scrubbed and trimmed
2 tablespoons butter
2 tablespoons horseradish
1 tablespoon cider vinegar
1 tablespoon chopped fresh dill or 1 teaspoon dried dill

Steam beets in a covered medium-size saucepan for 30 minutes, or until tender. Drain, peel skins, and place in a serving dish. Keep warm.

Melt butter in a small saucepan, then stir in remaining ingredients. Pour mixture over beets and toss well.

Sautéed Radish and Arugula

8 servings

¼ cup butter
1 pound radishes, washed and trimmed
4 cups arugula leaves, firmly packed thinly sliced radishes, for garnish (optional)

Melt butter in a large skillet. Add radishes and sauté, uncovered, over medium heat until radishes are tender but still crisp, about 3 or 4 minutes. Using slotted spoon, transfer to a medium-size bowl.

Add arugula to skillet and sauté, uncovered, over low heat until wilted, about 2 or 3 minutes.

Return radishes to skillet, toss with arugula, and heat briefly. Place in a serving dish, garnish with sliced radishes, if desired, and serve immediately.

Carrot and Turnip Pancakes

Carrots and turnips can be cooked together and pureed with milk and butter as if you were making mashed potatoes. With the addition of potatoes, this combination makes excellent potato pancakes.

4 servings

4	small potatoes, scrubbed and quartered
5	carrots, scrubbed and coarsely chopped
1	turnip, scrubbed and coarsely chopped
2	tablespoons butter
¼	cup milk
¼	cup flour
¼	cup grated Parmesan or Asiago cheese
1	tablespoon finely chopped fresh parsley
1	egg, well beaten
	oil for frying

Place potatoes in a medium-size saucepan, cover with water, and boil for 25 minutes, or until tender. Drain.

Place carrots and turnips in a medium-size saucepan, cover with water, and boil for 10 minutes, or until tender. Drain.

Put potatoes, carrots, and turnips in a food processor or blender and process briefly until mixture reaches consistency of mashed potatoes. Transfer to a large bowl.

Add butter, milk, flour, cheese, parsley, and egg and mix well. Form into small pancakes, ½ inch thick.

Sauté pancakes in a skillet with a small amount of oil until they are golden brown on both sides.

Steamed Broccoli Raab

Slow cooking enhances the flavor of broccoli raab; quick cooking makes it bitter. This makes a good side dish for pork chops and applesauce. If you should have leftovers, try the Cold Broccoli Raab (see recipe below).

4 servings

1	broccoli raab, washed
¼	cup olive oil
2	cloves garlic
¼	cup tarragon vinegar
	grated Parmesan or Asiago cheese

Preheat oven to 300°F.

Place broccoli raab (with water still clinging to leaves from washing), oil, and garlic in a large baking dish or casserole. Cover and cook for 30 minutes, or until tender, stirring occasionally. Add tarragon vinegar. Top with cheese and serve immediately.

Cold Broccoli Raab

Makes 1 cup

2	cups cooked broccoli raab
1	tablespoon low-sodium soy sauce
1	tablespoon sesame oil

In colander, gently press moisture from broccoli raab. Chop coarsely and place in serving bowl. Mix soy sauce and oil in cup. Pour over broccoli raab, toss, and chill before serving.

Grilled Baby Eggplant

4 servings

2   to 4 small eggplants
3   tablespoons olive oil
1   tablespoon butter
1   small onion, chopped
2   Roma tomatoes, seeded and chopped,
      or 1 tablespoon chopped sun-dried
      tomatoes*
1   tablespoon chopped fresh basil or
      1 teaspoon dried basil

Slice eggplants in half.

Heat oil in a large skillet over medium-low heat. Place eggplants face down and cook until golden brown, about 10 minutes. Remove eggplants and keep warm.

Melt butter in a large skillet. Add onions and sauté until soft. Add tomatoes and cook until liquid has evaporated.

Place eggplants cut side up on serving plate, top with onion and tomato mixture, and sprinkle with basil.

*For a less expensive alternative to store-bought sun-dried tomatoes, try the recipe Oven-Dried Tomatoes found in the box on page 205.

Marinated Yellow Tomatoes

For years we added a pinch of sugar to tomato dishes to counteract their natural acidity. Then we found out about yellow tomatoes, which are low in acid and naturally sweet.

4 servings

2   large yellow tomatoes, sliced
2   tablespoons chopped fresh basil
3   tablespoons olive oil
2   tablespoons fresh lemon juice
      freshly ground black pepper to taste

Arrange tomato slices on a platter in single layer. Sprinkle with basil.

Combine oil, lemon juice, and pepper in a small bowl. Pour over tomatoes and let stand at room temperature for 1 hour before serving.

SEED SOURCE LIST

Abundant Life Seed Foundation
P.O. Box 772
Port Townsend, WA 98368
(206) 385-5660
Catalog $1
Table Code AL

Bountiful Gardens
5798 Ridgewood Road
Willits, CA 95490
Table Code BG

W. Atlee Burpee Company
300 Park Avenue
Warminster, PA 18974
Catalog free
Table Code BP

The Cook's Garden
P.O. Box 65
Londonderry, VT 05148-0065
(802) 824-3400
Catalog $1
Table Code CG

Companion Plants
Route 6, Box 88
Athens, OH 45701
(614) 592-4643
Catalog $2
Table Code CP

DeGiorgi Company
P.O. Box 413
1411 Third Street
Council Bluffs, IA 51502
(712) 323-2372
Catalog $1
Table Code DG

Farmer Seed and Nursery
818 N.W. Fourth Street
Faribault, MN 55021
(507) 334-1623
Table Code FM

Good Seed Company
P.O. Box 702
Tonasket, WA 98855
Catalog $2
Table Code GS

Gurney Seed and Nursery Company
Second and Capitol
Yankton, SD 57079
(605) 665-4451
Table Code GY

Harris Seeds
Moreton Farm
3670 Buffalo Road
Rochester, NY 14624
(716) 594-9411
Table Code HM

H. G. Hastings Company
P.O. Box 4274
Atlanta, GA 30302-4274
(404) 524-8861
Table Code HS

Henry Field Seed and Nursery
2176 Oak Street
Shenandoah, IA 51602
(712) 246-2110
Table Code HF

Herb Gathering
5742 Kenwood Avenue
Kansas City, MO 64110
Catalog $2
Table Code HG

High Altitude Gardens
P.O. Box 4238
Ketchum, ID 83340
(208) 726-3221
Catalog $2
Table Code HA

Horticultural Enterprises
P.O. Box 810082
Dallas, TX 75381-0082
Table Code HT

Johnny's Selected Seeds
310 Foss Hill Road
Albion, ME 04910
(207) 437-43041
Table Code JS

Kalmia Farm
P.O. Box 3881
Charlottesville, VA 22903
Table Code KM

Le Jardin du Gourmet
P.O. Box 30
West Danville, VT 05873
Catalog $1
Table Code LJ

Le Marche Seeds International
P.O. Box 190
Dixon, CA 95620
(916) 678-9244
Catalog $2
Table Code LM

Moose Tubers/Fedco Seeds
52 Mayflower Hill Drive
Waterville, ME 04901
Table Code MT

Nichols Garden Nursery
1190 N. Pacific Highway
Albany, OR 97321
(503) 928-9280
Table Code NG

Park Seed Company
Highway 254 North
Greenwood, SC 29647-0001
(803) 223-7333
Table Code PK

The Pepper Gal
10536 119th Avenue North
Largo, FL 33543
Table Code PG

Pinetree Garden Seeds
New Gloucester, ME 04260
(207) 926-3400
Table Code PT

Redwood City Seed Company
P.O. Box 361
Redwood City, CA 94064
(415) 325-7333
Catalog $1
Table Code RC

Richters
Box 26
Goodwood
Ontario
L0C 1A0
(416) 640-6677
Catalog $4
Table Code RT

S & H Organic Acres
P.O. Box 1531
Watsonville, CA 95077
Table Code SH

Seeds Blum
Idaho City Stage
Boise, ID 83706
Catalog $2
Table Code SB

Shepherd's Garden Seeds
7389 West Zayante Road
Felton, CA 95018
(408) 335-5400
Catalog $1.50
Table Code SS

Southern Exposure Seed Exchange
P.O. Box 158
North Garden, VA 22959
Catalog $2
Table Code SX

Stokes Seeds
P.O. Box 548
Buffalo, NY 14240-0548
(416) 688-4300
Table Code ST

Thompson and Morgan
P.O. Box 1308
Farraday and Gramme Avenues
Jackson, NJ 08527
(201) 363-2225
Table Code TM

Tomato Grower's Supply Company
P.O. Box 2237
Fort Myers, FL 33902
Table Code TG

Vermont Bean Seed Company
Garden Lane
Fair Haven, VT 05743-0250
(802) 265-4212
Table Code VB

William Dam Seeds
P.O. Box 8400
Dundas
Ontario
L9H 6M1
(416) 628-6621
Catalog $1
Table Code WD

INDEX

Note: Page references in *italic* indicate tables.

I

K